25.00
9.50

D0912697

CROSSING OVER
SEA *and* LAND

CROSSING OVER SEA and LAND

Jewish Missionary Activity in the Second Temple Period

MICHAEL F. BIRD

Crossing Over Sea and Land: Jewish Missionary Activity in the Second Temple Period, by Michael F. Bird
© 2010 by Hendrickson Publishers Marketing, LLC
P. O. Box 3473
Peabody, Massachusetts 01961-3473

ISBN 978-1-59856-434-1

All rights reserved. No part of this book may be reproduced or transmitted in any form or by any means, electronic or mechanical, including photocopying, recording, or by any information storage and retrieval system, without permission in writing from the publisher.

BWHEBB [Hebrew] Postscript® Type 1 and TrueTypeT fonts Copyright © 1994–2009 BibleWorks, LLC. All rights reserved. These Biblical Hebrew fonts are used with permission and are from BibleWorks, software for Biblical exegesis and research.

Printed in the United States of America

First Printing — January 2010

Hendrickson Publishers is strongly committed to sustainability and environmentally responsible printing practices. The pages of this book were printed on 30% post consumer waste recycled stock using only soy or vegetable content inks.

Cover Art: Harbor of Classe. Early Christian mosaic. 6th C.E.
Location: S. Apollinare Nuovo, Ravenna, Italy
Photo Credit: Scala / Art Resource, N.Y.

Library of Congress Cataloging-in-Publication Data

Bird, Michael F.
    Crossing over sea and land : Jewish missionary activity in the Second Temple period / Michael F. Bird.
        p. cm.
    Includes bibliographical references and indexes.
    ISBN 978-1-59856-434-1 (alk. paper)
    1. Proselytizing—Judaism—History. 2. Judaism—History—Post-exilic period, 586 B.C.–210 A.D. 3. Judaism—Relations. 4. Jews—History—586 B.C.–70 A.D. I. Title.
    BM729.P7B57 2010
    296.6'90937—dc22
                                        2009031144

CONTENTS

PREFACE

This project began during my doctoral work at the University of Queensland where I originally set out to write a chapter on Jewish missionary activity as a precursor to the advent of early Christian missionary efforts. I naïvely assumed that it would take me about four weeks to do so. In fact, it took me eight months to research the topic, and that was only scratching the surface of the extant evidence and scholarly debate. Several years after completing my doctoral studies I have finally acquired the opportunity to return to this scintillating topic and to pursue several loose threads from my earlier publications. This exercise has occasioned a joyous exploration of the various Jewish writings relevant to the designated period: the Hebrew Bible, the Apocrypha, Pseudepigrapha, Dead Sea Scrolls, Philo, Josephus, Greek and Latin authors, the New Testament, Church Fathers, Rabbinic writings, the Targums, and also archaeological evidence. The purpose of such a mammoth undertaking was to identify and analyze the extent of Jewish missionary activity among Gentiles in and around the apostolic era. In this volume I offer the results of my foray into this subject. In the course of my research I have benefited from the earlier work of several scholars, especially Martin Goodman, Scot McKnight, Louis Feldman, John Dickson, Eckhard Schnabel, and Terence Donaldson. I consider these authors to be the primary dialogue partners in my study of the ancient sources and texts, and I acknowledge my indebtedness to them.

Along the way, of course, there are several people that I need to thank. First, and once again, Dr. Rick Strelan, my *Doktorvater*, who has continued to provide me with sound advice and stern warnings when I was first writing on this subject. Second, Martin Cameron of the Highland Theological College was able to track down several important and obscure works for me, and his assistance was quite crucial for the completion of this project. Third, as always, my dear wife Naomi and our children, Alexis, Alyssa, and Markus, who inspire and encourage me in my scholarly endeavors. Fourth, Paul Barnett (former Anglican

Bishop of North Sydney) read a much earlier edition of this work and offered some helpful comments. My thanks also go to Brandon Wason and Danny Zacharias who proofread the complete manuscript in meticulous fashion. Fifth, at the later stages of this project the advice of Jörg Frey was most helpful, rigorous, and made the book much better than it was to begin with. Sixth, I wish to express my gratitude to Anya Tilling who checked my German translations and I fully agree with her protest in an e-mail that, "I wish German academics would write straight forward sentences and not fancy twisted things as they do." Seventh, my deepest appreciation goes to Eilidh Wilkinson who kindly (and perhaps naively) agreed to do most of the indexing. Eighth, I am also grateful to Scot McKnight and Joel Willitts both of North Park University. Scot was an examiner for my doctoral thesis, and I have developed a wonderful relationship with him ever since. He has become not only a good friend, but also a mentor whose counsel I value and esteem. Scot keeps me aware of the necessity of doing good scholarly work and the goal for why we do it in the first place. In many ways my volume here is an update, revision, and sometimes a challenge to his work on Jewish missionary activity written some fifteen years ago. I sincerely hope that it is a worthy sequel to his own contribution to the debate. I first came across Joel Willitts when he was a PhD candidate at Cambridge University. I initially wrote him a letter from Australia after hearing a cassette recording of a conference paper that he gave entitled, "Why I Decided Not to Be an Historical Jesus Scholar." I was intrigued by his presentation precisely because I was doing research on the historical Jesus myself. Correspondence ensued through various letters and e-mails, and we finally met in person a few years later and have since shared a close relationship at both the personal and professional level. He has agreed to participate in several projects that I have roped him into, and Joel always has a wise word to offer as well, especially when I'm dreaming up yet another major project for us to tackle together. We have developed a scholarly partnership that I hope continues to blossom in the future. If I am Oscar Hammerstein then Joel is my Richard Rodgers. This volume is appropriately dedicated to these two scholars who have graced me with their friendship and encouragement.

ABBREVIATIONS

GENERAL

Aram.	Aramaic
b.	ben (= son of)
B.C.E.	before the Common Era
C.E.	Common Era
ed.	Edition, editor
frg.	fragment
FS	Festschrift
Heb.	Hebrew
vols.	volumes

ANCIENT SOURCES

'Abot R. Nat.	*Avot of Rabbi Nathan*
Adfin. Vocab.	*De Adfinium Vocabulorum Differentia*
Apoc. Pet.	*Apocalypse of Peter*
Asc. Isa.	*Martyrdom and Ascension of Isaiah*
Augustine	
Civ. D.	*De civitate Dei*
De Cons.	*De consensu evangelistarum*
Babylonian Talmud	
b. 'Abod. Zar.	*Avodah Zarah*
b. B. Bat.	*Bava Batra*
b. Ber.	*Berakhot*
b. Ker.	*Kerithot*
b. Meg.	*Megillah*
b. Me'il.	*Me'ilah*
b. Ned.	*Nedarim*
b. Nid.	*Niddah*
b. Pesah.	*Pesahim*

b. Qidd.	*Qiddushin*
b. Šabb.	*Shabbat*
b. Sanh.	*Sanhedrin*
b. Yebam.	*Yevamot*
Bar	Baruch
Barn.	*Barnabas*
Callimachus	
Epigr.	*Epigrammata*
CD	Cairo Genizah copy of the *Damascus Document*
1–2 Chron	1–2 Chronicles
Clement of Alexandria	
Strom.	*Stromata*
Col	Colossians
1–2 Cor	1–2 Corinthians
Dan	Daniel
Dem. Chr.	*Demonstratio de Christo et Antichristo*
Deut	Deuteronomy
Did.	*Didache*
Dio Cassius	
Hist.	*Historiae*
Diogn.	*Diognetus*
Ep. Arist.	*Epistle of Aristeas*
Epictetus	
Diss.	*Dissertationes*
Esth	Esther
Exag.	*Exagōgē* of Ezekiel the Tragedian
Exod	Exodus
Exod. Rab.	*Exodus Rabbah*
Eusebius	
Eccl. Hist.	*Historia ecclesiastica*
Prep. Ev.	*Praeparatio evangelica*
Ezek	Ezekiel
Gal	Galatians
Gen	Genesis
Gen. Rab.	*Genesis Rabbah*
Gos. Thom.	*Gospel of Thomas*
Herodotus	
Hist.	*Historiae*

Hippolytus
  Refut.   *Refutatio omnium haeresium (Philosophoumena)*
Hos   Hosea
Ignatius
  Magn.   *To the Magnesians*
  Phld.   *To the Philadelphians*
Irenaeus
  Adv. Haer.   *Adversus haereses*
Isa   Isaiah
Jdt   Judith
Jer   Jeremiah
Jerusalem Talmud
  y. Qidd.   *Qiddushin*
John Chrysostom
  Epic. Theod.   *Letter to Theodore*
Jon   Jonah
Jos. Asen.   *Joseph and Aseneth*
Josephus
  Ag. Ap.   *Against Apion*
  Ant.   *Jewish Antiquities*
  J.W.   *Jewish War*
  Life   *The Life*
Josh   Joshua
Jub.   *Jubilees*
Justin
  1 Apol.   *Apologia i*
  Dial. Tryph.   *Dialogus cum Tryphone*
Juvenal
  Sat.   *Satirae*
1–2 Kgs   1–2 Kings
Lev   Leviticus
LXX   Septuagint
1–4 Macc   1–4 Maccabees
Mal   Malachi
Mart. Pol.   *Martyrdom of Polycarp*
Martial
  Epigr.   *Epigrams*
Mic   Micah

Mishnah
m. Bik.	*Mishnah Bikkurim*
m. 'Ed.	*Mishnah Eduyyot*
m. Git.	*Mishnah Gittin*
m. Ker.	*Mishnah Kerithot*
m. Ned.	*Mishnah Nedarim*
m. Pesah.	*Mishnah Pesahim*
m. Yad.	*Mishnah Yadayim*
Num	Numbers
Num. Rab.	*Numbers Rabbah*
Obad	Obadiah

Petronius
| *Sat.* | *Satyricon* |

Philo
Abr.	*De Abrahamo*
Cher.	*De cherubim*
Conf. Ling.	*De confusione linguarum*
Decal.	*De decalogo*
Deus Imm.	*Quod Deus sit immutabilis*
Flacc.	*In Flaccum*
Gai.	*Legatio ad Gaium*
Her.	*Quis rerum divinarum heres sit*
Leg.	*Legum allegoriae*
Leg. Gai.	*Legatio ad Gaium*
Migr. Abr.	*De migratione Abrahami*
Op. Mundi	*De opificio mundi*
Quod Omn. Prob.	*Quod omnis probus liber sit*
Poster. C.	*De posteritate Caini*
Praem. Poen.	*De praemiis et poenis*
Quaest. in Ex.	*Quaestiones et solutiones in Exodum*
Quaest. in Gen.	*Quaestiones et solutiones in Genesin*
Sacr.	*De sacrificiis Abelis et Caini*
Som.	*De somniis*
Spec. Leg.	*De specialibus legibus*
Virt.	*De virtutibus*
Vit. Cont.	*De vita contemplativa*
Vit. Mos.	*De vita Mosis*

Pliny the Elder
   Nat. Hist.   *Naturalis historia*
Plutarch
   Cic.   *Cicero*
   Conv.   *Quaestionum convivialum libri IX*
Porphyry
   Abst.   *De abstinentia*
Pss   Psalms
Pss. Sol.   *Psalms of Solomon*
4Q174   *Florilegium*, also *Midrash on Eschatology*[a]
4Q175   *Testimonia*
4Q381   Non-Canonical Psalms B
1QapGen   *Genesis Apocryphon*
1QH   *Hodayot* or *Thanksgiving Hymns*
1QM   *Milhamah* or *War Scroll*
1QpHab   *Pesher Habakkuk*
4QpNah   *Pesher Nahum*
4QPrNab   *Prayer of Nabonidus*
11QPs[a]   *Psalms Scroll*[a]
1QS   *Serek Hayahad* or *Rule of the Community*
1QSb   *Rule of the Blessings* (Appendix b to 1QS)
Seneca the Younger
   Ep. Mor.   *Epistulae morales*
Sib. Or.   *Sibylline Oracles*
Sifre Num.   *Sifre Numbers*
Sir   Sirach/Ecclesiasticus
Strabo
   Geog.   *Geographica*
T. Benj.   *Testament of Benjamin*
T. Gad   *Testament of Gad*
T. Jos.   *Testament of Joseph*
T. Jud.   *Testament of Judah*
T. Levi   *Testament of Levi*
T. Naph.   *Testament of Naphtali*
T. Mos.   *Testament of Moses*
T. Zeb.   *Testament of Zebulun*
Tacitus
   Ann.   *Annales*
   Hist.   *Historiae*

Tertullian
  Test.   *De testimonio animae*
Tob   Tobit
Tosefta
  t. B. Mes.   *Bava Metzi'a*
  t. Qidd.   *Qiddushin*
  t. Sanh.   *Sanhedrin*
  t. Sukk.   *Sukkah*
  t. Yad.   *Yadayim*
Wis   Wisdom of Solomon
Zech   Zechariah
Zeph   Zephaniah

MODERN SOURCES

ABD   *Anchor Bible Dictionary* (ed. David Noel Freedman)
ABRL   Anchor Bible Reference Library
AJEC   Ancient Judaism and Early Christianity
BAR   *Biblical Archaeology Review*
BDAG   A Greek-English Lexicon of the New Testament
               and Other Early Christian Literature (ed. Walter
               Bauer, et al., 4th ed.)
Bib   *Biblica*
BIS   Biblical Interpretation Series
BRS   Biblical Resource Series
BZNW   Beihefte zur Zeitschrift für die neutestamentliche
               Wissenschaft
CBQ   *Catholic Biblical Quarterly*
CBR   *Currents in Biblical Research*
CIJ   *Corpus inscriptionum judaicarum* (ed. J. B. Frey)
DNTB   *Dictionary of New Testament Background* (eds.
               Craig A. Evans and Stanley E. Porter)
EQ   *Evangelical Quarterly*
GLAJJ   *Greek and Latin Authors on Jews and Judaism* (ed.
               Menahem Stern)
HTR   *Harvard Theological Review*
ICC   International Critical Commentary
JBL   *Journal of Biblical Literature*

JJS	*Journal of Jewish Studies*
JQR	*Jewish Quarterly Review*
JSHJ	*Journal for the Study of the Historical Jesus*
JSJ	*Journal for the Study of Judaism in the Persian, Hellenistic, and Roman Period*
JSNT	*Journal for the Study of the New Testament*
JSNTSup	Journal for the Study of the New Testament Supplement
JSPSup	Journal for the Study of the Pseudepigrapha Supplement
JTS	*Journal of Theological Studies*
LCL	Loeb Classical Library
LNTS	Library of New Testament Studies
NA^{27}	*Novum Testamentum Graece,* Nestle-Aland, 27th ed.
NIDNTT	*The New International Dictionary of New Testament Theology* (ed. Colin Brown)
NIGTC	New International Greek Testament Commentary
NRSV	New Revised Standard Version
NSBT	New Studies in Biblical Theology
NTS	*New Testament Studies*
OTP	*The Old Testament Pseudepigrapha* (ed. James H. Charlesworth)
PBM	Paternoster Biblical Monographs
PGM	*The Greek Magical Papyri in Translation* (ed. H. D. Betz).
RB	*Revue biblique*
RTR	*Reformed Theological Review*
SBT	Studies in Biblical Theology
SJT	*Scottish Journal of Theology*
SNTSMS	Society of New Testament Studies Monograph Series
ST	*Studia Theologica*
TANZ	Texte und Arbeiten zum neutestamentlichen Zeitatler
TAPA	*Transactions of the American Philological Association*
TDNT	*Theological Dictionary of the New Testament* (eds. Gerhard Kittel and Gerhard Friedrich)
TNTC	Tyndale New Testament Commentary
TSAJ	Texte und Studien zum antiken Judentum
TZ	*Theologische Zeitschrift*

UBS	United Bible Society
UBS[4]	United Bible Society Greek New Testament, 4th edition.
VC	*Vigiliae Christianae*
WBC	Word Biblical Commentary
WUNT	Wissenschaftliche Untersuchungen zum Neuen Testament
ZPE	*Zeitschrift für Papyrologie und Epigraphik*

Chapter One

Introduction

This volume is essentially a prequel to my earlier monograph *Jesus and the Origins of the Gentile Mission*[1] where I attempted to identify the impact that the historical Jesus exerted upon the rise and development of later Christian missions to the Gentiles. There I concluded that, in accordance with several strands of Jewish restoration eschatology, Jesus believed that a transformed Israel would transform the world, and because Israel's restoration had already begun it was becoming possible for Gentiles to experience the blessings of Israel's restoration and the advent of the kingdom as an embryonic foretaste of what was to come. Although I had engaged in concerted research and investigation into Jewish missionary activity of the Second Temple period during the writing of that volume, I did not have the opportunity to properly disseminate my conclusions which had to be largely presupposed and reduced to a mere footnote. It is here, however, that I intend to make that footnote come to life on its own and to tackle the subject afresh because it has such great significance for understanding Second Temple Judaism and early Christianity. What follows in this chapter is an introduction to the nature of the problem in plotting Jewish missionary activity in the Second Temple period and setting forth my own plan for how to go about such a study.

I take as my starting point the observation that Christianity was a missionary religion that crossed significant geographical, ethnic, religious, and political lines in the first centuries of the Common Era.[2] In the words of the Jewish scholar Martin Goodman: "Christianity

---

[1] (LNTS 331; London: T&T Clark, 2006)

[2] On mission and universalism in the Old Testament and ancient Israel see Eckhard J. Schnabel, *The Early Christian Mission* (2 vols.; Downers Grove, Ill.: InterVarsity, 2004), 1.55–91.

spread primarily because many Christians believed that it was positively desirable for non-Christians to join their faith and accrete to their congregations."[3] Similar is Ramsay MacMullen: "The impulse to reach out from the inside was a part of belief itself."[4] Martin Kähler went so far as to say that mission was "the mother of all theology."[5] I have found these points to be reinforced by my own study of Christian exegesis of Isa 42:6 and 49:6 that attaches to Jesus and the church a divine calling to take the message of the gospel to the entire world.[6] In the developing church of the second and third centuries the spread of Christians all over the world was frequently mentioned as part of the proclamation, exhortation, and apologetics of Christian authors.[7] The missionary ethos of Christianity filtered into its theology and drove the praxis of many Christians so that we may legitimately speak of Christianity as a self-consciously missionary movement.

That is not to say that this ancient religious movement with its missionary thrust was not without complexity and context. It is worth pointing out that Paul was not the first or the only Christian missionary to Gentiles active in the first half of the first century, and one should resist reducing the early Christian mission to the Pauline mission.[8] It is apparent that other Jewish Hellenistic Christian missionaries were active concurrently and cooperatively with Paul, but often independently of Paul's own mission.[9] There was also a Jewish Christian proselytizing

---

[3] Martin Goodman, "Jewish Proselytizing in the First Century," in *The Jews among Pagans and Christians in the Roman Empire* (ed. J. Lieu, J. L. North and T. Rajak; London: Routledge, 1992), 53.

[4] Ramsay MacMullen, *Christianizing the Roman Empire (A.D. 100–400)* (New Haven, Conn.: Yale University Press, 1986), 105.

[5] Martin Kähler, *Schriften zur Christologie und Mission* (Munich: C. Kaiser, 1971 [1908]), 190.

[6] Michael F. Bird, "'A Light to the Nations' (Isa 49:6): Intertextuality and Mission Theology in the Early Church," *RTR* 65 (2006): 122–31.

[7] *Diogn.* 11.1–3; Aristides, *Apologia* 2 (Syriac); Justin, *1 Apol.* 1.39; Tertullian, *Apologeticus* 21; Hippolytus, *Dem. Chr.* 61; Origen, *Against Celsus* 3.28; *Asc. Isa.* 3:13–21.

[8] Michael F. Bird, "The Early Christians, the Historical Jesus, and the Salvation of the Gentiles," in *Jesus from Judaism to Christianity* (ed. Tom Holmén; WUNT; Tübingen: Mohr/Siebeck, forthcoming); Abraham J. Malherbe, *Social Aspects of Early Christianity* (2d ed.; Eugene, Ore.: Wipf & Stock, 2003), 65.

[9] Barnabas (Acts 15:35–39), Priscilla and Aquila (Acts 18:2–3, 18, 24–26; Rom 16:3; 1 Cor 16:19), Apollos (Acts 18:24–26; 19:1; 1 Cor 16:12); and the list of names in Rom 16 might also include Jewish Hellenistic Christian missionaries in Rome early on.

mission underway in the Diaspora that competed with Paul for converts (e.g., Phil 1:15–18) and at times formed a loose confederation of opposition against him. Furthermore the subject of who, when, how, where, and why missionizing took place by Christians is quite difficult to answer from our scant sources. Consequently the question of whether "evangelism" was carried out by specific individuals or corporately by these newly established congregations in large urban cities is a subject of ongoing dispute.[10]

What is certain, however, is that the rise of early Christian missions to Jews[11] and Gentiles did not occur in a vacuum and it was indebted to several important contexts, factors, and precedents in the Greco-Roman world of antiquity. One may look towards Jesus as providing part of the propulsion for this phenomenon since post-Easter missionary activity has pre-Easter antecedents in Jesus' own aims and activities.[12] One can also look towards the philosophical schools of antiquity where conversion and defection were already well known occurrences.[13] In addition,

---

[10] Cf. the debate in Michael Green, *Evangelism in the Early Church* (Grand Rapids, Mich.: Eerdmans, 1970), 274; I. Howard Marshall, "Who Were the Evangelists?" in *The Mission of the Early Church to Jews and Gentiles* (ed. Jostein Ådna and Hans Kvalbein; WUNT 127; Tübingen: Mohr/Siebeck, 2000), 251–63; Reidar Hvalvik, "In Word and Deed: The Expansion of the Church in the Pre-Constantinian Era," in *The Mission of the Early Church to Jews and Gentiles* (ed. Jostein Ådna and Hans Kvalbein; WUNT 127; Tübingen: Mohr/Siebeck, 2000), 265–87; John P. Dickson, *Mission-Commitment in Ancient Judaism and in the Pauline Communities: The Shape, Extent and Background of Early Christian Mission* (WUNT 2.159; Tübingen: Mohr/Siebeck, 2003); James Ware, *The Mission of the Church in Paul's Letter to the Philippians in the Context of Ancient Judaism* (Leiden: Brill, 2005); Robert L. Plummer, *Paul's Understanding of the Church's Mission: Did the Apostle Paul Expect the Early Christian Communities to Evangelize?* (PBM; Bletchley: Paternoster, 2006).

[11] I have persisted in using the term "Jews" to describe those who, regardless of their geographical location, identified with the rites, beliefs, and customs of Israel's Yahwistic religion. For more on the use and definition of this term, please see the Excursus at the end of the chapter.

[12] Cf. Dale C. Allison, *Resurrecting Jesus: The Earliest Christian Tradition and Its Interpreters* (London: T&T Clark/Continuum, 2005), 32.

[13] I would add that along with Greco-Roman philosophies and Judaism, one should consider the missionary efforts of Buddhism as a precursor to the early Christian mission. Clement of Alexandria (*Strom.* 1.15) wrote:

Thus philosophy, a thing of the highest utility, flourished in antiquity among the barbarians, shedding its light over the nations. And afterwards

there is also the activity of Jews among pagan polytheists that provides crucial insights into the challenges that Jews faced living either under pagan hegemony or else in pagan cities. For various Jewish groups this environment had several different results including acculturation to the values and norms of Greek and Roman culture (e.g., Philo), defection which can be either political (e.g., Josephus) or religious (Tiberius Alexander).[14] Of course, many Jews tried to creatively maintain their Jewish identity and carefully engage in the wider fabric of society without completely being overwhelmed by the pagan environment in which they lived. This last option, all things being equal, was probably the default position of most Jews living in the Diaspora. We also know that as a direct result of Jews interacting with pagans, some pagans converted to Judaism. However, we cannot always say where, why, how, and by what medium. We do not always know the motivation and circumstance of such conversions, but the fact remains that many pagans adopted Jewish customs, remained sympathetic to Jewish beliefs, and some even went as far as to renounce their ancestral customs and become proselytes to Judaism. Such acts prompted curiosity and outrage from the pagan side and a host of questions and issues on the Jewish side as to what to do with proselytes.

---

it came to Greece. First in its ranks were the prophets of the Egyptians; and the Chaldeans among the Assyrians; and the Druids among the Gauls; and the Sramanas among the Bactrians; and the philosophers of the Celts; and the Magi of the Persians, who foretold the Saviour's birth, and came into the land of Judaea guided by a star. The Indian gymnosophists are also in the number, and the other barbarian philosophers. And of these there are two classes, some of them called Sramanas, and others Brahmins.

Origen (*Comm. on Ezekiel* [cited from Donald A. Mackenzie, *Buddhism in Pre-Christian Britain* {Glasgow: Blackie and Son, 1928} 42]) stated that Buddhists coexisted with Druids in pre-Christian Britain and he sees them as paving the way for the arrival of Christianity: "[T]he island [Britain] has long been predisposed to it [Christianity] through the doctrines of the Druids and Buddhists, who had already inculcated the doctrine of the unity of the Godhead." Cyril of Jerusalem (*Catechetical Lecture* 6.23) said of one of his pupils, "But Terebinthus, his disciple in this wicked error, inherited his money and books and heresy, and came to Palestine, and becoming known and condemned in Judaea he resolved to pass into Persia: but lest he should be recognized there also by his name he changed it and called himself Buddha."

[14] On Jewish apostasy and defection, see Stephen G. Wilson, *Leaving the Fold: Apostates and Defectors in Antiquity* (Minneapolis: Fortress, 2004), 23–65.

What informed Jewish views, activities, attitudes, and relationships with non-Jews was the inherent tension in the Jewish belief matrix about Israel and the nations. Early Christian disputes about jurisdictions of mission, the rite of passage for non-Jews entering into salvation and the church, and the socioreligious praxis for adherents to the Jesus movement must be seen against the complex backdrop of two seemingly contradictory thoughts in Judaism. On the one hand, Jews understood their God to be the one God of creation, not simply a national deity, but a universal deity, who exercised sovereignty over the inhabited world and over all of the nations. At the same time, they believed that God had uniquely chosen them to be his people from all the nations of the world and this creator God was uniquely related to Jerusalem and the Israelite cultus. Either way, the story of Israel could not be told without reference to the nations.[15] Herein lies the tension: the universalism of monotheism and the particularity of Israel's election. But what was the natural corollary of this tension in terms of day-to-day living beside Gentiles or at least under their political hegemony? If God had made the world for Israel, then why were Gentiles oppressing Israel? For those Jews with eschatological hopes, would the Gentiles be converted religiously to Yahweh worship, be admitted as aliens to Israel, be subjugated to a Jewish ruler, or simply be destroyed at the final day? Thus, monotheism, election, and eschatology provided a smelting pot for developing perspectives on how to relate to Gentiles. It invited reflection and thought on the fate of the Gentile nations vis-à-vis Israel, and this process had already begun in the Hebrew Bible itself, as a contrast of Jonah, Ezra, Ezekiel, and Isaiah illustrates. That could promote a range of social arrangements and ideological convictions about how Israel should coexist within a majority Gentile world. In some cases, there was only room for rank hostility towards non-Jews and an extreme emphasis on separation, while other Jews (not necessarily "liberal") were more inclined to engage positively with their neighbors, defend themselves against philosophical critique precisely through a shared philosophical discourse, and commend the Jewish way of life to outsiders. It is the nature of that commendation, which seems to have occurred in some

---

[15] Cf. Michael F. Bird, *Jesus and the Origins of the Gentile Mission* (LNTS 331; London: T&T Clark/Continuum, 2006), 26–29, 125–30; Terence L. Donaldson, *Judaism and the Gentiles: Jewish Patterns of Universalism (to 135 CE)* (Waco, Tex.: Baylor University Press, 2007), 1–2.

Jewish communities as attested in extant literature, that is the matter for discussion here. The details of why, who, how, where, when, and what impact this had upon the rise of early Christian missions are up for debate as well.

In light of that, my aim is to explore the nature of Jewish proselytizing activity and to ask whether it is possible to speak of a Jewish mission among Gentiles and how did that set the stage for the origins and development of later Christian missionary activity to the Gentiles. In sum, I am inquiring whether the primitive Christian mission to the Gentiles represents a continuation and revision of ongoing Jewish proselytizing efforts or whether it constitutes a genuine *novum*. Can we speak of a concerted effort, at least by some individuals and communities, to convert Gentiles to Judaism? If they did, is early Christianity's mission to the Gentiles merely an extension of such an activity? Did early Christianity win over paganism by using Jewish weapons?[16] Or did early Christianity succeed because it presented a more inclusive brand of Judaism than its rabbinic counterpart?[17] These are the questions that require resolution.

Let me also add a caveat here. We must remain conscious of the biases and ideologies that many persons bring to a study of this nature. Those of the Christian tradition (to which I admit that I belong) may want to advocate the "evangelical" uniqueness of Christianity over Judaism in order to demonstrate the superiority of Christianity over Judaism or perhaps to highlight the triumphal succession of Christianity from Judaism. Alternatively, those of the Jewish tradition may wish to retort that in the "evangelical" stakes the Jews of antiquity were equally up to the task and Christianity's success depends almost entirely on standing on the shoulders of those early Jewish teachers who had made effective inroads into pagan territory. For others a mission to convert those of another religion is something of an embarrassment as it can conjure up thoughts of intolerance and self-assured superiority which are inimical to religious pluralism or for fostering good interfaith rela-

---

[16] Cf. S. Safrai, and M. Stern, eds., *The Jewish People in the First Century: Historical Geography, Political History, Social, Cultural and Religious Life and Institutions* (2 vols.; Amsterdam: Van Gorcum, 1974–1976), 2.1097–98.

[17] Cf. Gerd Theissen, *Sociology of Early Palestinian Christianity* (trans. John Bowden; Philadelphia: Fortress, 1978 [1977]), 55, 58, 114; John Dominic Crossan, *The Historical Jesus: The Life of a Mediterranean Jewish Peasant* (San Francisco: Harper Collins, 1991), 418–22.

tions.[18] For that reason some scholars may wish to downplay any "evangelical" zeal to convert others. I wish to say, quite emphatically, that I am not trying to argue for the superiority of Christianity over Judaism, nor am I trying to make the Judaism of the Diaspora a kind of a John the Baptist–like forerunner to the Christian heralding of the gospel. I suspect that this is probably the view of many today and is arguably indicative of Adolf von Harnack's popular thesis on the rise of the Christian religion.[19] Also, I do not operate with the assumption that a religion that tries to convert people is evidently superior to a religion that does not. The various expressions of Judaism and Christianity in antiquity both accepted converts and to varying degrees sought them out. What concerns me is the historical, sociological, and ideological factors that made this so and what relationship existed between the two religious movements in regards to their interactions with Gentiles. The question I am pursuing is whether or not conversions to Judaism stemmed from activities that we would call "missional" and if that carried over into Christianity.

Thus, with those caveats aside, I am pursuing the topic of precisely how "missionary" Judaism[20] was prior to the advent of the early Christian movement and what influences Jewish proselytizing activity had upon the early Christian mission. This issue is, as will be seen later, exceptionally problematic and highly disputed. A serious problem is the fragmentary nature of the evidence which derives from sources that mention the topic only in passing and with little comment. Moreover, there is the difficulty of definition and the danger of presupposing and then imposing later Christian categories of mission on to Second Temple Judaism. Steven Mason points out the ambiguity of the terms used: "Judaism (which kind? represented by whom?), missionary (does

---

[18] Rodney Stark (*Cities of God: The Real Story of How Christianity Became an Urban Movement and Conquered Rome* [San Francisco: Harper Collins, 2006], 5) levels this charge against S. J. D. Cohen and Martin Goodman in their respective studies on the grounds that, as secular Jews, they want to prohibit all religious proselytizing.

[19] See S. J. D. Cohen, "Adolf Harnack's 'The Mission and Expansion of Judaism': Christianity Succeeds Where Judaism Fails," in *The Future of Early Christianity: Essays in Honor of Helmut Koester* (ed. Birger A. Pearson; Minneapolis: Fortress, 1991), 163–69.

[20] For a discussion of the term "Judaism," please see the Excursus at the end of the chapter.

mission require a central body or character?), and religion (how was ancient religion distinct from ethnic culture? from philosophy?)."[21] This is a subject that will have to be explored later.

Previous scholarship on this topic is relatively easy to divide up into a taxonomy of views. Essentially there are those who maintain that Judaism was a missionary religion and those who argue that it was not.[22] Around the turn of the twentieth century, it was common to argue that Judaism was indeed a missionary religion. This view found notable expression in the works of Adolf von Harnack, Emil Schürer, Julius Wellhausen, and T. Mommsen.[23] The position was reinforced by several scholars well versed in Jewish sources, including G. F. Moore, B. J. Bamberger, W. G. Braude, and S. Sandmel.[24] This perspective was virtually canonized with Karl Kuhn's article in *Theological Dictionary of the New Testament* and A. D. Nock's early work on conversion in antiquity.[25]

---

[21] Steve Mason, "The *Contra Apionem* in Social and Literary Context: An Invitation to Judean Philosophy," in *Josephus' Contra Apionem: Studies in its Character and Context with a Latin Concordance to the Portions Missing in Greek* (eds. Louis H. Feldman and John R. Levison; Leiden: Brill 1996), 187.

[22] See a historical survey of the debate in Rainer Riesner, "A Pre-Christian Jewish Mission," in *The Mission of the Early Church to Jews and Gentiles* (eds. J. Ådna and H. Kvalbein; Tübingen: Mohr/Siebeck 2000), 211–20.

[23] Adolf von Harnack, *The Expansion of Christianity in the First Three Centuries* (trans. James Moffatt; 2 vols.; London/New York: Williams & Norgate/G. P. Putnam's Sons, 1904–1905), 1.1–18; Emil Schürer, *The History of the Jewish People in the Age of Jesus Christ* (edited and revised by G. Vermes, F. Millar and M. Black; 3 vols.; Edinburgh: T&T Clark, 1973–1987 [1886]), 3.1.150–76; T. Mommsen, *Römische Geschichte V: Die Provinzen von Caesar bis Diocletian* (5th ed.; Leipzig: Weidmann, 1904), 492; Julius Wellhausen, *Israelitische und Jüdische Geschichte* (2d ed.; Berlin: Walter de Gruyter, 1895), 152.

[24] G. F. Moore, *Judaism in the First Centuries of the Christian Era: The Age of the Tannaim* (3 vols.; Cambridge, Mass.: Harvard University Press, 1927–1930); B. J. Bamberger, *Proselytism in the Talmudic Period* (2d ed.; Cincinnati/New York: Hebrew Union College/Ktav, 1968); W. G. Braude, *Jewish Proselytizing in the First Five Centuries of the Common Era: The Age of the Tannaim and Amoraim* (Providence: Brown University Press, 1940); Samuel Sandmel, *The First Christian Century in Judaism and Christianity: Certainties and Uncertainties* (New York: Oxford University Press, 1969).

[25] K. G. Kuhn, "προσήλυτος," *TDNT* 6.727–44; A. D. Nock, *Conversion: The Old and the New in Religion from Alexander the Great to Augustine of Hippo* (Oxford: Oxford University Press, 1933), 61–62. See also works by Harry J. Leon, *The Jews of Ancient Rome* (rev. Carolyn A. Osiek; Peabody, Mass.: Hendrickson, 1995 [1960]), 250–56; Dieter Georgi, *The Opponents of*

Despite some occasional dissenters,[26] acceptance of widespread Jewish missionary activity remained the dominant viewpoint so that Joachim Jeremias could state: "Jesus thus came on the scene in the midst of what was par excellence the missionary age of Jewish history."[27] However, in the last twenty-five years this consensus has been contested and has arguably been overturned.[28] The primary contributors who have overturned the old consensus are Scot McKnight and Martin Goodman who, in works published between 1991 and 1994, have arguably convinced the majority of academics working in the field of Christian origins and Judaism of the Greco-Roman period that postexilic Judaism cannot be properly characterized as a missionary religion. McKnight concludes, "it is my contention, contrary to a great deal of Christian and Jewish scholarship today, that Judaism was not truly a 'missionary religion' except in the most general of definitions of missionary."[29] Goodman states: "The missionary here in search of converts to Judaism is a phenomenon first approved by Jews well after the start of the Christian mission, not before it."[30] While McKnight and Goodman disagree on certain interpretations of evidence such as the extent of Jewish proselytizing in Rome (McKnight is more willing than

---

Paul in Second Corinthians (ed. John Riches; Edinburgh: T&T Clark, 1986); Peder Borgen, "The Early Church and the Hellenistic Synagogue," *ST* 37 (1983): 55–78; idem, *Early Christianity and Hellenistic Judaism* (Edinburgh: T&T Clark, 1996).

[26] Cf., e.g., Johannes Munck, *Paul and the Salvation of Mankind* (trans. Frank Clarke; London: SCM, 1959), 264–71; L. Goppelt, "Der Missionar des Gesetzes. Zu Röm. 2,21f," in *Christologie und Ethik: Aufsätze zum Neuen Testament* (Göttingen: Vandenhoeck & Ruprecht, 1968), 138–39, n. 5.

[27] Joachim Jeremias, *Jesus' Promise to the Nations* (trans. S. H. Hooke; SBT 24; London: SCM, 1958), 12. See the similar statement made by Moore, *Judaism in the First Centuries*, 1.324: Judaism was "the first great missionary religion of the Mediterranean world." How far this view filtered into non-biblical scholarship is observed by how it is reflected in the conclusion of sociologists Patrick Nolan and Gerhard Lenski in their textbook on sociology (*Human Societies: An Introduction to Macrosociology* [9th ed.; Boulder, Colo.: Paradigm, 2004], 170–71) where they stated that: "For a time, Judaism was a missionary religion and won converts in many parts of the Roman world."

[28] Cf. Cohen, "Adolf Harnack," 166–67.

[29] Scot McKnight, *A Light among the Gentiles: Jewish Missionary Activity in the Second Temple Period* (Minneapolis: Fortress, 1991), 117.

[30] Martin Goodman, *Mission and Conversion: Proselytizing in the Religious History of the Roman Empire* (Oxford: Clarendon, 1994), 90.

Goodman to admit more rigorous conversion efforts on the part of Jews in Rome), they are nonetheless in general agreement about the lack of a universal proselytizing drive in Judaism as a whole in the Greco-Roman period prior to the rise of early Christianity. In the resurgence of interest in the subject, much of it stimulated by the monographs of McKnight and Goodman, there has been an abundance of publications on this topic that have endeavored to either defend[31] or reject[32] the notion of extensive pre-Christian Jewish missionary activities among Gentiles.

---

[31] Louis H. Feldman, "Was Judaism a Missionary Religion in Ancient Times?" in *Jewish Assimilation, Acculturation and Accommodation* (ed. M. Mor; Lanham, Md.: University Press of America, 1992), 24–37; idem, *Jew and Gentile in the Ancient World: Attitudes and Interactions from Alexander to Justinian* (Princeton: Princeton University Press, 1993); Peder Borgen, "Proselytes, Conquest, and Mission," in *Recruitment, Conquest, and Conflict* (eds. Peder Borgen, Vernon K. Robbins and David B. Gowler; Atlanta: Scholars, 1998), 57–77; Reidar Hvalvik, *The Struggle for Scripture and Covenant: The Purpose of the Epistle of Barnabas and Jewish-Christian Competition in the Second Century* (WUNT 2.92; Tübingen: Mohr/Siebeck, 1996), 268–318; David Rokéah, "Ancient Jewish Proselytism in Theory and Practice," *TZ* 52 (1996): 206–24; Clifford H. Bedell, "Mission in Intertestamental Judaism," in *Mission in the New Testament: An Evangelical Approach* (eds. William J. Larkin Jr. and Joel F. Williams; New York: Marynoll, 1998), 21–29; James Carleton Paget, "Jewish Proselytism at the Time of Christian Origins: Chimera or Reality?" *JSNT* 62 (1996): 65–103; John P. Dickson, *Mission-Commitment in Ancient Judaism and in the Pauline Communities*, 11–85; Rodney Stark, *The Rise of Christianity: A Sociologist Reconsiders History* (Princeton: Princeton University Press, 1996), 52; idem, *Cities of God*, 5–7.

[32] Martin Goodman, "Proselytising in Rabbinic Judaism," *JJS* 40 (1989): 175–85; idem, *Mission and Conversion*, 60–90 (= Martin Goodman, "Jewish Proselytizing in the First Century"); Scot McKnight, *A Light among the Gentiles*; E. Will and C. Orrieux, *"Prosélytisme Juif"? Histoire d'une erreur* (Paris: Les Belles Lettres, 1993); A. T. Kraabel, "The Roman Diaspora: Six Questionable Assumptions," *JJS* 33 (1982): 445–64; idem, "Immigrants, Exiles, Expatriates, and Missionaries," in *Religious Propaganda and Missionary Competition in the New Testament World: Essays Honoring Dieter Georgi* (eds. L. Bormann, K. Eel Tredici and A. Standhartinger; Leiden: Brill, 1994), 71–88; S. J. D. Cohen, "Crossing the Boundary and Becoming a Jew," *HTR* 82 (1989): 13–33; idem, "Was Judaism in Antiquity a Missionary Religion?" in *Jewish Assimilation, Acculturation and Accommodation* (ed. M. Mor; Lanham, Md.: University Press of America, 1992), 14–23; Paula Fredriksen, "Judaism, the Circumcision of Gentiles, and Apocalyptic Hope: Another Look at Galatians 1 and 2," *JTS* 42 (1991): 532–64; Lester L. Grabbe, *Judaism from Cyrus to Hadrian* (London: SCM, 1992), 534–35; I. Levinskaya, *The Book of Acts in Its First Century Set-*

While the McKnight-Goodman view is clearly in the ascendancy, it has not gone unchallenged. Louis Feldman has responded to the views of McKnight and Goodman and contested their findings at every level. Based on the cumulative evidence from demographic data and literary sources, he argues that the proof for Jewish missionary activity in antiquity is in fact considerable. His argument moves in several stages.[33] First, Feldman contends that proselytism is at least one possible explanation for the drastic increase in the size of the Jewish population during the Hellenistic period. Second, after a review of literary evidence from the *Epistle of Aristeas*, *Sibylline Oracles*, *Testament of Levi*, *Wisdom of Solomon*, *Testament of Joseph*, the writings of Philo and Josephus, and from rabbinic literature, he claims that many Jews were very active in seeking to win proselytes. Third, he detects in Roman resentment of conversion to Judaism an indication that Jews were pursuing missionary activities. Fourth, Feldman believes that the expulsions of Jews from Rome in 139 B.C.E. and 19 C.E. were due to aggressive missionary activities based on the various reports of the expulsions. Fifth, the tradition of Jewish propaganda-apologetic literature was an effective medium for proselytizing given high rates of literacy and the widespread availability of books among libraries and book collectors in the Roman era. The Septuagint, Apocrypha, and Pseudepigrapha, along with the writings of Philo and Josephus very probably contributed to conversions in his view, given that some Greco-Roman authors (e.g., Alexander Polyhistor) knew the history and customs of the Jewish people. Sixth, Feldman supposes that oral proclamation in the agora or synagogue would have been a further element that facilitated conversions to Judaism. Seventh, Feldman appeals to various instances of Gentile conversions in Palestine, Phoenicia, Syria, Mesopotamia, and in Rome which are taken as being indicative of widespread missionary practices.

---

ting 5: The Book of Acts in Its Diaspora Setting (Grand Rapids: Eerdmans, 1996); Riesner, "A Pre-Christian Jewish Mission," 211–50; Paul Barnett, "Jewish Mission in the Era of the New Testament and the Apostle Paul," in *The Gospel to the Nations* (eds. Peter Bolt and Mark Thompson; Festschrift Peter T. O'Brien; Sydney: Apollos, 2000), 263–83; Andreas J. Köstenberger and Peter T. O'Brien, *Salvation to the Ends of the Earth: A Biblical Theology of Mission* (NSBT 11; Downers Grove, Ill.: InterVarsity, 2001), 55–71; Eckhard J. Schnabel, *Urchristliche Mission* (Wuppertal: R. Brockhaus, 2002), 174 (= *The Early Christian Mission*, 1.172); Donaldson, *Judaism and the Gentiles*, 491–92, 512–13; James Patrick Ware, *The Mission of the Church in Paul's Letter to the Philippians*.
[33] Feldman, *Jew and Gentile in the Ancient World*, 288–341.

Some might suggest that Feldman's study is an effort to place ancient Judaism on a philosophical par with ancient Christianity in the missionizing stakes. This cannot be said to motivate John Dickson, however, an Australian Anglican who concludes his 2003 monograph by saying, "Sporadic evidence of intentional missionizing activity on the part of some Jews was indeed found in the literature, and attempts in recent scholarship to call into question the reliability of the relevant texts or to minimize their significance failed to convince."[34] Dickson rejects the category of a "missionary religion" and instead believes that it is profitable to investigate the activities of some Jews who consciously sought, in diverse ways, to draw Gentiles under the wings of the Shekinah. He finds at the level of both ideology (i.e., "mindset") and praxis (i.e., "missionizing") a framework conducive to missionary activity that was translated into action by some Jewish teachers who took it upon themselves to instruct Gentiles in the way of Torah which is an analogous role to that of "missionary."[35]

It is against this background of scholarship that I intend to argue that the Christian Gentile missions, however indebted to their Jewish background, are not directly attributable to an on-going Jewish mission. It is my assessment that Jewish proselytizing activity was spasmodic, and that there was no concerted effort to convert Gentiles to Judaism on a wide scale. The primitive Christian mission arose principally out of a concoction of eschatology and Christology and reading the Jewish Scriptures in light of new perspectives in these areas.[36] These perspectives were fleshed out by Jewish Christians and Hellenistic Christians in contexts where the initiation and integration of Christian Gentiles into Jesus-believing groups were a matter of contention. The first Christians inherited intra-Jewish disputes about group boundaries, the means of proselytism, the status of proselytes and Gentile adherents to Judaism, and the problem of how to participate in pagan society. They engaged these matters from the vantage point of a specific eschatological and christological orientation. Given this framework, my contribution will be a fresh engagement with this issue and will represent a revision and update of earlier studies by McKnight and Goodman. I also intend to interact with more recent volumes that touch on the topic, as well as to

---

[34] Dickson, *Mission-Commitment in Ancient Judaism*, 309.
[35] Dickson, *Mission-Commitment in Ancient Judaism*, 11–50 (esp. 49–50).
[36] See further Bird, "A Light to the Nations," 122–31.

put forward my own understanding of certain pieces of evidence from the Pauline corpus (such as that derived from Galatians and Colossians) and how they relate to these very issues. This study will proceed by defining "mission" and "conversion" as they relate to antiquity (chapter two). It will then assess the various strands of evidence for Jewish proselytizing activity including a study of sources relating to both Palestine (chapter three) and the Jewish Diaspora of the wider Mediterranean (chapter four). I will follow that up with a study of further information from the New Testament and early Christian literature about Jewish missionary activity and missionary competition between Jews and Christians (chapter five). The matters discussed will cover a wide array of evidence drawn from Jewish, Christian, and pagan sources in addition to brief surveys of epigraphic and archaeological evidence. I conclude that, although proselytes to Judaism were made in significant numbers, there is no evidence for concerted, organized, or regular efforts to recruit Gentiles to Judaism via the process of proselytizing. Conversion to Judaism was a difficult affair, and was usually done at the initiative of the Gentile.

EXCURSUS: "JEWS" AND "JUDAISM"

I prefer to use the term "Jew," but several scholars prefer a translation of "Judean" for Ἰουδαῖος (see, e.g., BDAG, 478–79). K. C. Hanson and Douglas Oakman (*Palestine in the Time of Jesus: Social Structures and Social Conflicts* [Minneapolis: Fortress, 1998], 176; see also Steve Mason, "Jews, Judaeans, Judaizing, Judaism: Problems of Categorization in Ancient History," *JSJ* 38 [2007]: 457–512) list five possible meanings for the word depending on its context: (1) the inhabitants of Judah, distinct from the surrounding regions of Galilee, Samaria, Peraea, Idumaea, etc.; (2) all the inhabitants of Palestine, including Galilee, Samaria, Perea, Idumea, etc.; (3) all those in the Mediterranean and near east with ethnic connections to Judea; (4) all those professing allegiance to the state religion of Judah (even if proselytes); and (5) the ruling elites of Judea (as opposed to peasant classes). I am open to using "Judean" as the default setting for Ἰουδαῖος, as this seems necessary in certain places (e.g., Josephus, *Ant.* 18.196 and *Ag. Ap.* 1.179).

But against a universal correlation of "Judean" with Ἰουδαῖος, there are several things worth noting. (1) Epigraphic evidence indicates that the word Ἰουδαῖος designates someone who is ethnically a "Jew," but it can also designate a proselyte who has become a Jew by religious and social integration. In this later case, the designation can obviously be broader than a territorial or ethnographic affiliation because of its chiefly religious character (see Ross S. Kraemer, "On the Meaning of the Term 'Jew' in Greco-Roman Inscriptions," *HTR* 82 (1989): 35–53; Margaret H. Williams, "The Meaning and Function of *Ioudaios* in Graeco-Roman Inscriptions," *ZPE* 116 [1997]: 249–62). (2) One must wonder if the titles "Israelite" (ישראלי), "Hebrew" (עברי), and "Judean" (יהודי) are virtually synonymous. The interchangeability of some of these terms is highlighted by Josephus who calls himself both a "Hebrew" (*J.W.* 1.3) and a "Jew/Judean" (*Ant.* 1.4). These two designations are linked together in *Ant.* 1.146 as well (Ἕβερος ἀφ' οὗ τοὺς Ἰουδαίους Ἑβραίους ἀρχῆθεν ἐκάλουν Ἕβερος ["Heber, from whom they originally called the Jews Hebrews"]). Paul does something similar by referring to himself as ἐκ γένους Ἰσραήλ and Ἑβραῖος ἐξ Ἑβραίων (Phil 3:5), a Ἰουδαῖος and ὑπὸ νόμον (1 Cor 9:20), and as Ἰσραηλίτης (Rom 9:4). Paul, like Josephus, seems to use these terms flexibly and interchangeably. So while "Israelite" and "Hebrew" probably possess similar geographic or ethnographic connotations to "Judean," they also have a socio-religious component that cannot be eliminated. (3) In 2 Macc 2:21, 8:1, 9:17, and 14:38, Ἰουδαῖος appears to designate a religious disposition and is not a reference to one's place of origin or ethnic association. In fact, in 2 Macc 6:6, one can cease being a Jew by not performing the religious practices of keeping the Sabbath and festivals. (4) When adherents to the Israelite religion lived outside of Palestine, if they gained Roman citizenship, and if their first language was Greek and not Aramaic, then their identity became more complex and a single and simple identification of them as "Judean" does not do justice to the full complexity of their identity. Some Ἰουδαῖοι might have described themselves more as "Hellenists" than "Judeans." (5) Josephus describes the Idumaeans, who were from outside Judea, as becoming "Jews" (Ἰουδαῖος) because they adopted "circumcision" and the "customs of the Jews" (*Ant.* 13.258) and not because of their ethnicity or territorial proximity to Judea (see also *J.W.* 4.278 where the Idumaeans are labeled as those from the "kindred nations" [συγγενεστάτοις ἔθνεσιν]). We must also wonder if the vituperative term "half-Jew" used of Herod the Great (*Ant.* 14.403) refers to his ethnic descent or lax adherence to the Jewish way of life. (6) I am also unaware of there being any evidence for a non-Jew living in Palestine who did not follow the Jewish way of life being called a "Judean." Such persons were usually called "Syrians" instead (see Herodotus, *Hist.* 2.104.3; Clement of Alexandria, *Strom.* 1.15.72.5; Porphyry, *Abst.*, 2.260). In sum, the terms "Hebrew," "Israelite," and "Judean/Jew" can designate a wide variety of territorial, ethnic, and religious referents depending on the context and we should avoid boxing these terms into one exclusive referent. Yet the religious nature of being a Ἰουδαῖος does appear to be the most acute and frequent connotation. See especially Daniel R. Schwartz, "'Judaean' or 'Jew'? How Should We Translate *Ioudaios* in Josephus?" in *Jewish Identity in the Greco-Roman World* (ed. J. Frey, D. R. Schwartz, S. Gripentrog; AJEC 71; Leiden: Brill, 2007), 3–27 and S. J. D. Cohen, *The Beginnings of Jewishness: Boundaries, Varieties, Uncertainties* (Berkeley: University of California Press, 1999), 92–93 (my thanks to Loren Rosson and Chris Weimer for pointing me to some of this material).

By referring to "Judaism," I do not refer to it as a monolithic entity but rather use it to denote a common ethnicity and custom that unified the γένος ("race") or ἔθνος ("nation") of Jewish people. The diversity of beliefs among the Jewish people in the Second Temple period has led some to speak of "Judaisms." For example, Robert A. Kraft and George W. E. Nickelsburg (*Early Judaism and Its Modern Interpreters* [Atlanta: Scholars, 1986], 2) write, "early Judaism appears to encompass almost unlimited diversity and variety—indeed, it might be more appropriate to speak of early Judaisms." Similar is J. Andrew Overman (*Church and Community in Crisis: The Gospel according to Matthew* [Valley Forge, Penn.: TPI, 1996], 9): "So varied was Jewish society in the land of Israel in this period, and so varied were the Jewish groups, that scholars no longer speak of Judaism in the singular when discussing this formative and fertile period in Jewish history. Instead, we speak about Judaisms. In this time and place, there existed a number of competing, even rival Judaisms." However, this is not altogether helpful as it virtually denies any unifying traits within the Jewish national religion. I retain "Judaism" as a descriptive term because: (1) several scholars, while fully recognizing the varieties of Jewish belief, employ it as general term (e.g., E. P. Sanders, *Jewish Law from Jesus to the Mishnah: Five Studies* [London: SCM 1990], 255–56; Richard Bauckham, "The Parting of the Ways: What Happened and Why," *ST* 47 [1993]: 137–38; Martin Goodman, *Mission and Conversion: Proselytizing in the Religious History of the Roman Empire* [Oxford: Clarendon, 1994], 39; John M. G. Barclay, *Jews in the*

Mediterranean Diaspora from Alexander to Trajan (323 BCE–117 CE)
[Edinburgh: T&T Clark, 1996], 401); (2) "Judaism" (Ἰουδαϊσμός)
is a term that was used by Jews themselves in the Second Temple period and we can safely assume that these writers were well aware of
the diversity and complexity of their own religious beliefs, practices,
and nationality (2 Macc 2:21; 8:1; 14:38; 4 Macc 4:26; Gal 1:13–14);
(3) according to Jossa (Giorgio Jossa, *Jews or Christians?* [trans. Molly
Rogers; WUNT 202; Tübingen: Mohr/Siebeck, 2006], 23), the designation "Judaisms" results from seeing Judaism in primary intellectual
rather than social categories. Martin Hengel (*Judaism and Hellenism*
[2 vols.; trans. John Bowden; London: SCM, 1974], 1.1–2) defines
Ἰουδαϊσμός as follows: "The word means both political and genetic
association with the Jewish nation and exclusive belief in the one God
of Israel, together with observance of the Torah given by him." See for
futher discussion, Cohen, *The Beginnings of Jewishness*, 7–8, 105–6.

CHAPTER TWO

DEFINING "MISSION" AND "CONVERSION" IN THE ANCIENT WORLD

Any assessment regarding the extent and character of Jewish and Christian missionary activity in Second Temple Judaism depends entirely on how one defines "mission" and "conversion."[1] These are heavily freighted terms loaded with modern theological and cultural baggage. Furthermore, and as we will see, there are different definitions of mission and various models of conversion that have been proposed by historians and sociologists. To speak of a religious mission immediately conjures up questions about *what* the purpose of the mission is—to inform people, to change peoples' morals, to enlarge the membership of a religious association—*who* the people are, *why* the mission is needed, and by *what* means the mission will be pursued. To speak of religious conversion also elicits questions about rites of passages, medium and message, public recognition, psychological disposition, and varieties of conversion (partial, full, intellectual, cultural, social, etc.). Hence, it is necessary to define these terms in order to develop a religious pattern against which one can weigh and assess the evidence for purported Jewish missionary activity. The substance of this chapter is to engage the

---

[1] See definitions and comments offered by Moore, *Judaism in the First Centuries*, 1.324; McKnight, *A Light among the Gentiles*, 4–7; Paul R. Trebilco, *Jewish Communities in Asia Minor* (Cambridge: Cambridge University Press, 1991), 164–66; Goodman, *Mission and Conversion*, 38–59; Eckhard Schnabel, "Jesus and the Beginnings of the Mission to the Gentiles," in *Jesus of Nazareth, Lord and Christ* (eds. Joel B. Green and Max Turner; Grand Rapids, Mich.: Eerdmans, 1994), 47–49; idem, *Early Christian Mission*, 1.10–12; Barclay, *Jews in the Mediterranean Diaspora*, 408, n. 11; Paget, "Jewish Proselytism," 69–70, 76–79; Hvalvik, *Struggle for Scripture and Covenant*, 267–73; Barnett, "Jewish Mission," 263–64; Riesner, "A Pre-Christian Jewish Mission," 221–23; Dickson, *Mission-Commitment in Ancient Judaism*, 7–10.

historical, theological, religious, and sociological issues related to defining "mission" and "conversion" as the groundwork for what follows.

MISSION AND CONVERSION: SOCIOLOGICAL AND IDEOLOGICAL ELEMENTS

A distinctive element of all the major missionary religions (Christianity, Judaism, and Islam) is that they all hold to some great "unveiling" of ultimate truth that is said to be of universal importance for the human race. Judaism claims that Yahweh was at work in creating the nation of Israel and he gave the Torah as the charter for God's covenant people. Christianity of course refers to the incarnation of Jesus Christ and pouring out of the Holy Spirit as the central nodes of history and the means of reconciliation between human beings and the triune God. In Islam there is the claim that Allah's final and definitive revelation has been given to Mohammed in the form the Qu'ran. There are of course different ways of trying to convert people to another religion such as through oral proclamation, military conquest, the written medium, cultural inducements, or via social integration into a new group. As will be seen, all of these missionary methods (if we can call them that) can be related to events and episodes in ancient Judaism. A central matter, though, is how the phenomenon of conversions relates to the ethos and identity of those who practiced the Jewish religion. In the ancient world various Gentiles became sympathizers to Judaism, and some even went as far as becoming proselytes. But does that alone justify a description of Second Temple Judaism as a "missionary religion"? According to Scot McKnight, a missionary religion is one that includes an element of religious self-definition whereby members believe that it is their purpose to undertake concerted efforts to persuade non-adherents to convert to their beliefs and adopt their patterns of behavior.[2] That opens up the question as to which beliefs and what patterns of behavior matter the most and how does one go about persuading non-adherents to join them.

The Problem with Definitions

Arguments about definitions could go on *ad nauseum* and yet they are also unavoidable. This book hasn't the space for a full engagement

---

[2] McKnight, *A Light among the Gentiles*, 4–5.

with the secondary literature on conversion and mission. Instead, I'll content myself with noting some of its more significant elements before offering my own definitions. To begin with, Martin Goodman distinguishes four different types of "mission" activity: information, education, apologetic, and proselytization. He describes the latter category in the following way:

> Those who approved of proselytizing mission believed that, as members of a defined group, they should approve of those within their number who might choose to encourage outsiders not only to change their way of life but also to be incorporated within their group.[3]

In contrast, some argue for less activist definitions of mission. For instance, Clifford Bedell argues that Jewish synagogues emitted an attractive presence to Gentiles, a kind of "sacred magnetism," and that is itself a legitimate form of missionary activity.[4] J. C. Paget criticizes McKnight and Goodman on the grounds that mission can be conceived of in terms other than centrifugal and aggressive activity. It may manifest itself in openness to outsiders or even in a desire to publicize its beliefs.[5] However, Paget's own definition of a missionary religion as "one which, in a variety of ways, makes it clear that conversion to that religion is a good thing"[6] is so broad as to be meaningless. Was there in the first century a religion where the members thought that conversion to its beliefs and teachings was a bad thing? I say that, doubtlessly, members of the mystery cults such as Mithraism and Isis would not have thought so, but we do not find in them recruiting practices that are analogous to Jewish or Christian proselytism.[7] Thus, Paget loads the dice of definition just as much as he accuses McKnight and Goodman of doing.

---

[3] Goodman, *Mission and Conversion*, 4.

[4] Bedell, "Mission in Intertestamental Judaism," 25.

[5] Paget, "Jewish Proselytism," 76–77.

[6] Paget, "Jewish Proselytism," 77.

[7] Cf. Nock, *Conversion*, 122–37; David E. Aune, "Expansion and Recruitment among Hellenistic Religions: The Case of Mithraism," in *Recruitment, Conquest, and Conflict* (eds. Peder Borgen, Vernon K. Robbins, and David B. Gowler; Atlanta: Scholars, 1998), 39–56; Goodman, *Mission and Conversion*, 20–37; Stark, *Cities of God*, 187–88. On the spread of Mithraism, Luther H. Martin writes ("Performativity, Narrativity, and Cognition: 'Demythologizing' the Roman Cult of Mithras," in *Rhetoric and Reality in Early Christianities* [ed. Willi Braun; Toronto: Wilfrid Laurier University Press, 2005], 196): "Although Mithraism was characterized by a widespread

In actuality, conceptions of mission are likely to prove fruitless unless they are anchored in an adequate definition of conversion. This deficiency is evident in John Dickson's work on mission-commitment in Judaism where he defines mission as *"the range of activities by which members of a religious community desirous of the conversion of outsiders seek to promote their religion to non-adherents."* Dickson, though cautious of maximalist and minimalist approaches, regards mission as a continuum so that a variety of activities geared towards Gentiles can still be accommodated under the umbrella of "mission." This is based upon his suggestion that certain practices (e.g., apologetic literature, ethical apologetic) though not *"directly intended"* to cause conversion were still *"oriented"* towards conversion. The underlying assumption is that almost anything that promotes the beliefs and reputation of the group becomes in some sense missional. Notwithstanding the validity of his assumption that practices such as apologetic writings necessarily contributed to conversions, his definition of conversion as *"a new socio-religious allegiance"* fails to discriminate between adherence and incorporation or between the varying levels of commitment that a target audience may respond with.[8] On such a definition there is no distinction between activities designed to induce political sympathy, evoke philosophical respect, propagate moral superiority, or even urge God-fearers to go the final yard and become proselytes. I would say that promotion and proselytism, though closely linked together, are not necessarily on the same trajectory or seeking the same outcomes. Rainer Riesner is probably correct when he asserts that a definition of mission should include both "intentionality and activity."[9] Dickson focuses far too much on intention

---

dissemination throughout the Roman Empire, its spread can be attributed to socio-political factors other than the 'religious' character of the Mithraic groups themselves. Even as the mobility of Egyptian merchants and immigrants facilitated the spread of the Isis cult, so the mobile character of the Roman military and of its civil servants, both of which dominated the demography of Mithraic membership, provides the 'strings of contagion' [citing L. Michael White] for the spread of Mithraism, a spread facilitated more by militarily and politically motivated 'acts of patronage and benefaction than on patterns of conversion of recruitment' [citing L. Michael White] . . . For Mithraism, in other words, as for Greco-Roman religions in general, there was no roving apostles or missionaries who represented and transmitted an approved or orthodox set of beliefs."

[8] Dickson, *Mission-Commitment in Ancient Judaism*, 8–10 (italics original).
[9] Riesner, "A Pre-Christian Jewish Mission," 223.

in his definition of a missionary religion without detailing exactly what that intention might be, and whether the end product is a circumcised proselyte or a pagan philosopher with a greater appreciation for Judaism. To proceed in a logical fashion, then, a more precise definition of mission will follow on from a suitable definition of conversion.

Defining Conversion in Judaism

Broadly put, religious conversion means transferring one's religious allegiance from one religion to another. In the ancient world conversion, though relatively infrequent, was not an unknown occurrence. In the philosophical sects, oriental cults, Judaism, and in Christianity conversions did take place.[10] A. D. Nock's idea of conversion as "a reorientation of the soul" and turning from "an earlier form of piety to another" fails to grasp the sociological dimension of conversion to Judaism.[11] Importantly, conversion to Judaism was more than an alteration of piety but involved joining a new ἔθνος akin to socialization or nationalization.[12] By converting to the Jewish religion one was also becoming a subject of the Judean state. It meant, in most cases, joining a group of people whose way of life was governed by the law of Moses and were distinguished from Greeks and Barbarians by that very fact. This transference required not merely adding Jewish beliefs to one's current religious framework, but jettisoning all, or at least a hefty part, of one's previous religious beliefs and redefining one's social identity around a particular social network with its various religious symbols, language, boundaries, and praxis. Conversion to Judaism (much like

---

[10] The classic study is Nock, *Conversion*.

[11] Nock, *Conversion*, 7.

[12] Cf. Moore, *Judaism in the First Centuries*, 1.327; G. B. Caird, *The Apostolic Age* (London: Duckworth, 1955), 84; Jeremias, *Jesus' Promise to the Nations*, 17; Ferdinand Hahn, *Mission in the New Testament* (trans. Frank Clarke; London: SCM, 1965 [1963]), 24; S. J. D. Cohen, "Respect for Judaism by Gentiles according to Josephus," *HTR* 80 (1987): 410–12; Alan F. Segal, "The Cost of Proselytism and Conversion," in *SBL 1988 Seminar Papers* (ed. D. Hull; Atlanta: Scholars Press, 1988), 346, 348; McKnight, *A Light among the Gentiles*, 7, 47; J. J. Scott, *Customs and Controversies: Intertestamental Jewish Backgrounds of the New Testament* (Grand Rapids, Mich.: Baker, 1995), 342; Barclay, *Jews in the Mediterranean Diaspora*, 408–9; Köstenberger and O'Brien, *Salvation to the Ends of the Earth*, 67.

Christianity) required displacing other forms of piety and religious devotion in favor of a new disposition. That is not to say that conversion
was always instantaneous or complete; converts rarely make a clean and
decisive break with their religious past, and many social arrangements
like family or business could obviously remain intact depending on the
circumstance. But conversion to Judaism by its very nature tended towards exclusion in the religious and social senses. Whereas pagans could
add the devotion of Isis or Dionysius to their web of preexisting religious activities, this was theoretically impossible for a Jewish convert, as
Judaism was an exclusively monotheistic faith.[13] Conversion to Judaism
was never purely a matter of a change in one's inward disposition, but
it required a social dislocation in leaving one community and joining
another. For this reason, we should study conversion and defection as
part of a sociological phenomenon in antiquity. It is crucial then to
underscore the sociological nature of religious conversion in relation to
pagans converting to Judaism.[14] Persons do not necessarily convert because they have found the doctrine or philosophy of a certain religion to
be intellectually superior.[15] There are an abundance of other factors in-

---

[13] That is not to say that the ideal always matched the reality as acculturation, assimilation, and even syncretism were not unknown among Jews
in antiquity. Furthermore, it was certainly possible to reinterpret Judaism to
make it far more permeable and malleable to the culture of the Hellenistic
polis and pantheon.

[14] Cf. L. R. Rambo, *Understanding Religious Conversion* (New Haven,
Conn.: Yale University Press, 1993); Zeba A. Crook, *Reconceptualising Conversion: Patronage, Loyalty, and Conversion in the Religions of the Ancient Medi-
terranean* (Berlin: Walter de Gruyter, 2004); Thomas M. Finn, *From Death to
Rebirth: Ritual and Conversion in Antiquity* (New York: Paulist, 1997); Rod-
ney Stark and Roger Finke, *Acts of Faith: Explaining the Human Side of Reli-
gion* (Berkeley: University of California Press, 2000); James G. Crossley, *Why
Christianity Happened: A Sociohistorical Account of Christian Origins (26–50
CE)* (Louisville: Westminster John Knox, 2006), 142–72; N. H. Taylor, "The
Social Nature of Conversion in the Early Christian World," in *Modelling Early
Christianity: Social Scientific Studies of the New Testament in Its Context* (ed.
Phil F. Esler; London: Routledge, 1995), 128–36.

[15] Josephus in *Life* presents himself as being on a spiritual pilgrimage
within Judaism, and he tried various sects and philosophies and evaluated
their doctrines until he settled on Pharisaism, which he regarded as the most
superior. It is fair to say that the genuineness of Josephus's Pharisaism is open
to question. He may have identified himself as a Pharisee since they were the
ruling party after 70 C.E. and then projected his allegiance to his youth. Justin

cluding religious experience, economic state, social status, and networks of relationships that facilitate conversions from one religion to another. We should not discount the importance of intellectual persuasion in the conversion process, but it is clearly subordinated to contact with a new religious movement through networks and relationships.[16] Determinative for conversion is social interaction where potential converts begin to share a group's identity and values, and only then are they formally initiated into the group. It is the convert's relationship with the group or with one of the group's members that affects the convert's eventual decision to join the group and to adhere to its beliefs and practices. In many cases, belonging precedes believing. In the words of Rodney Stark, "conversion is primarily about bringing one's religious behavior into alignment with that of one's friends and relatives, not about encountering attractive doctrines" and "conversion to new, deviant religious groups occurs when, other things being equal, people have or develop stronger attachments to members of the group than they have to non-members."[17] I contend that without these sociological models the conversion of entire "households" or large portions of synagogues to Christianity become impossible to understand.[18]

Martyr also utilizes the same form of the spiritual quest in evaluating various philosophies until he came to Christianity. We should not doubt the intellectual curiosity of educated and literate religious persons of antiquity, but the narration of the quest for religious truth was more of a literary genre than a historical occurrence. The real significance of doctrine according to Rodney Stark (*Cities of God*, 113–14) is that it determines if the term conversion even applies to the shift in the religious orientation of the convert.

[16] As anecdotal evidence for intellectual conversion, a friend of mine once told me the story of an atheist he knew who was converted to Christianity by reading from cover to cover Louis Berkhof's textbook on Systematic Theology. As an undergraduate I recollect that reading Berkhof's book was like swimming through tar, and yet it convinced one particular atheist of the coherence and comprehensiveness of a Christian worldview.

[17] Stark, *Cities of God*, 11; idem, *Rise of Christianity*, 18.

[18] Wayne A. Meeks (*The First Urban Christians: The Social World of the Apostle Paul* [New Haven, Conn.: Yale University Press, 1983], 77) writes: "If the existing household was the basic cell of the mission, then it follows from that motivational bases for becoming part of the *ekklēsia* would likely vary from one member to another. If a household became Christian more or less en bloc, not everyone who went along with the new practices would do so with the same understanding or inner participation. Social solidarity might be more important in persuading some members to be baptized than would their

As important as the social dimension of conversion is, however, we cannot escape its ideological and behavioral aspects. Peder Borgen delves into Philo and Paul to formulate a paradigm of conversion comprising three elements: religious, ethical, and social.[19] The primary advantage of this paradigm is that it stems from two first-century Jews who were familiar with proselytizing and its surrounding controversies, as opposed to purely sociological models that are either anachronistic or else culturally estranged from Second Temple Judaism and Greco-Roman culture.[20] I think this model is worth following up although it needs some social nuancing. Thus, I define conversion to Judaism as *aligning one's beliefs and practices with the religious framework and social fabric of a Jewish community, which involves (1) an ideological re-orientation of existing beliefs and/or the adoption of new beliefs, (2) an ethical transformation of commitment and values, in accordance with perceived norms, resulting in altered behavior, and (3) identification with and incorporation into the Jewish ethnē.* In other words, conversion to Judaism involves monotheism, Torah, and synagogue.

Conversion and Circumcision

Regarding the full integration of non-Jews into the Jewish community, how does one formally shift from adherent (understood as one who undertakes partial adoption of beliefs and practices) to convert (understood as one who becomes a bona fide member who transfers in)? What signifies that transference has taken place, and what is the authenticating signature of this moment? Specifically, we have to ask

---

understanding or convictions about specific beliefs. Differential qualities and degrees of engagement with the group would not be surprising."

[19] Borgen, "The Early Church and the Hellenistic Synagogue," 61; idem, *Early Christianity and Hellenistic Judaism*, 56–59; idem, "Proselytes, Conquest, and Mission," 63–64, 69–70; and see similarly Cohen, "Crossing the Boundary and Becoming a Jew," 26, 31; Finn, *Death to Rebirth*, 95–96; Donaldson, *Judaism and the Gentiles*, 488.

[20] A significant problem with sociological models of conversion (esp. post L. R. Rambo) is that they often assume a universal and transferable phenomenon of conversionism. However, the contours of conversion are more likely to be relative and specific to the unique environment of the culture and group in question. What is true and paradigmatic for conversion to Judaism in Alexandria in the first century may not necessarily apply to conversions to Judaism in New York in the 1970s.

whether or not circumcision was a prerequisite for entry into the commonwealth of Israel; or as Borgen contends, was it sometimes perceived as a subsequent duty on admission?[21] Neil McEleney advocated that "there is some small evidence that the precept of circumcision was not always insisted upon if formerly Gentile adherents otherwise practiced the Law fully."[22] But does the evidence support this?[23]

Circumcision was the most essential marker of (male) Jewish identity since it connected persons with Israel's covenant history. Circumcision was linked to God's covenant with Israel in which circumcision defined one's identity and status within the Mosaic covenant.[24] Going back further, in Gen 17:9–14 circumcision is the sign of the covenant between Abraham and God. Furthermore, in Gen 17:14 anyone who is uncircumcised has broken the covenant and must be cut off. The link of uncircumcision with apostasy appears again in 1 Maccabees where circumcision became a symbol of national resistance to Hellenism.[25] According to rabbinic tradition circumcision was necessary for entering the covenant.[26] In reverse terms, the Jew who refused to circumcise his children or even attempted to reverse the procedure was regarded as an apostate.[27]

---

[21] Borgen, "The Early Church and the Hellenistic Synagogue," 67; cf. John J. Collins, "A Symbol of Otherness: Circumcision and Salvation in the First Century," in *"To See Ourselves as Others See Us": Christians, Jews, Others in Late Antiquity* (eds. J. Neusner and E. S. Frerichs; Chico, Calif.: Scholars Press, 1985), 174, 178–79.

[22] N. J. McEleney, "Conversion, Circumcision and the Law," *NTS* 20 (1974): 328.

[23] Note that Paul states in Galatians: "I testify to every man who lets himself be circumcised that he is obliged to obey the entire law" (Gal 5:3). Similar are the Christian Pharisees reported in Acts, "It is necessary for them to be circumcised and ordered to keep the law of Moses" (Acts 15:5). The upshot of this is that obedience to the law followed on from circumcision and not vice-versa. Neither Paul nor Luke knew of uncircumcised proselytes who kept the entire law save its regulations about being circumcised. Note also that Justin represents the Jewish view as being basically the same (*Dial. Tryph.* 8). See further Schürer, *History of the Jewish People in the Age of Jesus Christ*, 3.1.164, 175.

[24] Cf. Exod 4:24–26; Lev 12:3; Josh 5:2–9; Sir 44:20; *Jub.* 15:28; Philo, *Quaest. in Gen.* 3.51–52; *m. Ned.* 3.11; Acts 7:8.

[25] 1 Macc 1:48, 60; 2 Macc 6:10; cf. Josephus, *Ag. Ap.* 1.171; *Ant.* 1.192–193, 214.

[26] *b. Ker.* 9a.

[27] 1 Macc 1:14–16; Josephus, *Ant.* 12.241; and Seutonius, *Domitian,* 12.2 (Stern, *GLAJJ* 2: §320). As Blaschke (*Beschneidung*, 360) points out, circumcision was a key part of being Jewish in post-Maccabean times.

Alternatively, it should be remembered that if the covenantal dimension of circumcision is abandoned, then its importance is clearly undermined and the necessity of the practice for conversion to Judaism is diminished. This is observable in Philo, whose tendency to allegorize the law often drove him to minimize any ethnocentric implications of the law.[28] In *Quaest. in Ex.* 2.2, Philo asserts that what constitutes a proselyte is not circumcision, but submission to God "because the proselyte is one who circumcises not his uncircumcision but his desires and sensual pleasures and the other passions of the soul (ὅτι προσήλυτός ἐστιν, οὐχ ὁ περιτμηθεὶς τὴν ἀκροβυστίαν ἀλλ᾽ ὁ τὰς ἡδονὰς καὶ τὰς ἐπιθυμίας καὶ τὰ ἄλλα πάθη τῆς ψυχῆς). For in Egypt the Hebrew nation was not circumcised."[29] John J. Collins believes that Philo's remark here shows how much room there was for debate about who actually was a proselyte. Collins infers from this text from Philo: "The implication of this passage is surely that circumcision is not an essential prerequisite for membership of the Hebrew nation"[30] which presents us with two tiers of proselytes: circumcised and uncircumcised. Others advocate that it is not conversion that is being referred to by Philo at all, but only the phenomenon of being a partial adherent or philosophical sympathizer to Judaism. As such, Louis Feldman believes that Philo is talking here only of the "sympathizer" and Shaye Cohen identifies a type of "monotheistic proselyte" who assents to monotheism.[31] Yet placing *Quaest. in Ex.* 2.2 against the phenomenon of adherence does not match the language that Philo uses because "proselyte" and "circumcised" are value-laden terms that are applied only to an elite few. According to John Nolland, Philo's statement presupposes the necessity and normality of circumcision for proselytes. Philo's remark is hardly dispensing with the practice of circumcision, rather Philo identifies true proselytes as a subgroup of circumcised proselytes. Philo believes that a deeper reality resides in the circumcision of the mind than in

---

[28] Cf. Barclay, *Jews in the Mediterranean Diaspora*, 170–76.

[29] The text of Philo here cited is based on the Greek rather than the Armenian version where the word order differs slightly.

[30] Collins, "A Symbol of Otherness," 173; cf. McEleney, "Conversion, Circumcision and the Law," 329; Feldman, *Jew and Gentile in the Ancient World*, 299.

[31] Feldman, *Jew and Gentile in the Ancient World*, 348; Cohen, *The Beginnings of Jewishness*, 151.

mere physical circumcision.[32] Similar is Andreas Blaschke, "The necessity of the physical circumcision of proselytes is presupposed here and . . . not disputed."[33] However, the reason given by Philo—"For in Egypt the Hebrew nation was not circumcised"—shows that he did not regard physical circumcision as the most important element of being an incomer or proselyte. Israel was "Israel" before the Exodus and prior to the giving of the law with its regulations about circumcision. Intellectual transformation ("circumcision of your desires") seems to be at least as important as physical circumcision, and perhaps even more so. So physical circumcision is comparatively devalued rather than denied as normative for conversion by Philo. This is attributable to the philosophical rather than covenantal character of Philo's thought.[34] Thus, contra Collins, if this is an adverse statement against the necessity of circumcision for proselytes it is quite subdued and does not intimate the redundancy of the ritual.[35]

On initiation into Judaism more generally, Philo is incredibly circumspect when it comes to the role of circumcision. He speaks of the necessity of being initiated into the law without stipulating how, thus leaving open the possibility that circumcision might not be required for full conversion.[36] Philo makes reference to true or fuller proselytes, as does Josephus, implying that there was an inferior level of attachment to Judaism, but what marked the inferiority is not stated.[37] Philo and Josephus both see some didactic elements of the law being reserved exclusively for the initiated, but that can obviously accommodate a wide

---

[32] John Nolland, "Uncircumcised Proselytes?" *JSJ* 12 (1981): 174–79; cf. Donaldson, *Judaism and the Gentiles*, 268–71.

[33] Andreas Blaschke, *Beschneidung: Zeugnisse der Bible und verwandter Text* (TANZ 28; Tübingen/Basel: Francke, 1998), 219 ["Die Notwendigkeit der physischen Beschneidung von Proselyten wird dabei vorausgesetzt und . . . nicht bestritten"].

[34] Cf. Barclay on Philo (*Jews in the Mediterranean Diaspora*, 170): "This move from history to philosophy represents a shift from the particular to the universal; to dehistoricize is to deJudaize."

[35] Ellen Birnbaum (*The Place of Judaism in Philo's Thought: Israel, Jews, and Proselytes* [Providence: Brown University Press, 1996] 200) notes: "His comments, however, do not address the practical issue of whether or not circumcision is required of proselytes, and it is difficult to know how to apply his remarks to real proselytes."

[36] Philo, *Virt.* 178.

[37] Philo, *Vit. Mos.* 1.147; Josephus, *Ant.* 20.38–42.

sway of initiation processes.[38] When Philo does speak of those who are "incomers" (οἱ ἐπηλύται)[39] he emphasizes their moral change and denunciation of idolatry, we find nothing that is particular to Jewish identity and no initiation rites.[40] To be sure, Philo emphasizes the importance of rejecting idols and upholding the law, but he never explicitly mentions circumcision as being necessary to enter Israel; though neither does he deny it. In a nutshell, Philo does not adjudicate on the necessity of circumcision for proselytes. He only declares the inferiority of circumcision to genuine worship of God.

There are other instances, however, where Philo implies the legitimacy and necessity of circumcision as a key part of Jewish identity. Philo is quite emphatic that those who reduce circumcision to an allegory have gone too far and though it connotes a wider philosophical reality it cannot be easily laid aside.[41] Elsewhere Philo defends the literal practice of circumcision for hygienic, procreative, and spiritual reasons[42] motivated no doubt by pagan revulsion and mockery against the practice.[43] In *Spec. Leg.* 4.176–178 he refers to the converts who have turned away from their own families, left their idolatrous practices, and become pilgrims of the truth and procurers of a better home in Judaism. The content is clearly concerned with social transference from one community to another, and there is no reference to Jewish markers of circumcision, food laws, and Sabbath keeping that are necessarily taken on board by proselytes. Yet we should keep in mind the very next paragraph where

---

[38] Philo, *Cher.* 42, 48–49; *Sacr.* 60; Josephus, *Ag. Ap.* 2.209–210.

[39] Cf. L&S 247.

[40] Philo, *Virt.* 182; 219.

[41] Philo, *Migr. Abr.* 89–94; cf. *Quaest. in Gen.* 3.48 (and 52) where circumcision is a "symbol, as if to show that it is proper to cut off superfluous and excessive desire by exercising continence and endurance in matters of the Law."

[42] Philo, *Spec. Leg.* 1.4–7; *Quaest. in Gen.* 3.48.

[43] Philo, *Spec. Leg.* 1.1–3 ("The ordinance of circumcision of the genitals is mocked, though it is an act which is practiced to no slight degree among other nations also"); Tacitus, *Hist.* 5.5.2 ("the other customs of the Jews are base and abominable . . . they adopted circumcision to distinguish themselves from other peoples by this difference"); Martial, *Epigr.* 7.30 ("nor do you shun the lecheries of circumcised Jews"); 7.82 ("the sheath unluckily fell off: lo, he was circumcised!"); ("Your overflowing malice, and your detraction everywhere of my books, I pardon, circumcised poet, you are wise!") 11.94 (Stern, *GLAJJ* 1: §§240, 243; 245); see also Juvenal, *Sat.* 14.99 (Stern, *GLAJJ* 2: §301); Petronius, *Satirae* 68.4–8; 102.14; frg. 37 (Stern, *GLAJJ* 1: §§193, 194, 195); Suetonius, *Domitian*, 12.2 (Stern, *GLAJJ* 2: §320).

he refers to the "peculiarity of its laws and customs" of the nation of the Jews and how these laws are "of necessity strict and rigorous, as they are intended to train them to the greatest height of virtue."[44] It would be difficult to imagine Gentile converts finding a comfortable home in the Jewish community without living under the same peculiar and rigorous laws that defined the Jewish people. On top of that, in *Quaest. in Gen.* 3.62 we read: "Why does Abraham circumcise those of foreign birth? The wise man is helpful and at the same time philanthropic. He saves and calls to himself not only his kinsmen and those of like opinions but also those of foreign birth." Although Philo starts off with the topic of circumcision in relation to the purchase of slaves (from Gen 17:12, 17), he also applies it more generally to those of "foreign birth" which seems to include the experience of proselytes by implication. If that implication holds true then we have grounds for suspecting that Philo expected proselytes to be circumcised.[45] Though Philo may, for the most part, wish to emphasize the proselyte's acceptance of monotheism, rejection of idolatry, and avoidance of immorality, he does not completely extinguish the particularity of Jewish ethnic identity that proselytism involves. He might highlight a form of ethical monotheism in his various discussions of proselytes, but he also emphasizes the social dislocation that converts experience from their own people and their integration into the Jewish commonwealth.[46] All in all, while the evidence from Philo sometimes appears to be at odds with itself, on balance it seems best to conclude that he did not exempt proselytes from being circumcised, but he attached only relative importance to it compared to what other Jewish groups thought about circumcision.

Josephus assumes that circumcision is the distinguishing mark of a Jewish male.[47] But he is also aware of the complications of circumcising non-Jews. Consequently, Josephus also preserves several stories dealing with circumcision and conversion and he narrates their often complex circumstances. The most significant and interesting of these stories is the conversion of the house of Adiabene where King Izates and his mother Helena adopted Jewish practices. Yet as to whether or not he should be circumcised, Izates is given two conflicting pieces of advice by, firstly, the Jewish merchant Ananias who tells him that he need not be circumcised,

---

[44] Philo, *Spec. Leg.* 4.179.
[45] Cf. Donaldson, *Judaism and the Gentiles*, 267.
[46] Donaldson, *Judaism and the Gentiles*, 243.
[47] Josephus, *Ant.* 1.192–193, 214; *Ag. Ap.* 1.171.

then, secondly, the Galilean Eleazar informs him that circumcision is completely obligatory. After his initial conversion Izates wanted to be circumcised in order to be "assuredly Jewish" (βεβαίως Ἰουδαῖος).[48] Yet, Josephus depicts the Jewish merchant Ananias as stipulating that Izates "could worship God without being circumcised."[49] But is this a position that most Hellenistic Jews would agree with? Collins thinks that in the context given by Josephus, "to worship God" means to do all that is necessary to ensure salvation (though what salvation means is not spelled out).[50] Ananias (or Josephus) justifies this practice by claiming that worship of God "counted more than circumcision"[51] which may reflect a general Hellenistic Jewish attitude indicative of Philo's comment in *Quaest. in Ex.* 2.2. When Ananias adds that God would forgive Izates for not being circumcised it is unclear whether it refers to forgiveness for failing to be circumcised as a condition of conversion, or forgiveness for failing to meet a subsequent obligation of conversion.[52] At this point we might think that Ananias's attitude indicates that it was indeed possible for a Gentile to convert to Judaism without circumcision. But that is a rather selective way of viewing the narrative. Although it can be said that some Jews evidently were more flexible on the issue of circumcision than others, it would be a mistake to conclude from the story of Izates that circumcision was not linked with conversion and integration into Israel for several reasons: (1) Ananias never says that remaining at this penultimate stage of commitment to Judaism makes Izates a Jew.[53] (2) King Izates did not regard himself as a Jew unless he was circumcised.[54] (3) The reasons given for not circumcising

---

[48] Josephus, *Ant.* 20.38; see also the report of the conversion of Izates's brother Monobazus and his relatives in *Ant.* 20.75. A later rabbinic midrash states: "Once Monabaz and Izates, the sons of King Ptolemy, were sitting and reading the book of Genesis. When they came to the verse, 'And you shall be circumcised' [Gen 17:11] one turned his face towards the wall and commenced to weep, and the other turned his face to the wall and commenced to weep. Then each went and had himself circumcised" (*Gen. Rab.* 46.10).

[49] Josephus, *Ant.* 20.41.

[50] Collins, "A Symbol of Otherness," 179.

[51] Josephus, *Ant.* 20.41.

[52] Josephus, *Ant.* 20.42; contra Collins ("A Symbol of Otherness," 178–79) who thinks that it can be taken to imply that circumcision was only a subsequent obligation upon admission. However, either could be possible here.

[53] Nolland, "Uncircumcised Proselytes?" 193.

[54] Josephus, *Ant.* 20.38.

Izates are exceptional; first, the need to avoid an uprising from public resentment at having a Jewish ruler, and second, Ananias's desire for self-preservation. (4) When Eleazar the Pharisee arrived on the scene he reproved Izates for failing to be circumcised, implying it was hardly pardonable or optional.[55] Eleazar regarded Jewish practices as a matter of law, not *ethos*, even for Gentiles.[56] Accordingly, Izates consents to undergo the procedure of circumcision. Josephus's comments that the dangers that Izates feared did not eventuate because of God's providence in protecting the faithful, indicates Josephus's own approval of Izates's decision to be circumcised.[57] Alan Segal is perhaps correct that for Josephus, all things being equal, being Jewish is better than being a God-fearer.[58] Of course it is open to question whether "God-fearer" was the category that Josephus had in mind. Even so, Izates's status is initially that of a non-Jew taken to observing some Jewish customs and proceeding on towards full conversion. Izates wanted to convert like his mother and that required circumcision. The tension in this vignette is whether Izates would in fact take that step. Josephus reports most favorably that he did.[59] In light of all this the summary of Blaschke seems correct:

> (1) In *Ant.* 20.34–48 circumcision is the crucial step from merely sympathizing with Judaism as a God-fearer to living as a "proper Jew." (2) The text provides no evidence for the inclusion of uncircumcised non-Jews as proselytes. (3) It seems likely, on its basis, that there was a Judean position, esp. in Diaspora Judaism, which advocated that uncircumcised God-fearers possibly have a share in the salvation of Israel ("God-fearer model"), whereas others inseparably connected participation in salvation for non-Jews to circumcision and conversion ("proselyte model"). (4) Ananias and Eleazar used their professions to propagate the Jewish faith, and they may not have been a singular phenomenon. Above all, pagan women were approached by them. (5) In pagan eyes circumcision is strange, alien, and unseemly.[60]

---

[55] Cf. Philo, *Quaest. in Gen.* 3.52.

[56] Daniel R. Schwartz, "God, Gentiles, Jewish Law: On Acts 15 and Josephus' Adiabene Narrative," in *Jewish Identity in the Greco-Roman World* (eds. J. Frey, D. R. Schwartz, S. Gripentrog; AJEC 71, Leiden: Brill, 2007), 271.

[57] Josephus, *Ant.* 20.43–48.

[58] Segal, "The Cost of Proselytism and Conversion," 357.

[59] Schwartz, "God, Gentiles, Jewish Law," 271.

[60] Blaschke, *Beschneidung*, 240 [1] In *Ant* 20,34–48 ist die Beschneidung der entscheidende Schritt von Bloßen Sympathisieren mit dem Judentum als Gottesfürchtiger hin zum leben als »rechter Jude«. 2) Der Text ist kein Beleg

Elsewhere there is supplementary evidence from Josephus that indicates the same link between circumcision and conversion to Judaism. In providing an account of the subjugation of the Idumaeans under Hyrcanus I, Josephus notes how the Idumaeans (under duress) submitted to "circumcision and the Jewish way of life" and were "finally called Jews" (ὥστε εἶναι τὸ λοιπὸν Ἰουδαίους).[61] Josephus records that the Roman military leader Metilius who was captured in Jerusalem after the fall of the Antonian fortress was saved from death by "promising to judaize to the point of circumcision" (μέχρι περιτομῆς ἰουδαΐσειν ὑποσχόμενον).[62] Donaldson says that Metilius "in effect saved his skin by being willing to part with a small portion of it"![63] Here "Judaizing" represents a number of possible measures that involve imitating, sympathizing, and finally identifying with the Jewish people. While pragmatically Metillius was expressing his willingness to change sides in the conflict, we should not play off the political meaning (side with the Jews) against the cultural meaning (adopt Jewish way of life) of Judaizing as Cohen does.[64] While Judaizing can involve offering political support, it ordinarily means far more than this in practice (e.g., Gal 2:14). On the cultural side, I concur with Blaschke who writes: "According to *J.W.* 2.454 circumcision is the end process of ἰουδαΐζειν [Judaizing] and the beginning of Ἰουδαῖος εἶναι [being a Jew]."[65] Josephus also includes a report from Strabo that Aristobulus I joined the Ituraeans to Judea by the "bond of circumcision" (ᾠκειώσατο δεσμῷ συνάψας

---

für die Annahme unbeschnittener Nichtjuden als *Proselyten*. 3) Anhand seiner ist aber eine Haltung von Judea v.a. im Diasporajudentum wahrscheinlich zu machen, die auch unbeschnittenen *Gottesfürchtigen* u.U. Anteil am Heil Israels in Aussicht stellte (»Gottesfürchtigenmodell«), wohingegen andere Heilsteilhaben auch für Nichtjuden untrennbar mit Beschneidung und Konversion verbunden haben (»Proselytenmodell«). 4) Ananias und Eleazar haben ihren Beruf zur Propagierung des jüdischen Glaubens genutzt und sind damit eventuell keine singulären Erscheinungen gewesen. Vor allem heidnische *Frauen* wurden von ihnen angesprochen. 5) In heidnischen Augen ist die Beschneidung seltsam, fremd und unziemlich].

[61] Josephus, *Ant.* 12.258.

[62] Josephus, *J.W.* 2.454.

[63] Donaldson, *Judaism and the Gentiles,* 292.

[64] Cohen, *The Beginnings of Jewishness,* 183; see Donaldson, *Judaism and the Gentiles,* 293–94.

[65] Blaschke, *Beschneidung,* 226 ("Nach *Bell* 2,454 ist die Beschneidung Ende des bloßen ἰουδαΐζειν und Anfang des Ἰουδαῖος εἶναι").

τῇ τῶν αἰδοίων περιτομῇ) which emphasizes circumcision as the chief indicator of shared identity and mutual commitment.[66] The Herodians (whose commitment to Judaism was always suspect) insisted on circumcision for intermarriage with princes from pagan kingdoms.[67] If one was to rule the Jewish people then it made sense that one had to be Jewish and the key marker (and in some cases the main deterrent for would-be suitors) was circumcision. Furthermore, Cohen examines several instances of conversion in *Antiquities* and concludes that for converts, "circumcision is the crucial indicator of their new status."[68] Circumcision was the end point or the final bridge to be crossed in the movement towards the Jewish way of life. The implication is that Judaizing by Gentiles was a broad concept, but circumcision was the terminus of conversion.[69] In sum, Josephus understands and appreciates the pragmatic and political reasons why Gentile adherents who wish to convert to Judaism might not go ahead and be circumcised. But he evidently reflects the view that circumcision remains the normal and definitive mark of a Gentile becoming a Jew.

Outside of Josephus, we observe further evidence for the association between circumcision and conversion. In Judith the Gentile Achior believed in God and consequently, "he circumcised the flesh of his foreskin and he was added to the house of Israel" (περιετέμετο τὴν σάρκα τῆς ἀκροβυστίας αὐτοῦ καὶ προσετέθη εἰς τὸν οἶκον Ἰσραηλ).[70] In Esther it is reported that "many of the Gentiles were circumcised and became Jews" (πολλοὶ τῶν ἐθνῶν περιετέμοντο καὶ ἰουδάιζον).[71] These two texts from Esther and Judith, from books dealing with women as the central characters, show that circumcision was presupposed as part of Jewish identity in a Gentile environment and they have in their background the reception of proselytes in the Diaspora, Palestine, and the Orient, where circumcision was central to conversion.[72] In the *Epic of Theodotus* the author presents a narration of the massacre of the Shechemites from Gen 34 and states that: "Jacob

---

[66] Josephus, *Ant.* 13.319.

[67] Josephus, *Ant.* 16.225; 19.355; 20.139, 145–146.

[68] Cohen, "Respect for Judaism by Gentiles according to Josephus," 420; cf. Barclay, *Jews in the Mediterranean Diaspora*, 438–39.

[69] Cohen, "Respect for Judaism by Gentiles according to Josephus," 416.

[70] Jdt 14:10 (LXX).

[71] Esther 8:17 (LXX); cf. Josephus, *Ant.* 11.285.

[72] Blaschke, *Beschneidung*, 119, 130.

said that he would not give her [Dinah] until all the inhabitants of Shechem were circumcised and became Jews."[73] Along with most Jewish authors of the period, Greco-Roman authors also associated circumcision—even of proselytes—with Jewish identity. Juvenal describes how a son of an adherent would inevitably "take to circumcision" as the final step in his conversion to the Jewish way of life.[74] Tacitus saw circumcision as a distinguishing mark of Jewish males when he says that "they adopted circumcision to distinguish themselves from other peoples by this difference," and he adds that "those who are converted to their ways follow the same practice."[75] Petronius highlights the link of circumcision with Jewish identity: "The Jew may worship his pig-god and clamour in the ears of heaven, but unless he cuts back his foreskin with the knife, he shall go forth from the people and immigrate to Greek cities."[76] Petronius also states, with obvious sarcasm, that one can disguise oneself as a Jew by being circumcised.[77] According to the Acts of the Apostles, although Paul's traveling companion Timothy had a Jewish mother—and Jewish identity is matriarchal—because he had a Greek father, Paul was compelled to circumcise Timothy so as to dissolve any question of his status as a "Jew" during his missionary travels among Jews and pagans in the Mediterranean coastal cities.[78] Suetonius reports a case where a man was publicly inspected to determine if he was circumcised in order to ascertain if he was liable to pay the *fiscus Iudaicus* (the war reparation tax levied upon the Jews across the empire in lieu of paying the temple tax to Jerusalem).[79] Even for those external to Jewish communities circumcision was the primary ethnic and religious indicator that demonstrated acquisition or retainment of Jewish identity (or at least for males).

We seem to be led to the inevitable conclusion that circumcision was the ritual signifier that marks the difference between adherence and conversion. Pagans and Greeks, regardless of their adherence to Jewish customs or their association with Jewish communities, were still

---

[73] *Epic. Theod.* frg. 5.

[74] Juvenal, *Sat.* 14.96–106 (Stern, *GLAJJ* 2: §301); cf. Schürer, *History of the Jewish People in the Age of Jesus Christ*, 3.1.169.

[75] Tacitus, *Hist.* 5.5.2.

[76] Petronius, *Satyricon*, frg. 37 (Stern, *GLAJJ* 1: §195).

[77] Petronius, *Satyricon*, frg. 102.13–14 (Stern, *GLAJJ* 1: §194).

[78] Acts 16:3.

[79] Suetonius, *Domitian* 12.2. On the *fiscus Iudaicus* see Josephus, *J.W.* 7.218.

of the "nations" (גוים or ἔθνη) if they were uncircumcised. Only by circumcision could males become *de jure* Jews.[80] We can make room for exceptions, account for misinterpretation of Jewish views by outsiders, recognize the elastic nature of group boundaries in certain settings; even so, circumcision was the primary expression of entering into the commonwealth of Israel for converts. Overall, then, we possess here an array of evidence that clearly marks out circumcision as the ordinary rite of passage for Gentile males to join Israel and to enter into covenant with their God, Yahweh.

There could be two main reasons for circumcising Gentiles. First, the requirement for circumcision is intensified within *Eretz* Israel as part of the effort to protect the sacred space of the holy land. This is particularly evident in the forced circumcision of the Ituraeans and Idumaeans (see below) and other forced conversions noted by Josephus.[81] One of the first actions of the Maccabean revolt led by Mattathias was that they "forcibly circumcised all the uncircumcised boys that they found within the borders of Israel."[82] This was a counter-response to the forced Hellenization of Judea by the Syrian king and was aimed at both apostates (those who did circumcise their children) but also against any non-Jews living in the land of Judea. According to the Christian author Hippolytus, some Jewish groups would even forcibly circumcise a Jew or a Gentile if they heard them even discussing the law or God.[83] The circumcision of Gentiles here is not a matter of mission or conversion but of maintaining the holiness of the land and protecting it against defilement.[84] More zealous expressions of Judean nationalism at times of conflict or conquest seem to have dissolved the category of "resident alien" or "sojourner" (גר) and did not afford the liberality of Diaspora Jews in assigning a positive, even if limited status, to Gentile adherents and associates.

A second reason for circumcising Gentiles is that circumcision was often expressed in regards to the positive soteriological value of the ritual for Gentiles. Acts 15:1 reflects this debate in early Christianity: "Unless you are circumcised, according to the custom taught by Moses,

---

[80] Martin Hengel and Anna Maria Schwemer, *Paul between Damascus and Antioch* (trans. John Bowden; London: SCM, 1997), 62.

[81] Josephus, *Life* 112–113, 149–154; *J.W.* 2.454.

[82] 1 Macc 2:46.

[83] Hippolytus, *Refut.* 9.21.

[84] Hengel and Schwemer, *Paul between Damascus and Antioch*, 65.

you cannot be saved."[85] Paul vigorously opposed the view that Gentiles had to convert to Judaism in order to be "saved." Yet by going that route Paul did not simply opt for a liberalized Jewish view of salvation without circumcision, but rather, he advocated full inclusion into the people of God on the basis of faith in Christ, which itself is able to deliver believers. For Paul, in the new age that had dawned in Jesus Christ's resurrection, physical circumcision had been replaced by "circumcision of the heart" as the ultimate sign of covenant inclusion.

There are, however, several strands of evidence from Diasporan, rabbinic, and Greco-Roman literature that show that the designation "Jew" could be applied somewhat flexibly and beyond the marker of circumcision and integration into the Jewish community. In the Hebrew Bible physical circumcision could be spiritualized or subordinated to circumcision of the heart which provided fertile soil for the thoughts of Diaspora Jews and Christians about the conversion of Gentiles. That is, you can theoretically have a situation in which a Gentile is spiritually circumcised and yet a Jew is not.[86] In some writings from the Jewish Diaspora the ethno-specific obligations of the Torah are downplayed. For example, in the Pentateuch, aliens are not permitted to partake of Passover unless they have been circumcised,[87] yet in *Ezekiel the Tragedian* circumcision is not mentioned as a prerequisite for celebrating Passover and the matter was disputed in later rabbinic writings.[88] Michael Lattke[89] brings attention to the connection between the call to discipleship in Mark 10:28–30 (leaving family, houses, fields and receiving rewards etc.)[90] and Luke 14:26–27/Matt 10:37–38 (necessity of hating parents and carrying cross)[91] with Philo's account of the proselytes in *De specialibus legibus*.[92] In the Marcan and Philonic accounts there is a leaving

---

[85] On the soteriological benefits of circumcision see also *Jub.* 15:25–34; CD 16:4–6; *T. Levi* 6:3.

[86] Deut 10:16; 30:6; Lev 26:41; Jer 4:4; 9:25–26; Ezek 44:9; Philo, *Spec. Leg.* 1.304–306; *Quaest. in Ex.* 2.2; *Quaest. in Gen.* 3.46, 48; 1QS 5:5; 1QH 18:20; 1QpHab 11:13; cf. Rom 2:29; Col 2:11; *Barn.* 9:1–9.

[87] Exod 12:43, 48–49; Num 9:14.

[88] *Exag.* 175–192; cf. *m. Pesah.* 8.8.

[89] Michael Lattke, "The Call to Discipleship and Proselytizing," *HTR* 92 (1999): 359–62.

[90] Cf. Matt 19:27–29; Luke 18:28–30.

[91] Cf. *Gos. Thom.* 55, 101.

[92] Philo, *Spec. Leg.* 1.51–52.

of "house, brothers, sisters, mothers, fathers, children or fields" and the departure from "their country, their kinsfolk and their friends." This stands in contrast with a view to gaining family and eternal life (Mark), or another homeland, relatives, friends, protection and refuge (Philo). Whether or not this language of leaving/gaining signifies a "Hellenistic Jewish definition of a proselyte"[93] is not certain. Philo maintains *both* a literal and deeper meaning of circumcision, yet he transfers remarkable esteem and prestige to Gentile converts apart from circumcision.[94]

Rabbinic literature adds further ambivalence as to who could be counted as a Jew. To begin with, it is notable that in some rabbinic discussions anyone who denies idolatry is counted as a Jew, which casts the net very broadly.[95] Even so, in other rabbinic regulations converts were ordinarily required to make a sacrifice and made to undergo both baptism and circumcision.[96] Then there is the comical tradition of three Gentiles who wanted to convert to Judaism who were rejected by R. Shammai but then accepted by R. Hillel. A first Gentile comes to Shammai; he wants to convert to Judaism, but the Gentile insisted on learning the whole Torah while standing on one foot. Shammai rejected him, so he went to Hillel, who taught him: "What you dislike, do not do to your friend. That is the basis of the Torah. The rest is commentary: go and learn!" Then another Gentile who accepted only the written Torah came to Shammai for instruction. Shammai refused, so he went to Hillel. On his first meeting, Hillel taught him the correct order of the Hebrew Alphabet. The next day Hillel reversed the letters. The convert was confused and asked why the order of the letters was changed. Hillel's answer goes on to illustrate the need for the written and oral Torah. Then a third Gentile wanted to convert so that he could

---

[93] Lattke, "The Call to Discipleship and Proselytizing," 361.

[94] Philo, *Spec. Leg.* 1.2–11; *Quaest. in Ex.* 2.2; *Quaest. in Gen.* 3.46–52; *Migr. Abr.* 89–94; *Som.* 2.25. Lattke ("The Call to Discipleship and Proselytizing," 361, n. 13) candidly admits that: "There is no reason to assume that Philo does not speak of 'Ganzproselyten.'"

[95] *b. Meg.* 13a; *b. Ned.* 25a; *Sifre Num.* 111.

[96] *m. Ker.* 2.1; *b. Ker.* 8b–9a; *m. 'Ed.* 5.2; *m. Pesah.* 8.8; *b. Pesah.* 92a; *b. Yebam.* 46a–47b; cf. Moore, *Judaism in the First Centuries,* 1.331–32; Kirsopp Lake, "Proselytes and God-Fearers," in *The Beginnings of Christianity* (eds. F. J. Foakes Jackson and Kirsopp Lake; 5 vols.; London: Macmillan, 1922–1933), 5.78–79; Schürer, *History of the Jewish People in the Age of Jesus Christ,* 3.1.173–76; Cohen, *The Beginnings of Jewishness,* 198–238.

become the High Priest and wear the Priestly garments. Shammai turns him away, but Hillel accepted him. Subsequently the convert realized that even David, the King of Israel, did not qualify as a priest since he wasn't descended from Aaron's line.[97] Obviously the story contains exaggeration, hyperbole, and it is not offering casuistic case law about conversions to Judaism (it is probably legend not history). Even so, circumcision is strangely absent from the narrative, and in the interactions between Hillel and the three Gentiles, conversion is a process of education and gradual increase in commitment. In another story, R. Joshua b. Hananiah in his debate with R. Eliezer b. Hyrcanus around the end of the first century C.E. argued that baptism is sufficient for initiation into Judaism.[98] The fact that one rabbi held such a view is not evidence that others did, and in any case it did not become the majority rabbinic view. The general pattern of rabbinic tradition, then, is that in *halakic* rulings there seems to be pretty clear grounds for circumcision being normal and obligatory for conversion by Gentiles, whereas *haggadic* episodes appear to represent more flexible and muddied lines of demarcation.

Greco-Roman authors also seem to have fairly broad ideas as to who is a Jew. Epictetus refers to someone who oscillates between two positions as being like a person who "is not a Jew, but is only acting" (οὐκ ἔστιν Ἰουδαῖος, ἀλλ᾽ ὑποκρίνεται), in contrast to someone who has adopted "the attitude of mind of the man who has been baptized and made his choice (βεβαμμένου καὶ ἡρημένου) then he is both a Jew in fact and is also called one (ὄντι καὶ καλεῖται Ἰουδαῖος)."[99] In Epictetus's censuring of attitudes about acting versus commitment, he enlists the example of Jewish adherents and Jewish converts, yet he registers baptism as the difference between the two positions. This suggests knowledge of the practice of "baptism" for initiates in Rome (where Epictetus was) as a means of initiation into Judaism.[100] The question is, does Epictetus witness to a time in Rome when baptism

---

[97] *b. Šabb.* 31a; *ʾAbot R. Nat.* 24ab; see McKnight, *A Light among the Gentiles*, 87.

[98] *b. Yebam.* 46a; cf. *y. Qidd.* 3:12 where R. Joshua insists on circumcision and baptism.

[99] Epictetus, *Diss.* 2.9.20 (Stern, *GLAJJ* 1: §254).

[100] See other debated references to baptism as a form of initiation in *Sib. Or.* 4:165; Philo, *Spec. Leg.* 1.262; *Cher.* 95; *Deus Imm.* 7–8; *Som.* 1.210; *m. Pesaḥ.* 8.8; *T. Levi* 14:6. Alternatively, see Robert L. Webb (*John the Baptizer and Prophet: A Socio-Historical Study* [JSNTSup 62; Sheffield: Sheffield Academic

replaced circumcision as the signifier of conversion? Nolland rightly points out that what Epictetus is doing is decrying those who profess a set of beliefs but do not practice them. Judaism is the example here, but it could be applied *mutatis mutandis* to any religion, philosophy, or cult.[101] Suffice to say, circumcision, its necessity or negligibility, is simply not mentioned by Epictetus. Baptism may have been part of the process of conversion for proselytes, but it does not prove that it was the only necessary part of conversion or even a sufficient condition for entrance into the Jewish community. Nor should we read into Epictetus internal debates from among the Jewish community in Rome on this matter since we have no record of baptism replacing circumcision for proselytes in Judaism before the Apostle Paul. More conclusively, what the Epictetus comment indicates is that once people have taken the decisive step and fully adopted the Jewish belief matrix and way of life, they are regarded as Jews even by Gentile outsiders.[102] In addition to Epictetus, several other pagan authors also make sweeping remarks about who belongs in the Jewish constituency. Some pagan writers simply assumed that any person who participates in Jewish practices was a Jew. As an example, Plutarch refers to an event in Cicero's life during his prosecution of Verres who was praetor of Sicily (Verres is Latin for "pig" or "boar"). During the proceedings a freedman named Quintus Caecilius Niger attempted to intervene in the trial. Caecilius was "liable of Jewish practices" (ἔνοχος τῷ ἰουδαΐζειν) and Cicero sarcastically asked him: "What has a Jew to do with a pig?" (τί Ἰουδαίῳ πρὸς χοῖρον;).[103] Dio Cassius goes so far as to say that the name "Jews" (Ἰουδαῖοι) can apply "to all the rest of mankind, although of alien race, who are affected by their customs" (ἐπὶ τοὺς ἄλλους ἀνθρώπους ὅσοι τὰ νόμιμα αὐτῶν, καίπερ ἀλλοεθνεῖς ὄντες, ζηλοῦσαι).[104] This proves only that pagan writers thought that practicing some Jewish customs placed such a person in the Jewish constituency. There is nothing that demonstrates that such an identification was also made in the various Jewish

---

Press 1991], 122–30) for arguments that there was no proselyte baptism in the Second Temple period.

[101] Nolland, "Uncircumcised Proselytes?" 180–82; cf. McEleney, "Conversion, Circumcision and the Law," 332; Cohen, *The Beginnings of Jewishness*, 152.

[102] Donaldson, *Judaism and the Gentiles*, 391.

[103] Plutarch, *Cic.* 7.5 (Stern, *GLAJJ* 1: §263).

[104] Dio Cassius, *Hist.* 37.16.5–17.1 (Stern, *GLAJJ* 2: §406).

communities of the Diaspora who probably knew of a finer distinction between converts and adherents.[105]

In sum, views on the entrance of Gentiles into the Jewish fold were not uniform. Its complexity derives from the problem of Jewish self-identity in antiquity.[106] In some quarters, it was not deemed necessary for Gentiles to be circumcised because it was not necessary for Gentiles to convert to Judaism. However, when incorporation into the Jewish nation or full conversion was the issue, the dominating perspective was that circumcision was required. What distinguished sympathizers/ God-fearers from proselytes, in Jewish minds anyway, was circumcision. God would be glorified by pagans worshipping him; Gentile adherence to some Jewish customs created a sense of solidarity and sympathy with the Jewish people; and Jews had cause to rejoice at this. But Gentile conversion, understood as initiation and integration into a Jewish community, involved circumcision as the crucial indicator of new identity and new status. Thus, if Gentiles wanted to enter a Jewish community and join themselves to Judaism, then they had to undergo circumcision.

Adherence and Conversion

Ultimately, what separates adherence to Judaism from conversion to Judaism is the level of transformation of ideology, identity, and praxis with the resulting level of conformity to the beliefs and behavior of a Jewish community. Donaldson correctly notes that sympathizers could also progress along the three axes of monotheistic worship, adoption of Jewish practices, and association with a Jewish community to varying degrees, whereas a full convert undertakes full adoption of all three.[107] To flesh this out, for a Gentile to completely Judaize meant that he or she would assent to Jewish monotheism, accept the obligations of *Torah* as a way of life as opposed to the pagan way of life, and join the nation of Israel as a proselyte.[108] Another difference between adherents and

---

[105] See Cohen, "Crossing the Boundary and Becoming a Jew," 20–21.

[106] Cf. Cohen, *The Beginnings of Jewishness.*

[107] Donaldson, *Judaism and the Gentiles,* 488–89.

[108] In the Septuagint προσήλυτος translates the Hebrew word גר ("foreigner") seventy-seven times (elsewhere ξένος [once], γειώρας [twice], and πάροικος [eleven times] are used). It is common to translate προσήλυτος as "convert" since by the first century it did by and large hold that meaning in inscriptions (Margaret H. Williams, *The Jews among the Greeks and Romans:*

converts is the matter of inclusion, self-description, and public recognition of their transference. When a full conversion has taken place, the Jewish community claims the convert as one of its own full members; the convert self-identifies with the community more closely than with other competing associations and defines his or her biography in light of that association; and those outside of the Jewish community recognize that a transference of allegiance and identity has taken place. Put simply, conversion and adherence can be differentiated from each other in at least three ways. First, ritual initiation through circumcision (and perhaps marriage for women) is crucial in formalizing the shift of identity, values, and beliefs for the proselyte. There are degrees of sympathizing and types of adherence (e.g., philosophical admiration, ethical imitation, political support, benefaction of Jewish communities, adoption of some rituals, etc.), while conversion requires that a final and recognizable threshold must have been traversed at some point. Second, adherents can add Jewish practices (e.g., Sabbath observance, food laws, attending synagogue) to their current range of religious activities while remaining fully entrenched in Greco-Roman society; whereas converts consciously abandon and break from their prior way of life in paganism in favor of a new way of life defined by the Torah. Third, adherence consists of "alteration" or a limited range of changes that develops one's behavior towards the direction of Judaism, whereas conversion entails a "transformation" of one's social and religious identity to the point of reconfiguring one's biography in light of new social and religious allegiances.[109] Although conversion may take place through a gradual series of alterations, an alteration itself does not constitute conversion

---

A Diasporan Sourcebook [London: Duckworth, 1998], 171–72; P. Figueras, "Epigraphic Evidence for Proselytism in Ancient Judaism," *Immanuel* 24/25 [1990]: 194–206), the New Testament (Matt 23:15; Acts 2:11; 6:5; 13:43), Philo (*Som.* 2.273; *Spec. Leg.* 1.51, 308; *Quaest. in Ex.* 2.2) and the Septuagint as well (e.g., Exod 12:48–49; Deut 1:16; Pss 93:6; 145:9; Zech 7:10; Mal 3:5; Isa 54:15; Jer 7:6; Ezek 14:7; Tob 1:8). Nevertheless, its meaning in the Septuagint is not uniformly about "converts" since it also denotes resident aliens (Lev 19:10; 24:16) and even Israelites (Exod 22:20; Lev 19:34; Deut 10:19). See Nahum Levison, "The Proselyte in Biblical and Early Post-Biblical Times," *SJT* 10 (1957): 45–56; Kuhn, "προσήλυτος," 6.730–31; U. Becker, "προσήλυτος," *NIDNTT* 1.360; Paul F. Stuehrenberg, "Proselyte," *ABD* 5.503; BDAG, 880.

[109] Beverly Roberts Gaventa, *From Darkness to Light: Aspects of Conversion in the New Testament* (Philadelphia: Fortress, 1986), 12.

if it lacks initiation and some form of primary (though perhaps not exclusive) adherence to the Jewish way of life.

Women and Conversion

A significant but often overlooked factor to be taken into account in formulating a criteria and explanation of conversion to Judaism is the position of Gentile women vis-à-vis Judaism.[110] Women were obviously not circumcised, and this raises a whole host of questions about the means and identification of conversion for women to Judaism. The case of female converts to Judaism underscores how fluid and thin the division between adherent/associate and convert/initiate could be under certain circumstances. While Jewish community boundaries were distinct they were nonetheless permeable, and partial membership was available for men and women.[111] But the lack of the identifying act of circumcision for women makes it difficult to find verifiable proof for pagan women crossing the boundaries and becoming Jewish. There is no evidence of baptism as a fixed rite for initiation prior to 70 C.E.[112]

Two Jewish novellas, the book of Ruth (in Hebrew) and *Joseph and Aseneth* (in Greek), appear to make intermarriage the key mechanism for integration into the Jewish nation for women.[113] Prior to their respective marriages to Boaz and Joseph, Ruth is a resident alien from

---

[110] Cf. David Daube, "Conversion to Judaism and Early Christianity," in *Ancient Jewish Law: Three Inaugural Lectures* (Leiden: Brill, 1981), 1–47; Cohen, "Respect for Judaism by Gentiles according to Josephus," 430; Fredriksen, "Judaism, the Circumcision of Gentiles, and Apocalyptic Hope," 546, n. 42; Judith M. Lieu, "Circumcision, Women and Salvation," *NTS* 40 (1994): 358–70; Shaye J. D. Cohen, *Why Aren't Jewish Women Circumcised: Gender and Covenant in Judaism* (Berkeley: University of California Press, 2005); Daniel R. Schwartz, "Doing Like Jews or Becoming a Jew? Josephus on Women Converts to Judaism," in *Jewish Identity in the Greco-Roman World* (eds. J. Frey, D. R. Schwartz, and S. Gripentrog; AJEC 71, Leiden: Brill, 2007), 93–109.

[111] Tessa Rajak, "The Jewish Community and Its Boundaries," in *The Jews among Pagans and Christians in the Roman Empire* (eds. Judith Lieu, John North, and Tessa Rajak; London: Routledge, 1992), 19.

[112] Hengel and Schwemer, *Paul between Damascus and Antioch*, 66.

[113] Aseneth does have her own ritual initiation, as it were, involving consumption of bread, wine, oil, and honeycomb. Yet this is more of an idiosyncratic feature of the narrative rather than a common aspect of female conversion to Judaism as far as is known.

Moab and Aseneth is a pagan woman in Egypt. There is also the instance of Venturia Paula, the synagogue matron who became a proselyte at the age of 70 and took the name Sarah.[114] Providing benefaction for a synagogue and changing one's Roman praenomen to a Hebrew name has all the hallmarks of one who has undergone transference from one group into another given the outward presentation of the self (name change) and recognition by others (formalized synagogue association). There is no indication if this was normative, common, or an exceptional action for a woman to take in order to convert to Judaism. What can be said with more certainty is that the absence of circumcision made it far easier for women, especially for those from the upper echelons of society and with some degree of independence, to frequent synagogues and to observe Jewish rites. This brought them in closer proximity, religiously and socially, to Jewish communities and the line between adherent and convert was probably more flexibly drawn for women.

CONCLUSION

In light of the foregoing discussion, which links conversion with circumcision (at least for males), "mission" within Judaism may be defined as *the diverse array of activities that consciously attempts to draw, recruit, or persuade persons into conversion consisting of ideological, axiological (ethical), and social transformation.* A mission of this order meant trying to convince Gentiles of monotheism, bringing the values and behavior of Gentiles into alignment with those of a Jewish community, and formally recognizing them as members of their own religious and social identity after the appropriate rituals and rites have taken place. For most Jews this meant, as the desired end, seeing a Gentile circumcised and integrated into the Jewish community. It is not too much to say that circumcision (at least for men) was the rite of passage and *sine qua non* of conversion to Judaism. Thus, as Paul Barnett rightly asserts, mission in Judaism must be drawn in relation to circumcision.[115] Yet the question is, did pre-Christian Jews aspire and attempt to convert Gentiles into becoming Jews? This is the question that will now be addressed.

---

[114]Frey, *CIJ* 1: §523.
[115]Barnett, "Jewish Mission," 264; cf. Cohen, "Crossing the Boundary and Becoming a Jew," 24–27; Finn, *Death to Rebirth*, 96.

EXCURSUS 1: GOD-FEARERS

Relevant to the discussion is the significance of the so-called "God-worshippers/fearers" (σεβόμενοι/φοβούμενοι τὸν θεόν), particularly prevalent in Acts,[116] and what they contribute to the evidence for the extent of Jewish missionary activity. The existence and identity of these purported "God-fearers" is disputed by a small contingent of scholars. It is necessary, then, to provide some adjudication on the evidence as to whether or not such God-fearers existed and what kind of relationship they had to Judaism. Any judgments about the existence and identity of the "God-fearers" influences how the evidence cited in the following chapters is to be understood.

According to Kuhn, the "God-fearers" were a well defined group of Gentiles who, "attended synagogue worship, believed in Jewish monotheism, and kept some part of the ceremonial law, but who did not take the step of full conversion to Judaism by circumcision."[117] Yet the claim that σεβόμενοι and φοβούμενοι are technical terms for non-Jewish adherents is problematic[118] since the appellation "God-fearer/worshipper" can describe Jews,[119] proselytes,[120] and even

---

[116] Acts 10:2, 22, 35; 13:16, 26, 43, 50; 16:14; 17:4, 17; 18:7.

[117] K. Kuhn, "προσήλυτος," 6.731; cf. U. Becker, "προσήλυτος," *NIDNTT* 1.361.

[118] The problem of assuming such a technical meaning for the terms was pointed out long ago by Lake, "Proselytes and God-Fearers," 5.84–88 and Louis H. Feldman, "Jewish 'Sympathizers' in Classical Literature and Inscriptions," *TAPA* 81 (1950): 200–208. See further Max Wilcox, "The 'God-Fearers' in Acts: A Reconsideration," *JSNT* 13 (1981): 102–22; Trebilco, *Jewish Communities in Asia Minor*, 146–47; Judith M. Lieu, "The Race of God-Fearers," *JTS* 46 (1995): 483–501.

[119] LXX: Pss 113:17–19; 117:4–6; 118:74; 134:20; Sir 2:7–9, 15–17; 6:16–17; 10:24; Jon 1:9; Jdt 8:8; *Pss. Sol.* 13:12; 18:8; *Sib. Or.* 3:575; *Ep. Arist.* 159; *Jos. Asen.* 8:5–9; 3 Macc 3:4; 4 Macc 5:24; 15:8; *T. Benj.* 3:4; *T. Gad* 3:2; 5:4; *T. Jos.* 11:1; Josephus, *Ant.* 1.96; 7.130, 153; 12.284; John 9:31; the inscription from the theatre at Miletus could read "Jews who are also God worshippers" (Εἰουδαίων τῶν καὶ θεοσεβῶν) [Frey, *CIJ* 2: §748]. For argument that this inscription refers to ethnic Jews see Rick Strelan, *Paul, Artemis, and the Jews in Ephesus* (BZNW 80; Berlin: Walter de Gruyter, 1996), 185–86.

[120] Acts 13:43; an inscription from a sarcophagus in Vigna Randaini reads: "Jewish proselyte...God-fearer" (ἰουδέα προσήλυτος θεοσεβή) [Frey, *CIJ* 1: §202]. Cf. McEleney, "Conversion, Circumcision and the Law," 327.

Gentiles.[121] More recently, Bernd Wander has pointed out that "God-fearer" can be used in at least three different ways in ancient literature functioning as: (1) an honorary title for a specific Jew, (2) a makeshift designation for Gentiles who sympathize with Jewish customs and are attached to the peripheral edges of Jewish communities, and (3) an honorary title for Gentile benefactors of Jewish synagogues.[122] In addition, the existence of such adherents/sympathizers as represented by Luke in Acts was questioned by A. T. Kraabel who suggested that, "at least for the Roman Diaspora, the evidence presently available is far from convincing proof for the existence of such a class of Gentiles as traditionally defined by the assumptions of the secondary literature."[123] Kraabel grounds his thesis on two key lines of evidence: (1) The archaeological evidence fails to demonstrate the existence of a group of Gentiles loosely connected to a synagogue known as "God-fearers," and (2) the "God-fearers" in Acts are Luke's own literary creation that symbolically demonstrate "how Christianity had become a Gentile religion *legitimately* and without losing its Old Testament roots."[124] In any case, the words σεβόμενοι/φοβούμενοι τὸν θεόν are not frequent in inscriptions whereas "fearer" (*metuens*) and "God-worshipper" (θεοσεβής) are more common.

Despite the arguments of Kraabel, there exists substantial evidence for a group of Gentile adherents/sympathizers to Judaism who remained on the fringe of Diaspora synagogues and were known loosely as God-fearers/worshippers. Although much of the epigraphic evidence is ambiguous to varying degrees there are several inscriptions which imply a recognizable group of Gentiles attached to a Jewish community, but not actually part of it. In the Panticapaeum manumissions (ca. first century C.E.) a freedman is emancipated by the synagogue "of the Jews and God-worshippers" (τῶν Ἰουδαίων καὶ θεὸν σέβων).[125] At Deliler,

---

[121](1) Pagans: e.g., Herodotus, 2.37; Josephus, *Ag. Ap.* 2.140; and (2) Sympathizers: e.g., Sir 10:22; *T. Naph.* 1:10; *2 Enoch* 48:7–8; Josephus, *Ant.* 20.34, 41, 195; and disputably Acts 10:2, 22; 13:16–17, 50; 16:14–15; 17:4–9; 18:7.

[122]Bernd Wander, *Gottesfürchtige und Sympathisanten* (WUNT 104; Tübingen: Mohr/Siebeck, 1998).

[123]A. T. Kraabel, "The Disappearance of the God-Fearers," *Numen* 28 (1981): 121; cf. Goodman, *Mission and Conversion*, 87.

[124]Kraabel, "The Disappearance of the God-Fearers," 120.

[125]Cited in Levinskaya, *The Book of Acts in Its Diaspora Setting*, 74–75. Strictly speaking a translation of either "Jews and God-fearers" or "Jews who

Lydia, a memorial (ca. third century C.E.) is erected in a synagogue which reads "To the most holy synagogue of the Hebrews, Eustathios, the God-worshipper, in remembrance of my brother Hermophilos, I have dedicated together with my bride [or sister-in-law] Athanasia, the wash-basin" (Εὐστάτιος ὁ θεοσεβής).[126] The synagogues at Sardis and Acmonia could also be added as further instances of God-fearers being publicly recognized as constituent members of the synagogue.[127] At the synagogue in Sardis (ca. 270–320 C.E.) there is reference to several God-fearers including these:[128]

Aurelios Polyippos, God-Fearer, I, having made a vow, fulfilled it.
Αὐρ(ηλιος) Πολύιππος θεοσεβὴς εὐξάμενος ἐπλήρωσα.

Aurelios Eulogios, God-fearer, I have fulfilled my vow.
Αὐρ(ήλιος) Εὐλόγιος θεοσεβής εὐχὴν ἐτελεσα.

Aurelios Euphrosynos II, a citizen of Sardis, Councillor.
Αὐρ(ήλιος) Εὐφρόσυνος [β Σαρδ. βου]λ τὸ περιμασχάλον ἐκ τῶν τῆς [Προνοία]ς ἐσκούτλω[σα].

Leontios, God-fearer, from the gifts of Providence, in fulfillment of a vow. I gave the *skoutlosis* of the bay.

---

are also pious" are possible (the ambiguities are noted especially by Figueras, "Epigraphic Evidence for Proselytism in Ancient Judaism," 202). Trebilco (*Jewish Communities in Asia Minor*, 156–57) prefers the former option since the inscriptions are not lauding the piety of the Jewish members as much as they are demanding the synagogue attendance of the ex-slaves who enjoy the benefaction of the synagogue or synagogue members.
[126] Frey, *CIJ* 2: §754; for ambiguities see Figueras, "Epigraphic Evidence for Proselytism in Ancient Judaism," 202; Trebilco, *Jewish Communities in Asia Minor*, 162; Levinskaya, *The Book of Acts in Its Diaspora Setting*, 61–62. Eustathios may be an ethnic Jew who is simply performing a pious act in dedicating a memorial to his late brother, and such a self-description as "pious" (ὁ θεοσεβής) is not unheard of among Jews. The name "Eustathios" itself simply means "well-built, stable" and is little help in determining his ethnicity. Still, the phrase remains ambiguous either way and Eustathios may belong to a family of God-fearers/worshippers which also is not unprecedented.
[127] Andrew Overman, "The God-Fearers: Some Neglected Features," in *New Testament Backgrounds* (eds. Craig A. Evans and Stanley E. Porter; Sheffield: Sheffield Academic Press, 1997 [1988]), 260; John H. Kroll, "The Greek Inscriptions of the Sardis Synagogue," *HTR* 94 (2001): 5–55.
[128] Cited from Kroll, "Sardis," 20, 25, 27, 42.

Λέοντιος θεοσεβής ἐκ τῶν τῆς Προνοίας δομάτων τὸ
διαχώρον ὑπὲρ εὐχῆς ἐσκούτλωσα.

Aurelios Hermogenes, citizen of Sardis, God-fearer, from the gifts of
Providence, having made a vow, I gave the seven-branched candlestick.
Αὐρ(ήλιος) Ἑρμογένης Σαρδ. θεοσεβὴς ἐκ τῶν τῆς Προνοίας
εὐξαμενος τὸ ἑπταμύξιον ἐποίησα.

Kroll says of these inscriptions: "This dossier of preserved inscriptions from [the] . . . Sardis Synagogue reveals a congregation that
counted among its most active, supporting contributors a significant
number that, as members of the Sardis City Council, belonged to the
local economic elite. It also included a good number of adherent gentiles or Godfearers. The dossier gives us the personal names of nearly
forty members of the congregation, nine of whom are identified by
some professional title or by a title within the synagogue community."[129]
This picture of amiable relations between the Jewish community and
Roman civic leaders in Sardis is confirmed by Josephus who refers to
documents from Roman officials and the people of Sardis confirming
the rights and privileges of the Jews living there (*Ant.* 14.235, 259–262;
16.171). One of the rights of the Jews was, in Trebilco's words, "a place
to come together with their wives and children to perform their ancestral prayers and offerings."[130] Even amidst a growing Christianity in
the third and fourth centuries, civic leaders in Sardis still permitted
the Jews their place of worship and, to some degree, participated in
its upkeep, and perhaps even its service.[131] The synagogue at Acomia
in Phrygia refers to: "This building erected by Julia Severa; P(ublius)
Tyrronios Klados, the head for life of the synagogue, and Lucius, son of
Lucius, head of the synagogue, and Publius Zotikos, archon, restored it
with their own funds and with money which they had deposited."[132] The
restoration of the Acomian synagogue was made possible by a mixture
of Jewish and Gentile benefactors. While the word "God-fearer" is not
used, the social dynamics here are similar to other synagogues at Sardis
and Aphrodisias whereby pagan patrons contribute to the life and wel-
fare of a Jewish community through various gifts and deposits. What

[129] Kroll, "Sardis," 48.
[130] Trebilco, *Asia Minor*, 38–39.
[131] Kroll, "Sardis," 48.
[132] Frey, *CIJ* 2: §766 (trans. from Donaldson, *Judaism and the Gentiles*, 463).

is particularly interesting here is that Julia Severa was a Roman noble woman, well known from ancient coinage, and married to Servenius Capito who held a magistrates office some time around 58 to 59 C.E. In other inscriptions, she was also a high priestess (probably of the imperial cult) and president of the games. Her relationship to the synagogue may be no more than an act of patronage designed to enhance her honor and prestige in the city. However, as Donaldson correctly notes, it is difficult to envisage a woman of such prominence making a donation of such substance to a religious community of this order without possessing some appreciation of Judaism and its religious aspects.[133]

The strongest evidence for a more definable group of Gentile sympathizers known as "God-fearers" derives from the Aphrodisias synagogue inscription (ca. second–third century C.E.).[134] This inscription details on side "A" the benefactors of a soup kitchen including thirteen people consisting of Jews, three proselytes, and two "God-worshippers" (θεοσεβής). On side "B" are the names of seventy-four people and the lower list is entitled "and as many are God-worshippers" (καὶ ὅσοι θεοσεβῖς). The revisers of Schürer comment: "It would be difficult to imagine clearer evidence that *theosebeis* could be categorized as a formal group attached to a Jewish community, and distinguished from Jews and from full proselytes."[135] Feldman goes so far to state that the inscription "establishes once and for all that there was a special class" known as "God-fearers."[136] The qualification that needs to be made, as Murphy-O'Connor has pointed out, is not only the relative lateness of the Aphrodisias inscription compared to Luke-Acts (the inscription is ca. third century C.E.), but also that the appellation θεοσεβής is used to describe those Gentiles who follow Jewish customs on side "A" and civic officials who provided patronage but probably not religious adherence on side "B."[137] In which case, θεοσεβής refers to both genuine religious sympathizers and civic well-wishers and for the latter group

---

[133] Donaldson, *Judaism and the Gentiles*, 466.

[134] J. Reynolds and R. Tannenbaum, *Jews and God-fearers at Aphrodisias: Greek Inscriptions with Commentary* (Cambridge: Cambridge Philological Society, 1987); Trebilco, *Jewish Communities in Asia Minor*, 152–55.

[135] Schürer, *History of the Jewish People in the Age of Jesus Christ*, 3.1.166; Trebilco, *Jewish Communities in Asia Minor*, 153.

[136] Feldman, *Jew and Gentile in the Ancient World*, 367.

[137] Jerome Murphy-O'Connor, "Lots of God-Fearers? Theosebeis in the Aphrodisias Inscription," *RB* 99 (1992): 418–24.

the designation is really a gracious compliment to their moral character and generosity.[138] That qualification notwithstanding, the Aphrodisias inscription is reasonable proof for Gentiles associated with a Jewish community being called θεοσεβής even if the designation is not a technical nomenclature, nor does it presuppose a particular mode of sympathy, loyalty, and allegiance to the Jewish way of life.[139] The cumulative case for an indeterminate class of Gentile "God-fearers" grows when literary evidence is adduced.[140] In making a vituperative remark against the Jews, Juvenal refers to the "father who Sabbath-fears" (*metuentem sabbata patrem*) as different from his son who eventually converts.[141] Juvenal's comment clearly identifies Gentile figures that followed Jewish customs but did not go the whole way of being socialized into the Jewish community. In the Septuagint the phrase "the fearers" (οἱ φοβούμενοι) occurs in Mal 3:16 where it denotes pious Israelites, but in 2 Chron 5:6 (LXX) "fearers" appears to be distinguished from "all the congregation of Israel" (πᾶσα συναγωγὴ Ισραηλ). The inclusion of the "fearers" in 2 Chron 5:6 is probably a gloss by a Greek translator since no equivalent phrase occurs in the Hebrew text. The translator was highlighting the universal relevance of the temple as a house of prayer for the nations by giving these "fearers" a cameo appearance at its dedication (and note 2 Chron 6:32–33 where Solomon asks

---

[138] Kraabel, "Immigrants, Exiles, Expatriates, and Missionaries," 81.

[139] I would also point out that it would be strange to see θεοσεβής as simply designating someone who is pious. Surely all donors to a synagogue, Jewish or Gentile, were pious anyway, so why mention it only for a few? Moreover, in some inscriptions (like those at Sardis) there is a juxtaposition of God-fearers and those who took measures to emphasize their Jewish ancestry. For example, at Sardis two donors are called "God-fearers" but a third nominates himself as from "the Tribe of Levi." This is a case of a Jewish donor who wanted to distinguish himself from the adjacent Gentile donors (Kroll, "Sardis," 9–10, 21).

[140] Cf. Trebilco, *Jewish Communities in Asia Minor*, 147–52; Levinskaya, *The Book of Acts in Its Diaspora Setting*, 117–26.

[141] Juvenal, *Sat.* 14.96 (Stern, *GLAJJ* 2: §301). Juvenal uses *metuo* (to fear) twice: once in relation to the Sabbath and again in relation to the Jewish code, but not in relation to God (there is no *metuentes deum*). Even so, like others (e.g., Stern, *GLAJJ* 2: §§103–6), I still think that this is a relatively clear description of a type of socioreligious activity (as opposed to a well-defined religious class) that could adequately be described as being a "God-fearer." However, see in counter-point Feldman, *Jew and Gentile in the Ancient World*, 347–48; Donaldson, *Judaism and the Gentiles*, 408–9.

YHWH to hear the prayers of foreigners who come to the temple). It is difficult to assert Luke's invention of the term when it probably appeared in whatever version of the Septuagint he utilized.[142] Josephus knows of Gentiles who are involved in Jewish life in some way either by practicing Jewish rituals or by participating in the synagogue.[143] On one occasion, Josephus explains that the wealth of the temple originated from the gifts of Jews and God-worshippers (τὴν οἰκουμένην Ἰουδαίων καὶ σεβομένων τὸν θεόν) from Asia and Europe who contributed to it and this seems to suggest two distinct classes of persons committed to the veneration and adornment of the Jerusalem temple.[144] He also relates the account of how the Syrians contrived to "rid themselves of the Jews" but had to be wary of the fact that "each city still had its judaizers" (ἰουδαΐζοντας). When juxtaposed with "Jews," the term "judaizers" denotes some kind of Gentile attachment to Jewish practices but seems to fall short of full conversion.[145] These Judaizers remained "alongside" (παρ᾽ ἑκάστοις) rather than in the Jewish community in Syria. Cohen has argued that verbs of this type, when the ιζειν ending is added to an ethnic designator, indicate foreigners who accommodate themselves to or sympathize with the beliefs and boundaries of a particular ethnic group by giving political support, adopting some of their customs, and speaking their language (e.g., Romanize, Hellenize, Judaize).[146] Philo also refers to non-Jews who admire the Jewish laws and how the Jews welcome such admirers like their own countrymen.[147]

Finally, we should consider also the testimony of Luke to the presence of non-Jews associated with Jewish communities among the eastern Mediterranean cities of the Roman Empire. Luke's description of the centurion of Capernaum, the centurion Cornelius, the devout

---

[142] Overman, "The God-Fearers," 258–59.

[143] Josephus, *Ag. Ap.* 2.282; *J.W.* 7.45; *Ant.* 20.195.

[144] Josephus, *Ant.* 14.110; but see Lake ("Proselytes and God-Fearers," 5.85) who thinks it denotes "all the Jews worshipping God." Against Lake, Donaldson (*Judaism and the Gentiles*, 326) points out the incongruity of Lake's translation since Lake failed to take account of the conjunction καί ("and") and such a reading would require the article, i.e., the Jews, the ones revering God. See also accounts of the temple receiving foreigners in *J.W.* 4.262, 275, 324; 5.15–18.

[145] Josephus, *J.W.* 2.463.

[146] Cohen, *The Beginnings of Jewishness,* 175–93.

[147] Philo, *Virt.* 108; *Vit. Mos.* 2:17–44; *Leg. Gai.* 210–211.

women of high standing in Pisidian Antioch, Lydia the trader in purple fabric in Philippi, Jason and the devout Greeks in Thessalonica, and Titius Iustus in Corinth all refer to a phenomenon of Gentile association with Jews and Judaism that was well known to both himself and his readers.[148] Overall, the notion of some pagans being connected to Jewish communities in an "of-but-not-in" manner was not an incongruity in Greco-Roman antiquity, but was a familiar religious stance.[149]

Donaldson rightly draws the following concluding observations from the material in Luke-Acts regarding a class of Gentile "God-fearers": (1) Luke seems to know the difference between a full convert to Judaism and a pious sympathizer (like Cornelius in Acts 10); (2) Luke appears to assume that "proselyte" refers to full conversion; (3) Luke took it for granted that in a typical synagogue one would encounter a body of non-Jews associated with the synagogue community in some ongoing fashion; (4) this body contains both full converts (i.e., proselytes) and those whose association and identification with the Jewish community was less complete (e.g., Cornelius); (5) once the decisive breakthrough in the Gentile mission had taken place in Peter's ministry to Cornelius climaxing in Cornelius's conversion and acceptance, Luke ceases to be interested in differentiating converts from adherents; (6) Luke uses various terms to refer to this group and its members including attributive terms (e.g., pious [Acts 10:2]; righteous [Acts 10:22]; and worshipping [Acts 13:43, 50; 17:4]) and substantive terms (e.g., the one who fears God [Acts 10:35]; those who fear God [Acts 13:16, 26], and a worshipper of God [Acts 16:14; 18:7]); (7) the constructions οἱ φοβούμενοι τὸν θεόν ("those who fear God") and οἱ σεβόμενοι τὸν θεόν ("those who worship God"), cannot refer to a well-defined category of Gentile adherents because of the multiplicity of terms used and due to the diverse range of affinity levels that these Gentiles have with Jewish communities in Luke's narration; and (8) yet one cannot rule out the possibility that these terms already carried a Gentile connotation for Luke and his intended readers.[150]

In summary, when all of this epigraphic, archaeological, and literary evidence is placed beside the accounts in Acts about certain Gentiles

---

[148] Luke 7:1–10; Acts 10:1–48; 13:16–17, 43, 50; 16:14–15; 17:4–9; 18:7.

[149] Reynolds and Tannenbaum, *Jews and God-fearers at Aphrodisias*, 88; Donaldson, *Judaism and the Gentiles*, 475.

[150] Donaldson, *Judaism and the Gentiles*, 432–34.

associated with Jewish synagogues called "God-fearers," it is hard to avoid the inference that Luke is tapping into a well-known social phenomena of Gentile adherence to certain tenets of Judaism and association of some degree with local Jewish communities. Thus, there is reasonable evidence for the association of a "vague class"[151] of Gentiles with variegated levels of interest in and attachment to Jewish communities who could be designated with the equivocal term "God-fearers" or "God-worshippers" as found in Acts.[152]

EXCURSUS 2: PROSELYTISM AND DEMOGRAPHICS

The increase of the Jewish population from the exile to the Greco-Roman period is frequently attributed to Jewish proselytization activity.[153] For instance, Salo Baron estimated that at the time of the exile (ca. 586 B.C.E.), Israel had a population of around 150,000, but by middle of the first century C.E. it had reached approximately 8 million. Baron

---

[151] Lake, "Proselytes and God-Fearers," 5.88.

[152] Collins, "A Symbol of Otherness," 182–83; Schürer, *History of the Jewish People in the Age of Jesus Christ*, 3.1.168; Thomas M. Finn, "The God-fearers Reconsidered," *CBQ* 47 (1985): 83; Segal, "The Cost of Proselytism and Conversion," 350–53; Reynolds and Tannenbaum, *Jews and God-fearers at Aphrodisias*, 65; Cohen, "Respect for Judaism by Gentiles according to Josephus," 419; Figueras, "Epigraphic Evidence for Proselytism in Ancient Judaism," 201–3; Fredriksen, "Judaism, the Circumcision of Gentiles, and Apocalyptic Hope," 541–42; McKnight, *A Light among the Gentiles*, 113–14; Lieu, "The Race of God-fearers," 483; Levinskaya, *The Book of Acts in Its Diaspora Setting*, 51; Paget, "Jewish Proselytism," 93; Barclay, *Jews in the Mediterranean Diaspora*, 279; Hvalvik, *Struggle for Scripture and Covenant*, 249–57; Overman, "The God-Fearers," 261–62; Williams, *The Jews among the Greeks and Romans*, 163; Barnett, "Jewish Mission," 265; Schnabel, *Early Christian Mission*, 1.129–33; Donaldson, *Judaism and the Gentiles*, 433–34, 445–46.

[153] See Harnack, *The Expansion of Christianity*, 1.8–11; Moore, *Judaism in the First Centuries*, 1.348; Schürer [F. Millar], *History of the Jewish People in the Age of Jesus Christ*, 3.1.171; Safrai and Stern, *The Jewish People in the First Century*, 1.117–83; Georgi, *The Opponents of Paul in Second Corinthians*, 83–84; Feldman, "Was Judaism a Missionary Religion in Ancient Times?" 26–27; idem, *Jew and Gentile in the Ancient World*, 293; Paget, "Jewish Proselytism," 70–71, 82–83, 101; A. Wasserstein, "The Number and Provenance of Jews in Graeco-Roman Antiquity: A Short Note on Population Statistics," in *Classical Studies in Honor of David Sohlberg* (ed. R. Katzoff; Ramat Gan: Bar-Ilan University Press, 1996), 307–17.

wrote: "During the two centuries of Hasmonean and Herodian rule over Palestine the Jewish people expanded numerically to an unprecedented degree not only in Palestine but also in other lands, in part by active proselytization."[154] Similar is Harnack: "[I]t is utterly impossible to explain the large total of Jews in the Diaspora by the mere fact of the fertility of Jewish families. We must assume . . . that a very large number of pagans . . . trooped over to Yahweh."[155]

Several scholars have asserted that this dramatic increase in the Jewish population provides at least circumstantial evidence for Jewish missionary activity. Feldman advocates that "[o]nly proselytism can account for this vast increase."[156] More cautious is Paget: "An increase in the number of proselytes does seem the most likely explanation."[157] But the attribution of the increase in Jewish population to proselytism has come under severe criticism on several points.[158] First, it is simply not clear if there even were major increases in the Jewish population in the first century B.C.E. and C.E., since the available figures of ancient Jewish populations are far from exact.[159] In the case of the twelfth-century Syrian writer, Bar-Hebraeus, upon whom Baron relies, the figures are quite spurious.[160] The problem is accentuated by the fact that numbers

---

[154] Salo Baron, "Population," in *Encyclopaedia Judaica* (ed. Cecil Roth; 16 vols.; New York: MacMillan, 1971), 13.870.

[155] Harnack, *The Expansion of Christianity*, 1.10–11.

[156] Feldman, *Jew and Gentile in the Ancient World*, 293.

[157] Paget, "Jewish Proselytism," 83.

[158] Fredriksen, "Judaism, the Circumcision of Gentiles, and Apocalyptic Hope," 538; McKnight, *A Light among the Gentiles*, 33; Cohen, "Was Judaism in Antiquity a Missionary Religion?" 19–20; Goodman, "Jewish Proselytizing in the First Century," 55–56; idem, *Mission and Conversion*, 84; Williams, *The Jews among the Greeks and Romans*, 13; Riesner, "A Pre-Christian Jewish Mission," 220–21; Brian McGing, "Population and Proselytism: How Many Jews Were There in the Ancient World?" in *Jews in the Hellenistic and Roman Cities* (ed. John R. Bartlett; London/New York: Routledge, 2002), 88–106; Schnabel, *Early Christian Mission*, 1.124.

[159] Ezra 2:64–65; Philo, *Flacc.* 43; Josephus, *Life* 235; *Ag. Ap.* 1.197; *J.W.* 2.80; 6.420–425; 7.445; *Ant.* 11.133; 17.300; 18.83–84; Tacitus, *Hist.* 5.13; *Ann.* 2.85.4; *b. Pesah.* 64b. See also Schürer, *History of the Jewish People in the Age of Jesus Christ*, 2.1–19; 3.1.3–86.

[160] For an evaluation of Bar-Hebraeus see McGing, "Population and Proselytism," 92–94, who concludes from Bar-Hebraeus's errors elsewhere that: "It is high time that the evidence of Bar-Hebraeus was given decent burial and removed from our consideration."

in antiquity are often exaggerated for rhetorical purposes or else are symbolical. McKnight suggests we lack the demographic information on geographical population statistics, birth and survival rates, and immigration patterns to be able to make an informed judgment about the magnitude of Jewish population trends.[161] Brian McGing notes:

> I do not believe we have the first notion of how many Jews there were in the ancient world, even roughly speaking, nor do we have the means to discover it. This may sound like a counsel of despair, but pretending otherwise and basing important theories on wishful thinking, will get us nowhere.[162]

A second response to the view that Jewish population increases provide evidence for missionary activity is that even if a conservative estimate of 4–6 million Jews in the first century is accepted, there is no reason to postulate proselytization as a dominant cause for the increase. Other factors may account for the growth such as superior Jewish hygiene, Jewish refusal to engage in infanticide and abortion,[163] immigration, intermarriage, forced conversions in Ituraea and Idumaea by the Hasmoneans,[164] assimilation of the Phoenicians into Israel, and an increase in the agricultural output of Ptolemaic Egypt that could sustain larger populations. A third critique is that even if one assented to proselytization as causing a swelling of Jewish numbers, it tells us nothing of the *how* and *who* and *why* of proselytizing.[165]

---

[161] McKnight, *A Light among the Gentiles*, 33.

[162] McGing, "Population and Proselytism," 106; cf. Wasserstein, "The Number and Provenance of Jews in Graeco-Roman Antiquity," 312–14, who thinks that the Jewish population at the time was definitely large but also unquantifiable. Jonathan L. Reed, "Population Numbers, Urbanization, and Economics: Galilean Archaeology and the Historical Jesus," in *SBL Seminar Papers 1994* (ed. Eugene H. Lovering, Jr.; Atlanta: Scholars Press, 1994), 203–19, raises similar cautions.

[163] Tacitus. *Hist.* 5.5.3.

[164] Ptolemy in Ammonius, *Adfin. Vocab.* 243 (Stern, *GLAJJ* 1: §146); Strabo, *Geog.* 16.2.34 (Stern, *GLAJJ* 1: §115); Josephus, *Ant.* 13.257–258, 318–319, 395–397; 15.254–255.

[165] Cf. Paget, "Jewish Proselytism," 83.

JEWISH MISSIONARY ACTIVITY IN PALESTINE

No bifurcation should be made between Hellenistic and Palestinian Judaism, as all Judaism from the middle of the third century B.C.E. is "Hellenistic Judaism" to some degree. Even so a division between Palestinian and Diasporan attitudes and activities towards Gentiles is made here because: (1) The Jewish homeland had very different sociocultural conditions as compared to those of the Diaspora, and (2) Palestinian Judaism had a more ethnocentric tendency and was generally more susceptible to nationalistic and anti-Gentile sentiment than was its Diaspora counterpart.[1]

While interaction between Jews and Gentiles centers mainly on the cities of the Diaspora, encounters between Jews and Gentiles in Palestine also took place through military conquest, resettlement, and trade. What I intend to do in this chapter is to look at the phenomenon of forced conversions drawn principally from the Hasmonean period, examine evidence from Qumran, look at a key verse in Matthew (Matt 23:15), analyze inscriptions from Palestine, and touch briefly upon rabbinic literature as they all relate to proselytizing activity in Palestine. As will be clear at the end of the chapter, I detect no evidence of widespread proselytizing efforts in Palestinian Judaism.

FORCED CONVERSIONS IN PALESTINE

One way in which Gentiles converted to Judaism was through threat or by the application of military force. This model of "conversion" reaches back into the period of preexilic Israel and what was

---

[1] On the problems of stratifying the topics for such a study see McKnight, *A Light among the Gentiles,* 8–10.

specifically "forced" was usually circumcision.[2] Conversions out of fear or duress took place even in the Persian period as narrated in Esth 8:11–17 and this event was celebrated annually at the feast of Purim as a festive celebration of the triumph of Israel over the Gentiles.[3] The Hasmoneans provide the most epic and grand-scale accounts of forced conversions including the forced conversion of the Idumaeans by John Hyrcanus I,[4] the Ituraeans by Aristobolus I,[5] and probably portions of Syria and Phoenicia by Alexander Jannaeus[6] late in the second century B.C.E. In some cases these groups were only permitted to remain in the land if they consented to be circumcised and agreed to follow the Jewish law. While we do not have details of how these procedures were carried out and enforced, we do possess here evidence of a systematic attempt to convert Gentiles to Judaism on a mass level. It is the opinion of John J. Collins that these forced conversions constitute the "only evidence for an organized Jewish proselytizing campaign."[7]

It is important to place these forced conversions in their political and religious context. These conversions represent a form of political subjugation of the populace rather than comprising a theological act of converting Gentiles to belief and trust in Israel's God. The conversions are indeed theological in so far as they subjugate a pagan population beneath the reign of God's people in God's land, but on the whole conversions of this kind are more about winning battles for Yahweh than winning converts for Yahweh's kingdom. Viewed in this manner these forced conversions are akin to the mandatory acculturation and integration of the defeated peoples into the Judean nation. The military conquest of the Hasmonean dynasty over the surrounding nations and tribes was accompanied by a deliberate intent to subjugate the populace beneath Jewish rule and religion. Such efforts clearly illustrate the interweaving of political and religious activities together.

---

[2] Cf. 1 Sam 18:25–27; 2 Sam 3:14; 2 Kgs 17:24–28; 1 Macc 2:46; Jdt 14:10; Esther 8:17; Josephus, *Ant.* 11.285; *J.W.* 2.454; *Life* 113.

[3] *Ant.* 11.292–295.

[4] *Ant.* 13.257–258; 15.254–255; Strabo, *Geog.* 16.2.34 (Stern, *GLAJJ* 1: §115).

[5] *Ant.* 13.318–319.

[6] *Ant.* 13.395–397.

[7] John J. Collins, *Between Athens and Jerusalem: Jewish Identity in the Hellenistic Diaspora* (BRS; Grand Rapids, Mich.: Eerdmans, 1999), 262.

However, it is legitimate to ask whether forced conversions can count as an expression of mission given our earlier definitions. Borgen infers a form of military proselytism or "sword mission" from extant accounts.[8] He writes: "In Jewish history and tradition there is also another form of reaching out to the gentile world, that of military conquest."[9] The definition of mission that I set forth earlier clearly does not permit a form of "sword mission" to be a legitimate form of missionary activity given the parameters that were set out about the transformation of identity and values in conversion. Forced circumcision or "sword mission" certainly is a type of military proselytism, but it is not a form of "mission" as mission is ordinarily understood.

We might also note that the "forced" nature of the conversion of the Idumaeans and Ituraeans by the Hasmoneans has been questioned as has been the issue of whether the imposition of Judaism was really all that radical for other Near Eastern peoples of the region.[10] We know that Strabo (who relies on Timagenes) reports the same events, but does not explicitly mention the compulsory nature of the conversions.[11] There are a number of reasons for viewing these conversions as far from being "skin-deep"[12]: The Idumaeans started attending Jewish festivals;[13] Alexander Jannaeus appointed Herod Antipater—a native Idumaean— to his court as *strategos* for Idumaea;[14] Idumaeans figured prominently in the Jewish revolt against Rome 66–70 C.E.;[15] and some Idumeans became disciples of Shammai.[16] The cultural shift was not as vast, since Herodotus records that circumcision was already common among the "Syrians of Palestine" (Σύριοι οἱ ἐν τῇ Παλαιστίνῃ) so circumcision may not have been culturally foreign to the non-Jewish peoples of the region to begin with.[17] It is also unlikely that a relatively small

[8] Borgen, *Early Christianity and Hellenistic Judaism*, 46.
[9] Borgen, "Proselytes, Conquest, and Mission," 66.
[10] Aryeh Kasher, *Jews, Idumaeans and Ancient Arabs* (Tübingen: Mohr/ Siebeck, 1988), 45–85; Cohen, *The Beginnings of Jewishness*, 110–18.
[11] Strabo, *Geog.* 16.2.34 (Stern, *GLAJJ* 1: §115); Josephus, *Ant.* 13.319.
[12] Moore, *Judaism in the First Centuries*, 1.336.
[13] *Ant.* 17.254.
[14] *Ant.* 14.10.
[15] *J.W.* 2.566, 652–654; 4.224–304; 5.248.
[16] *Sifre Zutta* (ed. Epstein), *Tarbiz*, I (1930), p. 70; cited in Kasher, *Jews, Idumaeans and Ancient Arabs*, 63 n. 56.
[17] Herodotus, *Hist.* 2.104.2–3 (Stern, *GLAJJ* 1: §1); cf. Philo, *Spec. Leg.* 1.2; *Quaest. in Gen.* 3.47; Josephus, *Ant.* 8.262; *Ag. Ap.* 1.168–171; Jer 9:25–26.

Hasmonean state, rife with internal dissension, would be able to annex and assimilate an adjacent territory so quickly without prior Jewish influence.[18] Moreover, the story of forced circumcision may have arisen out of anti-Hasmonean propaganda emerging from circles associated with Nicolaus of Damascus.[19] Ayreh Kasher argues that such conversions were "a voluntary act, the culmination of a gradual, drawn-out process of convergence between eastern Semitic ethnic groups nursing shared hostility to the Hellenistic world, which threatened their independent existence."[20] In other words, the conversion of the Idumaeans might have been a gradual process covering years if not decades.[21]

Suffice to say, the interaction of Idumaeans and Ituraeans with Israel in political, social, religious, and economic affairs is probably more complex than the sources indicate.[22] Yet the accounts of forced conversion may not be without historical credence and they cannot be attributed purely to anti-Hasmonean propaganda. Strabo's testimony available from both his *Geographica* and from Josephus's *Antiquities* is a vital witness here.

> The Idumaeans are Nabataeans, but owing to a sedition they were banished from there, joined the Judaeans, and shared in the same customs with them (Ναβαταῖοι δ᾽ εἰσὶν οἱ Ἰδουμαῖοι· κατὰ στάσιν δ᾽

---

[18] Kasher, *Jews, Idumaeans and Ancient Arabs*, 56; Steven Weitzman, "Forced Circumcision and the Shifting Role of Gentiles in Hasmonean Ideology," *HTR* 92 (1999): 40.

[19] Cf. Grabbe, *Judaism from Cyrus to Hadrian*, 330.

[20] Kasher, *Jews, Idumaeans and Ancient Arabs*, 55; cf. Cohen (*The Beginnings of Jewishness*, 116–17) who contends that the rural Idumaeans joined out of anti-Hellenistic sympathy and to "make the best of the inevitable." Regarding Josephus's account, Cohen ("Respect for Judaism by Gentiles according to Josephus," 422–23) thinks he follows the tradition of forced conversions so as to assuage Roman fears that shared circumcision can lead to a voluntary political-military coalition. See also Morton Smith, "The Gentiles in Judaism 125 BCE–CE 66," in *The Cambridge History of Judaism: Volume Three* (eds. W. D. Davies, William Horbury, and John Sturdy (Cambridge: CUP, 1999), 199–213; but note the objections of Weitzman, "Forced Circumcision," 43–44.

[21] To the Jewish aristocracy, the Idumaeans, especially the likes of Herod, were only half-Jews (ἡμιιουδαίῳ) perhaps because their adherence was either relatively recent or simply a condition of a political alliance (*Ant.* 14.403). See similar polemics in Justin, *Dial. Tryph.* 52; Eusebius, *Eccl. Hist.* 1.7.11; *b. B.Bat.* 3b. However, in other sources he is regarded as a bona fide Jew, see discussion in Cohen, *Beginnings of Jewishness*, 15.

[22] Weitzman, "Forced Circumcision," 59.

ἐκπεσόντες ἐκεῖθεν προσεχώρησαν τοῖς Ἰουδαίοις καὶ τῶν νομίκων τῶν αυ-τῶν ἐκείνοισ ἐκοινώνησαν).[23] He [Aristobulus] was by nature a man of gentleness and exceeding modesty, as Strabo testifies, in the name of Timagenes; who says thus: "This man was a person of gentleness, and very beneficial to the Jews; for he added a country to them, and joined a part of the nation of the Itureans for them, and bound them to them by the bond of their circumcision (καὶ τὸ μέρος τοῦ τῶν Ἰτουραίων ἔθνους ᾠκειώσατο δεσμῷ συνάψας τῇ τῶν αἰδοίων περιτομῇ)."[24]

On reflection, the terms "joined" (ᾠκειώσατο)[25] and "joined the Jews" (προσεχώρησαν τοῖς Ἰουδαίοις) are quite circumspect.[26] Even so, Josephus's account of Strabo does imply the annexing and subjugation of the territory followed by the compulsory circumcision of the populace. That account of military aggression and forced circumcision is reinforced by Ptolemy who records that the Idumaeans were "forced to be circumcised" (ἀναγκασθέντες περιτέμνεσθαι).[27] Though Strabo is earlier than Ptolemy he may not necessarily be more reliable since Strabo mistakenly identifies the Idumaeans with the Nabataeans.[28] We can also trust Josephus's version because although he had a clear aversion to forced conversions (see *Life* 1.112–113), and despite being of Hasmonean descent himself,[29] he records the event regardless.[30] The entire account about the forced conversion of the Idumaeans also corresponds with later attitudes towards the surrounding peoples by Hasmonean and Herodian rulers. Alexander Jannaeus sacked Pella in Moab (ca. 83 B.C.E.) because it would not adopt Jewish customs.[31] The attempt of the Idumaean Governor Costobarus to rebel against Herod was anchored partly in a desire to be free of Jewish rites,[32] hardly indicative of a volunteer. This should cast doubt on the notion that the reports of forced circumcisions were fabrications arising from

[23] Strabo, *Geog.* 16.2.34 (Stern, *GLAJJ* 1: §115).
[24] *Ant.* 13.319.
[25] *Ant.* 13.319.
[26] Strabo, *Geog.* 16.2.34 (Stern, *GLAJJ* 1: §115).
[27] Ptolemy in Ammonius, *Adfin. Vocab.* 243 (Stern, *GLAJJ* 1: §146).
[28] Strabo, *Geog.* 16.2.34 (Stern, *GLAJJ* 1: §115).
[29] *Life* 2.
[30] Feldman, *Jew and Gentile in the Ancient World*, 325.
[31] *Ant.* 13.397.
[32] *Ant.* 15.253–255.

anti-Hasmonaean propaganda or that the circumcision of the Idumaeans and Ituraeans was simply attributable to a gradual assimilation of
Near Eastern peoples into a dominant Judean state.

Other instances of aggressive circumcising are found even earlier in
the initial phase of the Maccabean revolt where, according to 1 Macc 2:44–
48, Mattathias forcibly circumcised all the boys in Israel he could find.

> They organized an army, and struck down sinners in their anger and ren-
> egades in their wrath; the survivors fled to the Gentiles for safety. And
> Mattathias and his friends went around and tore down the altars; they
> forcibly circumcised all the uncircumcised boys that they found within the
> borders of Israel. They hunted down the arrogant, and the work prospered
> in their hands. They rescued the law out of the hands of the Gentiles and
> kings, and they never let the sinner gain the upper hand (1 Macc 2:44–48).

Kasher thinks that Mattathias's actions focused only on Jewish boys
and not those outside the Jewish community,[33] but the entire passage
focuses on both re-Judaizing/de-Hellenizing the land of Israel and also
subjugating Gentiles within it. The "sinners" targeted in the pogrom can
include both affluent Jews (e.g., *1 Enoch* 102:9–11; Sir 9:11; 41:6) and
Gentiles (e.g., 1 Macc 1:7–10, 34; 2 Macc 12:23; 14:42; Ps 9:15–16; Tob
13:6; Gal 2:15).[34] Note also the strong anti-Gentile sentiment about those
who "fled" to the Gentiles and how the law was "rescued" out of the hands
of Gentiles. This suggests that those circumcised "within the borders of Israel" probably consisted of a mixture of culturally compromised Jews and
remaining non-Jewish residents. The logic is that the land would not be
holy if uncircumcised males dwelled in it. A similar perspective is found in
Josephus who depicts some Judeans threatening to forcibly circumcise two
Gentiles "if they wished to live among them."[35] Thus, against Borgen, the
motivation behind such conversions is not mission but sacralization—a
desire to reverse the process of Hellenization in *Eretz* Israel, to reinforce
Jewish boundaries, to protect the sacred space of Jerusalem and its envi-
rons—and the motivation came out of zeal for the law.[36] Nonetheless,
the forced conversions did have a huge momentous and continuing ef-

---

[33] Kasher, *Jews, Idumaeans and Ancient Arabs*, 58–59; cf. Cohen, *The Beginnings of Jewishness,* 118.
[34] On "sinners" in Judaism see Crossley, *Why Christianity Happened,* 76–96.
[35] *Life* 113.
[36] Weitzman, "Forced Circumcision," 58; Ware, *Paul's Letter to the Philippians,* 49.

fect on the religious landscape of Palestine since Josephus notes that after the conversion of the Idumaeans by Hyrcanus I "from that time on they have continued to be Jews" (εἶναι Ἰουδαίους) and this is proved by Idumaean participation in the Jewish revolt against Rome.[37]

QUMRAN

Overall, the Dead Sea Scrolls contribute little to our knowledge of proselytization in Palestine, but they do provide an example of how some Judeans found it impossible to relate to the Gentile world in anything other than negative terms.[38] The problem of how to integrate Gentile proselytes into Judaism or into the community at Qumran was not a topic that merited attention in the Scrolls, since the Scrolls are focused on intra-Jewish sectarianism vis-à-vis other Israelites and not on the status Gentiles *per se*. Consequently, there are vituperative remarks against the "seekers after smooth things" (1QH 2:31–32; 4QpNah 1:2, 4; 4Q169 2:4; 3:3, 6–8; CD 1:18–20), the "men of power" (1QpHab 8:11–12), and the "wicked priest" (1QpHab 1:13, 8:8–13). The Qumran writings concentrate mostly on segregation from Gentile impurities and look forward to the defeat and subjugation of the pagan nations.[39] All the same, it is illuminating to note what the extant Qumran writings (especially the sectarian documents and unique biblical interpretations) say about the future of the Gentiles and about the intensification of regulations for avoiding Gentiles.

The Gentiles are expressly forbidden from participating in the temple of the new age according to several documents. The accent in Qumran exegesis falls on the exclusive nature of worship in the temple, which makes no provision for the participation of non-Jews in the worship of the covenant God. The distinctiveness of the Qumranites can be seen by contrasting the various textual versions of Isa 56:6:[40]

---

[37] *Ant.* 13.258; 17.254; *J.W.* 4.224–235, 258 etc.

[38] For an overview of attitudes towards Gentiles in the Dead Sea Scrolls see Schnabel, *Early Christian Mission*, 1.105–16; Donaldson, *Judaism and the Gentiles*, 195–215.

[39] Roland Deines, "Die Abwehr der Fremden in den Texten aus Qumran: Zum Verständnis der Fremdenfeindlichkeit in der Qumrangemeinde," in *Die Heiden: Juden, Christen und das Problem des Fremden* (eds. Reinhard Feldmeier and Ulrich Heckel (WUNT 70; Tübingen: Mohr/Siebeck, 1994), 64.

[40] I have cited the texts from Craig A. Evans, "From 'House of Prayer' to 'Cave of Robbers': Jesus' Prophetic Criticism of the Temple Establishment," in

MT   And the sons of a foreigner that join themselves to the Lord, to minister to him, to love the name of the Lord, and to be his servants, all who keep the Sabbath without profaning it, and hold fast my covenant.

וּבְנֵי הַנֵּכָר הַנִּלְוִים עַל־יְהֹוָה לְשָׁרְתוֹ
וּלְאַהֲבָה אֶת־שֵׁם יְהֹוָה לִהְיוֹת לוֹ לַעֲבָדִים
כָּל־שֹׁמֵר שַׁבָּת מֵחַלְלוֹ וּמַחֲזִיקִים בִּבְרִיתִי׃

LXX   And to the foreigners that join themselves to the Lord, to serve him, and to love the name of the Lord, to be to him servants and *handmaids*; and *as for* all that guard my *Sabbaths* from profaning *them*, and hold fast to my covenant.

καὶ τοῖς ἀλλογενέσι τοῖς προσκειμένοις κυρίῳ δουλεύειν αὐτῷ καὶ ἀγαπᾶν τὸ ὄνομα κυρίου τοῦ εἶναι αὐτῷ εἰς δούλους καὶ δούλας καὶ πάντας τοὺς φυλασσομένους τὰ σάββατά μου μὴ βεβηλοῦν καὶ ἀντεχομένους τῆς διαθήκης μου

Tg. Isa   And the sons of *Gentiles* who have *been added to the people of* the Lord, to minister to him, to love the name of the Lord, and to be his servants, everyone who *will* keep *the* Sabbath without profaning it, and hold fast my covenants.

וּבְנֵי עַמְמַיָּא דְּמִתּוֹסְפִין עַל עַמֵּיה דַּיְיָ לְשַׁמָּשׁוּתֵיה
וּלְמִרְחַם יָת שְׁמָא דַּיְיָ לְמִהְוֵי לֵיה לְעַבְדִּין
כָּל דְּיַטַּר שַׁבְּתָא מֵאֲחָלוּתֵיה וּמִתַּקְפִין בִּקְיָמַי׃

1QIsaª   Also the sons of a foreigner that join themselves to the Lord, *to be his servants, and to bless the name of the Lord*, that observe *the* Sabbath without profaning it, and hold fast my covenant.

ובני הנכר הנלויים אל יהוה להיות
לו לעבדים ולברך את שם יהוה ושומרים
את השבת מחללה ומחזיקים בבריתי

The Septuagint follows the Masoretic Text very closely. The Isaiah Targum emphasizes that the Gentiles who flock to Zion have first been "added to the people of the Lord" or become proselytes.[41] 1QIsaiah[a] presupposes that the Gentiles who come cannot serve as priests since the reading omits "to minister to him," significantly restricting the service offered by Gentiles. One finds elsewhere that Gentiles and even proselytes are expressly prohibited from participating in the future eschatological temple: "This is the House which [He will build for them in the last days] . . . never [enter, nor the uncircumcised], nor the Ammonite, nor the Moabite, nor the half-breed, nor the foreigner (בן נכר), nor the proselyte (גר), ever; for there shall My Holy Ones be."[42] The primary issue here is purity rather than membership in Israel, and the purity of the temple is reflected in the purity of the community, which functions as an interim temple of sorts until God's eschatological deliverance.[43] The halakic letter 4QMMT, possibly stemming from the Teacher of Righteousness himself and written to the High Priest Jonathan, censures priests operating in the temple for receiving grain offerings from Gentiles; they should not be eaten by priests or brought into the temple.[44] This narration of the restoration of Israel and the renewal of the temple does not accommodate the participation of the Gentiles in the operation of the cultus and in fact its renewal seems contingent upon their exclusion.

The negative attitude towards non-Jews is reinforced by the repeated emphasis on the impurity of Gentiles and the need for exhaustive separation from Gentiles. This is exhibited lucidly in 4Q266 frg. 5.II:5–7, where priests who come into contact with Gentiles are forbidden from performing liturgical activities. The Temple Scroll (which may or may not be a sectarian document) also regards as punishable by death the one who has "defected into the midst of the nations and has cursed his people and the children of Israel" (11QT 64:12–13). In any event, separation from Gentiles is clearly accentuated.

---

[41] Like the Targum, later rabbinic Midrashim could interpret Isa 56:3–6 as implying that the foreigners who join themselves to the Lord first became proselytes (*Exod. Rab.* 19.4; *Num. Rab.* 8.2). There is no salvation of Gentiles *as Gentiles* as became normative in early Christianity.

[42] 4Q174 1:3–5.

[43] Donaldson, *Judaism and the Gentiles,* 213–14.

[44] Cf. *J.W.* 2.409–416 where the High Priest Eleazar refused to offer sacrifices on behalf of the emperor and so provided a catalyst for conflict with Rome. Josephus himself says that if Eleazar's decision was allowed to stand then the Jews would be "the only people to allow no alien the right of sacrifice or worship" and become "open to the charge of impiety" (*J.W.* 2.414).

In other documents, it was the eschatological destruction of the Gentiles rather than the eschatological pilgrimage of the nations to Zion that is emphasized at several places. The visitation of divine vengeance upon the Gentiles is a key ingredient in hopes for the future. The *War Scroll* is the "rule" (סרך) for how the coming battles are to be fought between the "exiles in the wilderness" and the Gentile nations.[45] 1QM is arguably an apocalyptic version of the apologetic historiography of the Maccabean literature transposed to the future where the devastating destruction of the *kittim* (כתיים) marks the conquest of Yahweh and the "sons of light" over apostate Jews and the pagan world at large and over Greece and/or Rome in particular.[46] Other nations adjacent Israel are named (e.g., Edom, Moab, Ammon, Philistia, and Asshur),[47] but all the nations opposing God's elect will be conquered by a coalition of the community and heavenly combatants. The defeat of the local Gentile nations signals the coming of the "time of salvation" (עת ישועה) for the people of God.[48] The eschatological pilgrimage of the nations known from the Hebrew Scriptures (e.g., Isa 2:2–4, Mic 4:14, and Zech 8:22–23) has been ostentatiously transformed into a symbol of the humiliation and subjugation of the nations.[49] According to the commentary on Nahum, there will be no prophetic envoys to the nations, rather the prophet declares about Yahweh's emissaries: "And 'his messengers' are his envoys, whose voice will no longer be heard by the nations"[50] which is naturally contrasted with scriptural hopes articulated in passages such as Pss 18:49, 108:3, Isa 42:6, 49:6, and 66:19–20 where the nations hear the prophetic messengers. The future for the pagan nations is one of judgment, not redemption according to this framework.

The non-sectarian writings at Qumran (i.e., those not originating among the Qumranites themselves) contain ambivalent depictions of Gentiles. A copy of the second-century B.C.E. document *Jubilees* is extant at Qumran, and it includes an exhortation to avoid contact with

---

[45] See further on the defeat of the nations in Qumran literature Michael E. Fuller, *The Restoration of Israel: Israel's Regathering and the Fate of the Nations in Early Jewish Literature and Luke-Acts* (BZNW 138; Berlin: Walter de Gruyter, 2006), 133–48.

[46] See esp. 1QM 14:16–19:13.

[47] 1QM 1:1–2.

[48] 1QM 1:5.

[49] 1QM 12:11–16; 14:5–7; 19:3–7.

[50] 4QpNah 3–4, 2:1.

Gentiles, but also affirms that the nations of the earth will be blessed by Abraham.[51] The Psalms Scroll[a] states: "Instruct me, Lord, in your law, and teach me your precepts so that many may hear your deeds and nations may honor your glory" which mirrors the kerygmatic function of the Psalms in the Hebrew Bible.[52] Yet this was not a Qumran composition and reflects a more general view that Israel's preservation and deliverance will result in an effusion of the Torah to outsiders. 4Q159 frags. 2–4 affirms Lev 25 and the prohibition against selling Israelites as slaves to resident aliens. The Damascus Document contains historical allusions to the formation of the sect amid exhortations for conduct and precepts concerning discipline within the community. Though concerned principally with "insiders," it makes tacit reference to those persons who are a גר at certain points. At one place, the Damascus Document refers to the "poor, the needy, and the alien," and given the largely pentateuchal language here גר very probably means "alien" or "sojourner" as opposed to "proselyte."[53] Elsewhere the Damascus Document, much like rabbinic literature, knows of a generic categorization of Priests, Levites, Israelites, and Proselytes and such figures can be members of the community.[54] The question in this text is whether the word גר means Jewish proselyte, resident alien, or something else. The Damascus Document regards Jewish non-members of the community effectively as non-Jews. Here גר means one who is undertaking the entrance process on the way to becoming an "Israelite" or a member of the Damascene community.[55] Given this social setting, I find a translation of "neophyte" may be preferable. This is reinforced by the observation that 1QS 6:13–14 seems to assume that new members are drawn from Israel rather than from non-Jewish stock. Segregation from Gentiles is observed also in the Damascus Document: "Let no man rest in a place near Gentiles on the Sabbath."[56] There is a further proscription against selling circumcised foreign slaves to Gentiles since "they [the slaves] have entered into the covenant of Abraham."[57] Whereas

---

[51] *Jub.* 20:22–24; 12:23.

[52] 11QPs[a]/11Q5 24:8–9; cf., e.g., Pss 9:11; 18:49; 45:17; 57:9; 67:2–7; 96:3–10; 97:1; 105:1; 108:3; 119:46; 126:2–3; 145:11–12, 21.

[53] CD 6:14–21; cf. Lev 19:10; 23:22; Deut 14:29; 16:11, 14; 24:17–21.

[54] CD 14:5–6; *t. Qidd.* 5.1.

[55] Schnabel, *Early Christian Mission*, 1.111.

[56] CD 11:14–15.

[57] CD 12:10–11; cf. *m. Git.* 4.6.

Jews in the Diaspora and in Palestine sought to avoid excessive fraternizing with Gentiles, in the literature of Qumran this is intensified into absolute avoidance of Gentiles for risk of contamination. The most positive portrayal of a Gentile in the Scrolls is in the Qumranite version of the Prayer of Nabonidus. This story stands in some kind of tradition-historical relation to Dan 4 and it is about a Babylonian king who prays to the God of Israel for healing.[58] The king takes the initiative in praying to "the God Most High" after a Jewish exorcist forgave his sins and urged him to make a written proclamation as to what God had done for him. The prayer is reminiscent of 2 Kgs 5, Jonah 1, and Mal 1. Yet even there he never addresses God in the first person singular, and he does not become a proselyte.[59] The role of the exorcist or diviner is not that of a missionary, but more akin to Daniel from Dan 1–6 who is a Jewish sage used by God to force Gentile rulers to recognize that the reign and authority of Israel's God is infinitely superior to that of their own earthly realm.

There is a universalism in the Scrolls insofar as the elect are destined to rule over the world[60] and Yahweh's reign will encompass all the nations. However, the Qumran scrolls demonstrate that having an intense eschatology does not necessarily draw one into universalistic hopes affording a positive place for the Gentiles with a restored Israel.[61] For the most part, the Gentiles are associated with impurity, idolatry, and everlasting destruction. The Qumran writings do know of Gentile proselytes and foreigners, but not as members of their own community.

MATTHEW 23:15

A verse frequently cited from the New Testament in favor of the existence of Jewish missionary activity in the Second Temple period is Matt 23:15: "Woe to you, scribes and Pharisees, hypocrites! For you

---

[58] 4QPrNab.

[59] Schnabel, *Early Christian Mission*, 1.106–7; Donaldson, *Judaism and the Gentiles*, 201.

[60] 4Q381 76–77, 14–16 reads: "He chose yo[u] [from m]any [peoples] and from the great nations to be his people, to rule over all [. . .][. . . h]eavens and earth, and as most high over every nation of the earth."

[61] See further Lawrence H. Schiffman, "Non-Jews in the Dead Sea Scrolls," in *The Quest for Context and Meaning: Studies in Biblical Intertextuality in Honor of James A. Sanders* (eds. Craig A. Evans and Shemaryahu Talmon; BIS 28; Leiden: Brill, 1997), 153–71; Schnabel, *Early Christian Mission*, 1.330.

cross sea and land to make a single convert, and you make the proselyte twice as much a child of hell as yourselves." The logion is the second of seven woe oracles in Matt 23:13–36 which denounces the scribes and Pharisees.[62] The logion can be understood in several ways. (1) It can be understood as a reference to the proselytizing of Gentiles by Pharisees.[63] This is supported by the fact that περιάγω ("I cross") implies a sense of itinerancy and the same word is used in Matt 4:23 and 9:35 for Jesus' own mission activity.[64] The passage can be said to have mind the task of distant travel with a view to making converts. We also know that some Pharisees such as R. Hillel (ca. 110–10 B.C.E.) were purportedly willing to accept Gentiles and instruct them (later rabbinic discussions about proselytes may derive from first-century Pharisaic practices in this matter since the problem of proselytes was hardly unique to the post-135 C.E. period).[65] However, Davies and Allison caution that since Matt 23:15 is full of "hyperbolic invective" it cannot be used as evidence of Jewish missionary activity.[66] Did Pharisees *really* go on sea voyages to win over Gentiles for Yahweh? While an

---

[62] On the authenticity of the saying as an utterance of Jesus see Michael F. Bird, "Matthew 23:15—The Case of the Proselytizing Pharisees," *JSHJ* 2 (2004): 120–22.

[63] Jeremias, *Jesus' Promise to the Nations*, 19; Schürer, *History of the Jewish People in the Age of Jesus Christ*, 3.1.160; Daube, "Conversion to Judaism and Early Christianity," 11–12; John P. Meier, *Matthew* (Wilmington: Michael Glazier, 1986 [1980]), 269; Segal, "The Cost of Proselytism and Conversion," 356; Feldman, "Was Judaism a Missionary Religion in Ancient Times?" 29; idem, *Jew and Gentile in the Ancient World*, 298; Paget, "Jewish Proselytism," 94–97; Rokéah, "Ancient Jewish Proselytism," 212–13; Bedell, "Mission in Intertestamental Judaism," 28.

[64] Contra McKnight, *A Light among the Gentiles*, 154, n. 30; and with Levinskaya, *The Book of Acts in Its Diaspora Setting*, 39.

[65] *b. Šabb.* 31a.

[66] W. D. Davies and Dale C. Allison, *The Gospel according to Saint Matthew* (3 vols.; ICC; Edinburgh: T&T Clark, 1988–1997), 3.288; cf. Fredriksen, "Judaism, the Circumcision of Gentiles, and Apocalyptic Hope," 538; Kraabel, "The Disappearance of the God-Fearers," 123; idem, "The Roman Diaspora," 452; Wander, *Gottesfürchtige und Sympathisanten*, 218–27. M. Löhr (*Der Missionsgedanke im Alten Testament: Ein Beitrag zur alttestamentlichen Religionsgeschichte* [Freiburg: J. C. B. Mohr, 1896], 40) wrote: "Es ist schwer zu entscheiden, ob dieses Zeugnis ein Hyperbel ist, oder auf Tatsachen beruht, da uns andere Nachrichten über eine missionierende Tätigkeit der Juden aus jener Zeit vollständig fehlen."

intention to make converts from a certain group is clear, the zeal to do so is undoubtedly exaggerated.

(2) The passage can be understood as signifying the efforts of Pharisees to convert other Jews to Pharisaism.[67] Goodman suggests that "Matthew is here attacking Pharisees for their eagerness in trying to persuade other Jews to follow Pharisaic *halakah*."[68] This interpretation is supported by the fact that προσήλυτος ("proselyte") can be used flexibly and even be applied to Jews under certain circumstances (e.g., Exod 22:20 LXX where προσήλυτος translates גרים, which refers to the Israelites in Egypt).[69] Furthermore, the verse does imply that the convert became a Pharisee or at least adopted a Pharisaic interpretation of the Torah. That comports with accounts from Josephus and the Gospel of Mark that the Pharisees were eager to transmit their traditions to other Jews in Palestine.[70] At the horizon of Matthew's Gospel, however, the verse is quite probably employed against a background of competition and rivalry between Jewish Christians associated with Matthew's audience and post-70 C.E. pharisaic Jewish leaders over the socioreligious allegiances of Gentile sympathizers to Judaism or Jesus-believing Gentiles. The contest is whether these Gentiles will become and/or remain "Christians" or become "pharisaic Jews." Later Christian writings also know of Christians who took to Jewish ways,[71] and this might reflect the situation that called for Matthew to mention and expound this logion from the Jesus tradition. In other words, this verse seems to have Gentiles (of some kind) somewhere in the background rather than being a purely intra-Jewish debate about whose *halakah* Jews should follow.

(3) Matthew 23:15 can be understood as denoting the attempt of Pharisees to turn God-fearers into full Jews.[72] McKnight thinks that the

---

[67] Munck, *Paul and the Salvation of Mankind*, 266–67; Goodman, "Jewish Proselytizing in the First Century," 60–63; idem, *Mission and Conversion*, 69–74; Levinskaya, *The Book of Acts in Its Diaspora Setting*, 6–39; Köstenberger and O'Brien, *Salvation to the Ends of the Earth*, 64; Will and Orrieux, *Prosélytisme Juif?*, 119, 322; Donaldson, *Judaism and the Gentiles*, 412–15.

[68] Goodman, "Jewish Proselytizing in the First Century," 61; idem, *Mission and Conversion*, 70–71.

[69] Goodman, *Mission and Conversion*, 73.

[70] Josephus, *Ant.* 13.197; 17.41; 18.15; and implicitly in Mark 7:1–13.

[71] Cf. *Barn.* 3.6; *Did.* 8:1–2; Ignatius, *Phld.* 6:1; Justin, *Dial. Tryph.* 47.

[72] Kuhn "προσήλυτος" *TDNT* 6.742; McKnight, *A Light among the Gentiles*, 106–8; Davies and Allison, *Saint Matthew*, 3.289; D. A. Hagner, *Matthew* (2 vols.; WBC; Dallas, Tex.: Word, 1993–1995), 2.669; Paul Bar-

compounding of "make" (ποιῆσαι) and "convert" (προσήλυτον) implies the total conversion and circumcision of a Gentile. The activity envisaged corresponds remarkably with that of Eleazar the Galilean from *Ant.* 20.40–42 who compelled King Izates to be circumcised and attain a fuller and more acceptable conversion according to stricter interpretations of the law.[73] Thus the issue is making partial converts into full converts with extreme zeal for the Torah: "Torah proselytization."[74] Yet there is no definitive proof from Matt 23:15 itself that a shift from adherence to conversion is envisaged since we lack any reference to prior adherence to Jewish ways by these potential converts. Likewise, there is no allusion to circumcision and incorporation into Jewish communities or anything which could indicate "closing the deal" so to speak in their socioreligious transference. While a proselyte is clearly the end product spoken of we do not know if these hypothetical missional Pharisees began with pagan or with Jewish sympathizers. Either scenario is possible.

(4) Matthew 23:15 can be understood as representing the efforts of Pharisees in trying to recruit God-fearers into the cause of Jewish resistance to the Roman Empire.[75] This view is plausible on the grounds that: (i) Pharisaism had a militant wing and often exhibited a zealous theology for Israel's liberation by its members.[76] (ii) To "Judaize" (ἰουδαΐζειν) can include adopting Jewish customs but also embracing the Jewish political cause.[77] (iii) According to Josephus, several foreigners were fighting against the Romans for the Jews including members of

---

nett, *Jesus and the Rise of Early Christianity: A History of New Testament Times* (Downers Grove, Ill.: InterVarsity, 1999), 270; idem, "Jewish Mission," 271–72; Riesner, "A Pre-Christian Jewish Mission," 232–34; Ware, *Paul's Letter to the Philippians*, 53–55.

[73] Eleazar may have even been a Pharisee since his strictness on the law resembles Josephus's description of the Pharisees in *Life* 191 and *J.W.* 1.110; cf. Riesner, "A Pre-Christian Jewish Mission," 238.

[74] McKnight, *A Light among the Gentiles*, 107.

[75] See Bird, "The Case of the Proselytizing Pharisees" for further discussion.

[76] Cf. the refusal of 6,000 Pharisees to take an oath of loyalty to Herod and Caesar (*Ant.* 17.41–45; *J.W.* 1.571–573); the uprising of 6 C.E. led by Judas the Galilean and a Pharisee named Saddok (*Ant.* 18.1–10; *J.W.* 2.56, 118); according to Josephus the "fourth philosophy" (i.e., Zealots) is said to agree with Pharisaic notions (*Ant.* 18.23); and Simon b. Gamaliel, a Pharisee, was an associate of John of Gischala who led a faction of the Jewish uprising against Rome (*J.W.* 4.159; *Life* 189–198).

[77] Cf. Josephus, *J.W.* 2.454, 463; *Acts of Pilate* 2.

the Adiabenian royal family.[78] (iv) In *Dial. Tryph.* 122, Justin cites Matt 23:15 and then alludes to it again to refer to the violent acts that proselytes of the Jews do to Christians: "But the proselytes not only do not believe, but twofold more than yourself blaspheme His name, and wish to torture and put to death us who believe in Him; for in all points they strive to be like you." The implication is that replicating the hypocrisy of the Pharisees was not the sum meaning of the logion (though it is likely to be Matthew's primary perspective). Justin points out that the saying is relevant to sectarian violence between Jews and Christians.

It appears that despite comprising "the only ancient source that explicitly ascribes a missionary policy to a Jewish group,"[79] Matt 23:15 does not demonstrate the existence of Jewish missionary activity. Of the four options we have examined, only option one implies proselytizing activity, and yet the invective remarks expressed in the logion reflects rhetoric rather than reality about pharisaic activity. If we accept option two—converting other Jews to Pharisaism—then the passage does not refer to Jewish missionary activity either. If one accepts the evidence for the third or fourth option as the best explanation of Matt 23:15, then the making of proselytes is directed towards those who are already adherents to Judaism in some way. In these last options, the passage is about the Pharisaizing of God-fearers to a zealous brand of Judaism, not a mission of Pharisees to Gentiles.

INSCRIPTIONS FROM PALESTINE

The role of epigraphic evidence is much neglected in studies of Christian origins and Second Temple Judaism. Inscriptions about proselytes and God-fearers provide us with physical residue of the relations that Gentiles had with their Jewish neighbors, how they celebrated their association with Jewish communities, and how they even marked their integration into a Jewish community as proselytes. While the majority of inscriptions about proselytes and God-fearers come from the Diaspora (principally Rome and North Africa), there are a few extant inscriptions about proselytes from ossuaries found in Palestine which have been conveniently cataloged by Paul Figueras (and I have also provided a bilingual inscription from Gideon Avni and Zvi Greenhut in # 6).

---

[78] Josephus, *J.W.* 5.248–250; 7.191; *Ant.* 17.254–268; and *J.W.* 2.520; 5.474.
[79] Cohen, "Was Judaism in Antiquity a Missionary Religion?" 18.

1. שלום הגרית, "Shalom [or Salome] the Proselyte" (Mount of Olives, Jerusalem).

2. מריה הגרית הדולקת, "Maria [or Miriam] the fervent proselyte" (Necropolis, Jerusalem).[80]

3. ΔΙΟΓΕΝΗC ΠΡΟCΗΛΥΤΟC ΖΗΝΑ, "Diogenes the proselyte son of [or from] Zena" (Dominus Flevit, Jerusalem).

4. ΙΟΥΔΑΝ ΠΡΟCΗΛΥΤΟC ΤΥΡΑ, "Judah the proselyte from Tyre" (Dominus Flevit, Jerusalem).

5. ΙΟΥΔΑΤΟC ΛΑΓΑΝΙΟΝΟC ΠΡΟCΗΛΥΤΟΥ, "[Ossuary] of Judah son of [or from] Laganion, the proselyte" (Museum of St. Anne, Jerusalem).

6. ΑΡΙCΤΩΝ
ארסטון אפמי
יהודה הגיור
Ariston, Ariston of Apamea, Judah the proselyte (Kidron Valley, Jerusalem).

Post-death rituals are a good indicator of the religious ethos of the deceased, much in the same way that references to God and the afterlife in the preamble to wills, obituaries, and gravestones inscriptions tell us much about the faith of the people who wrote them. What does this contribute to our knowledge of proselytism in Palestine? First, in terms of origins, the Judah of inscription # 4 is named specifically as from Tyre and in # 6 Ariston is identified with Apamea of Syria. Otherwise, it is not known where the other proselytes came from unless some of the genitive modifiers refer to geographical origins rather than to paternity (see # 3 "of Zena" and # 5 "of Laganion"). While all of these inscriptions come from Jerusalem it is possible that the persons in fact lived outside of Jerusalem and were perhaps buried in ossuaries in the Holy City by request as a mark of piety on the part of the deceased. That would have been more likely for proselytes from the regions of Idumea, Perea, Galilee, Syria, or the Decapolis. The Gentile population of Jerusalem

---

[80] The translation of the participle הדולקת (*ha-doleqet*) is ambiguous. It derives from the verb דלק which means "to burn." It could mean here "zeal" or "fervor" (Figueras "Epigraphic Evidence for Proselytism in Ancient Judaism," 196) while Frey supposes that it refers to Maria's task as a lighter of lamps (Frey, *CIJ* 1390). See for discussion Donaldson, *Judaism and the Gentiles*, 438–39.

was probably quite small, and while the proselytes might have lived in Jerusalem for a time, they were probably not proselytized there (e.g., like "Nicolaus, a proselyte of Antioch" who was a member of the Jerusalem church [Acts 6:5]). Second, all the names on the ossuaries are Jewish with the exceptions of Diogenes and Ariston (Greek names) and this probably reflects the Jewish custom of converts sometimes taking a new name upon their conversion.[81] Third, nothing can be ascertained about how or why these individuals became proselytes. The inscriptions are indeed physical evidence that proselytism did occur in and around the regions of Palestine. But the inscriptions themselves tell us nothing about how or who or why, and they lead us no further into understanding the socioreligious factors resulting in Gentile conversions to Judaism. Fourth, given that out of the hundreds of ossuaries that have been excavated and restored, only half a dozen contain references to proselytes, this should naturally lead us to believe that the presence of proselytes in Judea was a rarity, and thus also was proselytism.

Rabbinic Literature

In contrast to the Qumran Scroll's silence on Gentile proselytization, rabbinic literature is distinguished by a plethora of content and a diversity of opinion on the subject. Although these rabbinic traditions postdate the Second Temple period, their utility for this study is that they may contain some degree of continuity with proselytizing in the Second Temple era, even if that continuity is now impossible to determine.

While Gentile impurity was a given (see the Mishnah tractate 'Abodah Zarah on idolatry),[82] ideas about the future of the Gentiles and attitudes towards proselytes were pluriform.[83] On the one hand, efforts were made to fully accept the proselytes. For instance, there was a debate

---

[81] Leonard Victor Rutgers, *The Jews in Late Ancient Rome: Evidence of Cultural Interaction in the Roman Diaspora* (Leiden: Brill, 1995) 172n111.

[82] On how attitudes towards purity and impurity affected attitudes towards the conversion and assimilation of Gentiles, see C. E. Hayes, *Gentile Impurities and Jewish Identities: Intermarriage and Conversion from the Bible to the Talmud* (Oxford: Oxford University Press, 2002).

[83] R. Shammai and R. Hillel are reported to have had very different opinions when it came to interacting with potential converts: b. Šabb. 31a; 'Abot R. Nat. 24ab.

between R. Gamaliel and R. Joshua b. Hananiah concerning whether or not the prohibition of Ammonites joining Israel from Deut 23:3 was still in force as occasioned by the request of Judah the Ammonite to enter Israel. At the conclusion of the debate, "They said to him, 'You have already heard the ruling of the elder. Lo, you are permitted to enter into the congregation.'"[84] R. Judah the Prince forbade anyone from reminding a proselyte's son of his origin probably because that would mark an attempt to diminish his status in the congregation of Israel.[85] In a midrash on Numbers it is stated that a proselyte is assured of a place in the age to come, and the Babylonian Talmud expects that Gentiles who keep the Noachide commandments will participate in the future age as well.[86] The standard Jewish liturgical prayer, the Amidah, includes a blessing for the גֵר צֶדֶק ("righteous proselyte"): "May thy compassion be stirred, O Lord our God, towards the righteous, the pious, the elders of thy people, the house of Israel, the remnant of their scholars, towards proselytes, and towards us also."[87]

On the other hand, we can find evidence of less than a warm reception of proselytes. R. Helbo reportedly said that "proselytes are as injurious to Israel as a scab" and "hinder the coming of the Messiah."[88] R. Eliezer b. Hyrcanus is said to have stated that "the children of the wicked among the heathen will not live [in the world to come] nor be judged." R. Eliezer says, "None of the Gentiles has a portion in the world to come, as it is said, *The wicked shall return to Sheol, all the Gentiles who forgot God* [Ps 9:17]."[89] That same belief is extant elsewhere and denies Gentiles entry into the messianic age: "Converts will not be accepted in the days of the Messiah, just as they did not accept proselytes either in the time of David or in the time of Solomon."[90] Less antagonistic texts still reflect the view that proselytes were insiders but not necessarily equals, as can be seen in the fact that members of priestly families were not permitted to marry proselytes or their daughters.[91]

---

[84] *t. Yad.* 2.17–18; cf. *m. Yad.* 4.4; *b. Ber.* 28a.

[85] *t. B. Mes.* 3.25 cited in Feldman, *Jew and Gentile in the Ancient World*, 338.

[86] *Numbers Rabbah* 8.9; *b. Sanh.* 105a.

[87] *Amidah*, bar. 13.

[88] *b. Qidd* 70b; *b. Yebam.* 47b; *b. Nid.* 13b.

[89] *t. Sanh.* 13.2.

[90] *b. Yebam.* 24b and *b. 'Abod. Zar.* 3b.

[91] *m. Bik.* 1.4; *b. Qidd.* 70b.

On the whole, rabbinic statements concerning proselytes are fairly
positive as compared to remarks about Gentiles and idolatry, which are
predominantly negative. According to Gary Porton there is a tension
exhibited in the rabbinic writings between granting converts full status
in Israel, while remaining cognizant of the fact that they shall never be
fully assimilated and are a subclass of Israelites.[92] That goes to show that
the theological ideal did not always match up to the pragmatic reality
and many rabbinic leaders were aware of the difference. Further proof
of that duality is the recognition that proselytes are often differentiated
from other Jews in funeral inscriptions. Proselytes were recognized as
members of the Jewish community, but their Gentile origins followed
them to the grave, and in inscriptions some Jews wanted their bonafide
status differentiated from proselytes and God-fearing associates.[93]

Goodman thinks that a more receptive attitude towards proselytes
is suggested by rabbinic depictions of Abraham, Joseph, and Jethro as
missionaries among pagans.[94] Nevertheless, he also points out that a
willingness to accept is distinct from a desire to acquire and the impulse for conversions remained with the prospective proselyte.[95] This is
epitomized in the tract *Numbers Rabbah* 8.3 and a midrash attributed
to Rabbi Judah the Prince on Isaiah found in *Canticles Rabbah* 1.15.2:

> The Holy One loves the proselytes exceedingly. To what is the matter like?
> To a king who had a number of sheep and goats which went forth every
> morning to the pasture, and returned in the evening to the stable. One
> day a stag joined the flock and grazed with the sheep, and returned with
> them. Then the shepherd said to the king, "There is a stag which goes out
> with the sheep and grazes with them, and comes home with them." And
> the king loved the stag exceedingly. And he commanded the shepherd, say-
> ing: "Give heed unto this stag, that no man beat it"; and when the sheep
> returned in the evening, he would order that the stag should have food
> and drink. Then the shepherds said to him, "My Lord, thou hast many
> goats and sheep and kids, and thou givest us no directions about these, but

---

[92] Gary Porton, *The Stranger within Your Gates: Converts and Conversion
in Rabbinic Judaism* (Chicago: University of Chicago Press, 1994), 192, 215;
cf. Finn, *Death to Rebirth*, 98.

[93] Donaldson, *Judaism and the Gentiles*, 444–45; Kroll, "Sardis," 21.

[94] Goodman, "Proselytising in Rabbinic Judaism," 178–79; cf. Rokéah,
"Ancient Jewish Proselytism," 213–14; Robert Hayward, "Abraham as Proselytizer at Beer-Sheba in the Targums of the Pentateuch," *JJS* 49 (1998): 24–37.

[95] Goodman, "Proselytising in Rabbinic Judaism," 181.

about this stag thou givest us orders day by day." Then the king replied: "It is the custom of the sheep to graze in the pasture, but the stags dwell in the wilderness, and it is not their custom to come among men in the cultivated land. But to this stag who has come to us and lives with us, should we not be grateful that he has left the great wilderness, where many stags and gazelles feed, and has come to live among us? It behooves us to be grateful." So too spoke the Holy One: "I owe great thanks to the stranger, in that he has left his family and his father's house, and come to dwell among us; therefore I order in the law: 'Love the stranger'" (Deut 10:19).

When a certain kind of dove is being fed, the other doves smell the food and flock to her cote. So when the elder sits and expounds, many strangers at that time become proselytes, like Jethro who heard and came, or Rahab who herd and came. So through Hananiah, Mishael, and Azariah many become proselytes. What is the reason? "For when he sees his children . . . they will sanctify my name," then, as it goes on, "those who err in spirit will come to understanding" (Isa 29:23–24).

In the first midrash on Numbers, the proselyte (stag) joins Israel at his own initiative and without any obvious attempt to draw or recruit him. The passage also assumes that proselytes are somewhat of an anomaly and regulations concerning them are ambivalent. In the second midrash on Isaiah, proselytes are likened to doves who come searching for food and then find it. This is at a piece with what we have observed elsewhere: openness towards Gentiles, but not active recruitment of Gentiles. The notion of a mission oriented towards making proselytes is nowhere in sight as the impetus falls upon the necessity of accepting proselytes who willingly attach themselves to the Jewish community.

Goodman writes: "The evidence for rabbinic approval of winning converts is indirect and allusive, but when it is laid out it may be seen to have some cumulative force."[96] Perhaps it is the case that the derivation of a more open attitude towards proselytes may have stemmed from rabbinic awareness of the success of Christian missionaries among Gentiles.[97] We must also be exceptionally cautious of reading rabbinic

---

[96] Goodman, *Mission and Conversion*, 144.

[97] Goodman, "Proselytising in Rabbinic Judaism," 185; Hayward, "Abraham as Proselytizer," 33; Hvalvik (*Struggle for Scripture and Covenant*, 291–95) rejects that idea that Judaism became a missionary religion in response to Christianity, rather, he advocates that missionary competition is detectable within the witness of the New Testament.

attitudes into the pre-Hadrian period. The destruction of the temple, the expulsion of the Jews from Judea, and the rise of the Christian movement, may have affected developing Jewish attitudes towards Gentiles and proselytizing in a way that did not previously exist.

In conclusion, the evidence from Palestinian sources including Qumran, the Gospel of Matthew, the Maccabean writings, rabbinic literature, and inscriptions does not support the existence of widespread proselytizing efforts. When non-Jews did convert to Judaism in Palestine it was often under duress, some groups thought of the pagan nations as suitable only for cosmic destruction as part of the restoration of Israel, some Pharisees may have been willing to proselytize God-fearers to Pharisaism but they appear the exception, and the status of proselytes in Jewish communities remained ambivalent and they did not always receive a warm welcome. In sum, the comment from Safrai and Stern appears correct: "there was in Palestine no active propaganda to further the cause of proselytism."[98]

---

[98] Safrai and Stern, *The Jewish People in the First Century*, 2.1095.

CHAPTER FOUR

JEWISH MISSIONARY ACTIVITY IN THE DIASPORA

Despite the extent of diversity within the Judaism of the first centuries of the Common Era, there was still a common web of social customs and religious beliefs among Jewish communities spread throughout the Mediterranean and Near East.[1] Payment of the temple tax, ancestral connections, and familial relation kept Jews outside of Palestine in relationship with the Jewish homeland. Arguably, the distinguishing features of the dispersed Jewish communities included a higher degree of acculturation than in Palestine, a more acute awareness of the problems and politics of Jewish-Gentile relations, the quandary of retaining Jewish identity while participating in the fabric of wider pagan society, the existence of synagogal communities, and the absence of two important Jewish symbols: temple and territory. Indeed, by virtue of being immersed in a majority-Gentile culture, Jews in the Greco-Roman Diaspora had a different, arguably more intense, interface with that culture than did their Palestinian counterparts. The sheer proximity of Jews to Gentiles throughout the Diaspora resulted in a larger number of Gentiles who exhibited interest in Jews and Judaism, often to the point of "conversion." The Diaspora, then, provides the largest amount of evidence of "conversion" to Judaism by non-Jews.

SOCIORELIGIOUS CONTEXT OF THE DIASPORA

We should appreciate the unique religious context of the Diaspora that meant that Jews were frequently exposed to and sometimes even

---

[1] For a sketch of Diaspora Judaism, see Barclay, *Jews in the Mediterranean Diaspora*, 401–42 and Erich S. Gruen, *Diaspora: Jews amidst Greeks and Romans* (Cambridge, Mass.: Harvard University Press, 2002).

embraced the religious pluralism of pagan cities.[2] For a start we find prohibitions about cursing God in the Hebrew Bible being applied equally to not blaspheming gods in pagan cities.[3] A clear instance of this is found in the Septuagint translation of Exod 22:27, which changes "You shall not curse God" (אֱלֹהִים לֹא תְקַלֵּל) to "You shall not curse gods" (θεοὺς οὐ κακολογήσεις), and this interpretive gloss probably functions to urge Hellenistic Jews not to foster religious tensions by blaspheming pagan deities.[4] Commenting on Lev 24:15, which also prohibits cursing God, Philo writes: "[I]t seems, he is not now speaking of the primary God the creator, but of those who are accounted gods in the different cities . . . of whom it is necessary however to abstain from speaking ill, in order that none of the disciples of Moses may ever become accustomed to treat the appellation of God with disrespect."[5] Josephus is similar: "Let no one blaspheme those gods which other cities revere; nor rob foreign temples, nor take treasure that has been dedicated to the name of a god."[6] Given common Jewish critiques against idolatry and the inferiority of the Greco-Roman pantheon to Yahweh (as found classically in Isa 44 and *Wis* 13), one can understand why many Jewish authors sought to avoid religious tensions by including pagan deities within the biblical commands not to curse [a] God.

The exclusive allegiance of Jewish persons to their religious traditions could vary considerably and some Jews found reason to participate, for civic or religious purposes, in the worship of other gods. For instance, there are a number of inscriptions found in the vicinity of a temple complex at el-Kanais in Egypt that are dedicated to "Pan of the Success-

---

[2] Religious pluralism was not unknown in Palestine as the Samaritans renamed their temple at Matt Gerizim "Jupiter Hellenius" or "Zeus-the-Friend-of-Strangers" (*Ant.* 12.257–264; 2 Macc 6:2). There are examples, both historical and legendary, of Gentile rulers offering sacrifices in Jerusalem including Alexander the Great, Ptolemy III, Antiochus VII Sidete, Marcus Agrippa, Vitellius, Ptolemy IV, and Heliodorus (*Ant.* 11.329–332; *Ag. Ap.* 2.48; *Ant.* 13.242–243; 16.14; 18.122; 3 Macc 1:9; 2 Macc 3:35).

[3] Louis H. Feldman and Gōhei Hata, *Josephus, Judaism, and Christianity* (Detroit: Wayne State University Press, 1987), 193.

[4] At the same time Feldman (*Jew and Gentile in the Ancient World,* 292) points out that the Septuagint could refer to idols in the most contemptuous terms such as Deut 7:25 which uses the term βδελύγματα which means "abominations," "filth," "nastiness," "nausea," or "sickness."

[5] Philo, *Vit. Mos.* 2.205.

[6] *Ant.* 4.207.

ful Journey" and can be dated ca. 150–80 B.C.E. Two such inscriptions read: (1) "Bless God! Theodotos [son] of Dorion, a Jew, rescued from the sea" where a Jew thanks the deity Pan for his fortunate rescue from a shipwreck;[7] and (2) "Ptolemaios [son] of Dionysios, a Jew, blesses the god" though here the occasion for the blessing is not given.[8] To give one final example, there is a pagan style Latin dedication to a group of deities made by an Italian freedwoman who describes herself as "Iuda" or Jewess.[9] Evidently some Jews were not only willing to participate in ad hoc pagan rituals, but were even willing to make a permanent memorial out of it. Thus, the degree of strictness attached to observance of the Torah and the exclusivity of devotion to Yahweh was hardly unanimous among Jews of the Diaspora.

From the perspective of the Greco-Roman world, monotheism was one of the more distinctive aspects of Jewish beliefs,[10] even if it was not entirely unique to them. Josephus states that "God as one is common to all the Hebrews."[11] But some Jews felt the need to lessen its obvious polemic implication against paganism by identifying their God with the supreme Greco-Roman gods. The *Epistle of Aristeas* states: "These people worship God the overseer and creator of all, whom all men worship including ourselves, O King, except that we have a different name. Their name for him is Zeus and Jove."[12] While the text could be attributed to a Gentile, it is far more probable that it represents a Jewish option that vied for a non-exclusivist claim for Judaism in a polytheistic religious environment. Similarly, in the fragments of Aristobulus, preserved by Eusebius, the author contends that Judaism is a philosophy on par with Hellenistic philosophy and both represent parallel routes to the same destination: the way of a virtuous life and monotheistic

---

[7] Frey, *CIJ* 2: §1537.

[8] Frey, *CIJ* 2: §1538.

[9] Frey, *CIJ* 1: §77.

[10] Tacitus, *Hist.* 5.5: "But their conception of heavenly things is different … the Jewish religion is purely a spiritual monotheism." See also *Ag. Ap.* 2.148; *Mart. Pol.* 3.2; Justin, *1 Apol.* 13.1.

[11] *Ant.* 5.112; cf. *Ep. Arist.* 132, 139; Philo, *Decal.* 65; *Sib. Or.* 3:629; 3 Macc 5:13; *Jos. Asen.* 11:10.

[12] *Ep. Arist.* 16. The pagan philosopher Celsus countered the exclusive claims of Christians by saying: "It makes no difference if one invokes the highest God or Zeus or Adonai or Sabaoth or Amoun, as the Egyptians do, or Papaios as the Scythians do" (Origen, *Against Celsus* 5.41). This is a claim that proto-orthodox Christianity rejected, see John 14:6 and Acts 4:12.

religious devotion.[13] Although some Jews might remove the name of "Zeus" from Greek pottery because it was offensive to them, nonetheless, Aristobulus says of the philosophers who refer to Zeus that "their intention refers to God."[14]

In addition, the cult of the *Theos Hypsistos* ("most high god") attested in Asia Minor and the Greek cities near the Black Sea provided an expression of monotheism that was ambiguous enough to accommodate Jews and pagans in a common worship if required.[15] Several inscriptions from the Bosporus region include an opening dedication to "the most high god" (ca. late first or early second century C.E.). To give an example from one of the inscriptions: "To the most high God, Almighty, blessed in the reign of king Mithridates . . . Pothos, the son of Strabo, dedicated to the prayer house in accordance with the vow of his house-bred slave-woman, whose name is Chrysa, on condition that she should be unharmed and unmolested by any of his heirs under Zeus, Ge, Helios."[16] This inscription has obvious Jewish elements. The reference to a prayer house (προσευχῆ), which also appears in other inscriptions from the region, connects the manumission of a slave to a Jewish community. Also, the adjectives "almighty" (παντοκράτωρ) and "blessed" (εὐλογψτός) are common Jewish doxological terms for God and occur frequently in Jewish inscriptions. Yet at the very end of the inscription we find reference to three pagan gods in Zeus, Ge, and Helios. Is it unthinkable that Jews could produce such an inscription? Is it included simply to appease the religious interests of a manumitted pagan slave? Could it be that Gorgippian Jews used the expression simply as a matter of legal form rather than religious devotion?[17] Was it produced by pagans or God-fearers instead?[18] The matter of Jewish provenance or Jewish influence is impossible to solve. Perhaps the *Theos*

---

[13] Donaldson, *Judaism and the Gentiles*, 107.

[14] Aristobulus, frg. 4 (Eusebius, *Prep. Ev.* 13.12.7).

[15] Cf. Stephen Mitchell, "The Cult of Theos Hypsistos between Pagans, Jews and Christians," in *Pagan Monotheism in Late Antiquity* (eds. P. Athanassiadi and M. Frede; Oxford: Oxford University Press, 1999), 83–148.

[16] Frey, *CIJ* 1: §690.

[17] Cf. Elizabeth Leigh Gibson, *The Jewish Manumission Inscriptions of the Bosporus Kingdom* (Tübingen: Mohr/Siebeck, 1999), 119.

[18] On attributing this inscription to Gentile sympathizers see Levinskaya, *The Book of Acts in Its Diaspora Setting*, 113 and Donaldson, *Judaism and the Gentiles*, 458.

Hypsistos cult evolved out of a Jewish mission to create sympathizers,[19] or else it was a pagan cult with Jewish influences.[20] In either case, the *Theos Hypsistos* cult made syncretism at least a possibility for Jewish communities.

One must keep in mind that the door of religious pluralism swings both ways and it is apparent that some pagans were willing to respect Judaism as a legitimate religious option. A statement attributed to Numenius the Pythagorean philosopher says: "For what is Plato, but Moses speaking in Attic?"[21] This shows that some pagan philosophers identified the best of the Jewish tradition with the best of Greek philosophy. As we have seen, this same identification was made by many Jewish intellectuals, for whom philosophical monotheism was more important than was cultic monotheism. It seems that there are expressions of Judaism that are monotheistic but also malleable, that contain a flattening out of Israel's unique status, and in which the parity of Jewish and Hellenistic ethical traditions are emphasized.

The Jewish encounter with Hellenism led some Jews like Tiberius Alexander,[22] Dositheus,[23] and Herod the Great's great-grandchildren[24] to abandon their ancestral customs altogether. Of course, Hellenism was not essentially inimical to Jewish belief, and it could on the one hand bring existing beliefs about the Torah into a new form of cultural expression, as in the case of Philo's platonic exegesis of the Jewish Scriptures. We should also note Hengel's dictum that all Judaism of the first century is a form of Hellenistic Judaism and an absolute bifurcation between these two cultural entities should not be pressed too formally.[25] Still, Hellenism could and did lead some Jews to question the literal meaning of the law and even to abandon it in favor of a more symbolic or allegorical approach where covenant markers such as circumcision are either degraded or disappear. Even Philo, who was no stranger to symbolic readings, warned against the dangers of an extreme allegorical approach to matters such as circumcision.[26]

---

[19] Levinskaya, *The Book of Acts in Its Diaspora Setting*, 83–103.
[20] Trebilco, *Jewish Communities in Asia Minor*, 127–44.
[21] Stern, *GLAJJ* 2: §§6–10.
[22] *Ant.* 20.100.
[23] 3 Macc 1:3.
[24] *Ant.* 18.141.
[25] Hengel, *Judaism and Hellenism*, 1.104.
[26] Cf. Philo, *Migr. Abr.* 86–93.

Jews encountering Hellenism did not always abandon their customs as there was a broad spectrum of Jewish responses to Hellenism. John Barclay has helpfully summarized five different levels of assimilation ranging from an enclave type mentality that rejected Hellenistic culture and restricted participation in wider pagan society through to a position that abandoned key Jewish distinctives and more comfortably embraced Hellenistic culture.[27]

1. Abandonment of key Jewish social distinctives

2. Gymnasium education

3. Attendance at Greek athletics/theatre

4. Commercial employment with non-Jews

5. Social life confined to the Jewish community

One would expect that, generally speaking, the attitudes and behaviors towards Gentiles and pagan religion would operate differently at each level of assimilation. A Jew living at scale # 5 may hold to the central importance of belief in the Jewish God and circumcision as the litmus test of belonging to the covenant people, however, his interaction and opportunity to engage with Gentiles are likely to be highly restricted. What is more, he may not even see the point of inviting other peoples to join the elect nation and be content with trying to maintain his covenant status in a challenging environment. Alternatively, those on the top of the scale at # 1 may encounter non-Jews frequently but they would be more likely to abandon Jewish practices and fail to see the need to persuade Gentiles to become Jews. Thus, if one operates with a framework that is somehow affirming of other religions, then one will emphasis the uniqueness not the exclusive absoluteness of one's own religious perspective. If infused with pluralistic attitudes, one may become more focused about winning intellectual respect rather than winning converts, and be more concerned with countering rumors about one's religious rituals than with integrating pagans into Jewish communities. If we all worship the same god, only by a different name, then there is little point in converting anybody to our religion except perhaps to inform others of the inherent virtue of our own practices and philosophy. This shows the way that the degrees of assimilation and acculturation of Jews in the Diaspora could have

---

[27] Barclay, *Jews in the Mediterranean Diaspora*, 93–97.

affected attitudes towards Gentiles. It also determined the type of intellectual and social exchange between them and influenced the form and degree of proselytizing that took place.

Thus, religious pluralism affected the political, social, and religious landscape of Jewish beliefs and practices in the Diaspora.[28] As shown above, that can be seen in Jewish sensitivity in not wanting to offend the religious scruples of their pagan neighbors, lessening the exclusive claims of their monotheistic worship, and sometimes expressed in syncretistic practices. Hellenistic culture did impact how Judaism was described and presented in the wider pubic forum. At the same time, there can be no denying the robust nature of Hellenistic Judaism and its ability to survive as a minority faith. Judaism was presented to Gentiles in such a way that there were conversions to Judaism in Greek cities and in sufficient enough numbers to earn the ire of the cultural elites. This leads us to the question of how Judaism was presented to Gentiles, that is, what did pagans see in Judaism that drew them to the national religion of the Jews? Furthermore, what did Jews of the Diaspora, as shown by their writings, think of conversions and converts in light of this socioreligious context? To these questions I now turn.

PAGAN ATTRACTION TO JUDAISM

An interesting subject for investigation is why some non-Jews found the Jewish way of life attractive and regarded the Jewish communities as a desirable social location. Why did pagans choose to convert to Judaism when Jews were not always welcomed and wanted in Greco-Roman cities? Robert Goldenberg writes: "The Jews and their religion were highly visible in the Greco-Roman world. The Jews were numerous (perhaps 20 percent of the population in the eastern Mediterranean basin), and they were aggressively proud of their distinctive monotheistic faith. Their rituals aroused fascination. The cohesion of their communities and the stability of their families were strongly appealing in a chaotic world."[29] This seems to be along the right lines, but

---

[28] Cf. P. Pratap Kumar, ed., *Religious Pluralism in the Diaspora* (Leiden: Brill, 2006).

[29] Robert Goldenberg, *The Origins of Judaism: From Canaan to the Rise of Islam* (Cambridge: CUP, 2007), 180.

we can say more. What pagans saw in Judaism would depend entirely on what they saw of it, and it would depend entirely on their encounters with the Jewish population of a city or village. From inscriptions and a few other pieces of literary evidence, we know that proselytes were made, but we know relatively little as to why or what motivated them to join themselves to the Jewish way of life. What can be said is that many pagans certainly found Judaism to be an attractive religious and social option. In fact, Hengel and Schwemer refer to the "power of attraction" of Judaism as opposed to a Jewish "mission" to non-Jews.[30] Bedell even thinks in terms of a "sacred magnetism" exuded by synagogues towards outsiders.[31] This element of attraction is important because, as Gaventa suggests, to inquire about conversion is to ask what attracts people to a faith, to look at what changes their understanding of themselves and their environment, and what supports them in their new social and religious disposition.[32] There were probably a number of factors that made Judaism an attractive socioreligious option for pagans.

First, Eastern practices and rites gained popularity in some circles in the Roman west. Many Romans had a fascination with rites and rituals from Greece, Egypt, and Persia. We can see the popularity of Eastern practices reflected in the response of the Romans; it was becoming widespread enough to make Romans fear that it would take over their own culture. Thus, a lot of the Roman criticism of Jews and Judaism came from a fear that the distinctive Roman gods and ancient customs were being polluted by foreign influences. Juvenal lamented the fact that Rome was becoming a Greek city, even worse an oriental city, a virtual Rome-on-the-Orontes.[33] This is why Seneca complained about the Jews that the vanquished had given laws to their victors, and why Tacitus said that the Jews teach others "to despise all gods, to disown their country."[34] Juvenal protests about the sons of God-fearers who take to circumcision and are "wont to flout the laws of Rome, they learn and practice and revere the Jewish law."[35] The spread of Judaism into Rome was part of a wider influx of non-Roman (or non-Romanized) religions into the

---

[30] Hengel and Schwemer, *Paul between Damascus and Antioch*, 75–76.

[31] Bedell, "Mission in Intertestamental Judaism," 25.

[32] Gaventa, *From Darkness to Light*, 3.

[33] Juvenal, *Sat.* 3.58–63.

[34] Seneca, *De Superstitione* cited in Augustine, *Civ. D.* 6.11; Tacitus, *Hist.* 5.5.2.

[35] Juvenal, *Sat.* 14.96–106 (Stern, *GLAJJ* 2: §301).

Latin West particularly during times of social upheaval. Between the late third century B.C.E. and the third century C.E., several Eastern cults, such as those of Isis, Cybele, and Mithras, penetrated various strata of Roman society. These cults presented Roman citizens with intriguing rituals and the promise of blessings, prosperity, and salvation in this world and even in the next. There was a tension in Roman religious philosophy. On the one hand Roman religion was pluralistic and the gods of annexed territories were added to the Roman pantheon. Since Roman religion was not exclusivist in principle or practice, it was relatively easy to establish new cults in the imperial capital itself and to worship in a variety of religious temples and associations. That is why a Roman noble woman such as Julia Severa could be a pagan high priestess and also the benefactor of a synagogue at Acomia in Phrygia.[36] At the same time, this could lead to a neglect of indigenous Roman rites and customs, which infuriated religious and civic leaders. The capacity of a religious tradition to endure depends entirely on a continual renewal and affirmation of its beliefs and practices. The observance of Roman rites was a civic duty and an expression of national loyalty especially in relation to the imperial cult. Some Romans were alarmed at the neglect of their own rites and rituals and what this meant in terms of the loyalty of the populace. The expansion of the Roman Empire eastwards (eventually as far as Parthia) brought with it a two-way interface as Rome and her provinces were gradually brought under the influence of Eastern religions that included the national religion of Judea.

Second, Judaism could also claim a high degree of authority because of its antiquity and distinguished history. This antiquity was acknowledged by Greek and Latin authors and even by bitter critics of Judaism.[37] Jewish authors like Philo and Josephus made much of the antiquity of their race and rituals in their respective apologies for the Jewish people. Philo's embassy to Gaius is predicated on the desire to honor both the emperor and the ancient customs of the Jewish people.[38] Book one of Josephus's *Against Apion* takes up this theme at length, and he purposes to respond to reproaches against the Jewish people including the allegation that the Jewish nation is relatively young. Josephus

---

[36] Frey, *CIJ* 2: §766; Trebilco, *Jewish Communities in Asia Minor*, 58–59; Donaldson, *Judaism and the Gentiles*, 463–66.

[37] Cf., e.g., Tacitus, *Hist.* 5.5.1.

[38] Cf., e.g., *Leg. Gai.* 305–315.

combs through evidence in Greek historiography to instruct others in the truth "of our great antiquity" (ἡμετέρας ἀρχαιότητος).[39] To outsiders this meant that the Jewish people and their way of life was not faddish, but was on par with the history of the Greeks, Phoenicians, and Egyptians and their associated traditions.

Third, practices of Judaism such as prayer, alms giving, calendrical observances, instruction in Scripture, purity laws, and Sabbath observance may have been especially attractive in a world that valued ritual to a high degree. In the ancient world ritual was the key mechanism by which one demonstrated one's piety and established connections with the divine realm. The Jewish traditions of prayer, alms giving, calendrical observances, instruction in Scripture, purity laws, and Sabbath observance all presented an organized way of life for continued communion with a divine being. The Jerusalem temple, besides being a splendid monument and a wonder of the ancient world, had laws detailing its operation and conduct for sacrifices that were regarded as effective to the point that non-Jews were able to worship in the outer precincts of the temple (what is often referred to in modern times as the "court of the Gentiles") and bring offerings as an act of cosmopolitan piety.[40] Some Jewish authors could even emphasize that the temple was available for worship by all.[41] In fact, many of the biblical and post-biblical expressions of universalism, universal access to the worship of God, that is, are centered on the temple. While that access was limited and policed, the temple remained a "house for all nations" (Isa 56:7).[42] In fact, Josephus makes this point at length at several places.[43]

---

[39] *Ag. Ap.* 1.4.

[40] Greek and Roman rulers could pay respects to the temple and even contribute to its building, upkeep, and adornment as a mark of such piety and good will towards the populace (cf., e.g., Philo, *Leg. Gai.* 157; Josephus, *J.W.* 2.340–341; *Ant.* 12.58; 13.78, 242–244; 18.122; *Ag. Ap.* 2.48). 1 Esd 2:3 has Cyrus declare that "the Lord of Israel, the Lord Most High, has made me king of the world and commanded me to build him a house at Jerusalem." In Josephus's summary this persuaded him that "the Most High God" had appointed him as "king of the entire world" (*Ant.* 11.6).

[41] Although the Dead Sea Scrolls in contrast emphasize exclusions from the worship of the temple, e.g., 4QMMT B 1–3, 8–9; 4Q174 3:3–6.

[42] Cf. Bird, *Jesus and the Origins of the Gentile Mission*, 134–43 for a summary of universalist and exclusivist ideologies about the temple and non-Jews.

[43] *Ant.* 11.87; 14.110; *J.W.* 4.272; and esp. *Ag. Ap.* 2.193.

Fourth, the Jewish religion was considered to be effective in petitioning God for healing and for defeating evil magic and evil spirits. The purpose of magic in the ancient world was to enable people to coerce the gods or divine powers to accomplish certain tasks, to manipulate certain people, or to exert power over the spiritual realm, and Jews were thought to excel in these practices. Jews were known to practice magic as evidenced by Bar-Jesus/Elymas who, according to Acts, was something of a personal attendant or chaplain to Sergius Paulus on the island of Cyprus and is called "a certain magician, a Jewish false prophet" by Luke (Acts 13:6).[44] The Roman procurator Felix similarly had a Jewish magician Simon the Cypriot as a friend who mediated in his affections for Drusilla.[45] The Samaritan Simon Magus (according to Christian tradition the first "gnostic") combined Samaritan Yahwism with magical practices and possibly gained followers through his various powers.[46] Moses was regarded as one of the greatest magicians to have ever lived.[47] P. S. Alexander writes: "Magic flourished among Jews despite strong and persistent condemnation by religious authority. Healing by this means was especially common, sickness being widely diagnosed as caused by malevolent invading spirits which could only be driven out by the appropriate incantations and spells."[48] Many Jewish rites, rituals, and names were often associated with deliverance from evil powers. Some Jews claimed that circumcision and obedience to the law could protect someone from evil angels.[49] Itinerant Jewish exorcists were known to operate in both Palestine and in the Diaspora as evidenced by several references to them in Christian writings, most notably the sons of Sceva in Ephesus described by Luke in Acts 19:13–14.[50] These exorcists probably provided services for non-Jews, as is described in the case of *The Prayer*

---

[44] Acts 13:6–12; cf. Lucian, *Philopseudes* 16 (Stern, *GLAJJ* 2: §372); *Tragodopodegra* 173 (Stern, *GLAJJ* 2: §374).

[45] Josephus, *Ant.* 20.142.

[46] Acts 8:9–24.

[47] Pliny the Elder, *Nat. Hist.* 30.11 (Stern, *GLAJJ* 1: §221); Apeleius, *Apologia* 90 (Stern, *GLAJJ* 2: §361).

[48] Schürer, *History of the Jewish People in the Age of Jesus Christ*, 3.1.342. Cf. also Clinton E. Arnold, *The Colossian Syncretism: The Interface between Christianity and Folk Belief in Colossae* (Grand Rapids, Mich.: Baker, 1996), 15–17.

[49] CD 16:4–6 and the "Angel of Obstruction"; *Jub.* 15:28–32 and the spirits who "rule so that they might be led astray."

[50] Luke 11:18/Matt 12:27; Acts 19:14–17; Justin, *Dial. Tryph.* 85; Irenaeus, *Adv. Haer.* 2.6.2.

of Nabonidus which, though fictitious, assumes a scenario in which a non-Jew would go to a Jewish גזר ("exorcist" or "diviner") for help.[51] A similar feat is attributed to Abraham in the Dead Sea Scrolls where he reportedly exorcized an evil spirit that afflicted Pharaoh.[52] Josephus gives an eyewitness account of an exorcism performed by a Jew named Eleazar that was done in the presence of Vespasian and his attendants.[53] In rabbinic tradition, the fourth generation tannaitic rabbi Simeon b. Yose allegedly exorcised a demon from the Roman Emperor's daughter.[54] Non-Jewish sources also provide records of the supernatural power of Judaism; Juvenal records that Jews were well-known for their capacity to interpret dreams.[55] In the Greek magical papyri there is reference to exorcism practices, where the words "by the God of the Hebrews" are invoked to effect an exorcism.[56] In fact, Hengel and Schwemer point out that around one third of the extant magical papyri and amulets are based on Jewish elements.[57] Thus, the effectiveness of Jewish rituals and exorcisms and other magic for dispelling demons and for curing illnesses was another reason for pagan attraction to Judaism.

Fifth, monotheism may have been another factor in the attractiveness of Judaism to Gentiles. Monotheism was known by Jews and pagans as one of the distinguishing beliefs of Judaism. Monotheism as a religious phenomenon was not, however, restricted to Judaism.[58] The philosophers Xenophanes and Antisthenes were monotheists, and other philosophical systems such as Platonism, Aristotelianism, and Stoicism argued variously for a supreme principle or prime mover behind the existence and operation of the cosmos. Origen's work *Contra Celsus* is arguably a debate between a Christian monotheist and a pagan monotheist.

Some authors found the monotheism of the Jews to be praiseworthy. According to Augustine, the Gentile author Varro (born 115 B.C.E.), could regard the "God of the Jews to be the same as Jupiter"

---

[51] 4QPrNab.
[52] 1QapGen 20:16–31.
[53] *Ant.* 8.46–48.
[54] *b. Me'il.* 17b.
[55] Juvenal, *Sat.* 6.547 (Stern, *GLAJJ* 2: §299).
[56] *PGM* IV.3019.
[57] Hengel and Schwemer, *Paul between Damascus and Antioch*, 70.
[58] Cf. P. Athanassiadi and M. Frede, eds., *Pagan Monotheism in Late Antiquity* (Oxford: Oxford University Press, 1999).

and "he perceived that the Jews worship the highest God."[59] Stoic henotheism and Jewish monotheism shared some similar philosophical terrain in positing the superiority of one god and regarding human life as the journey of the soul towards the virtuous life. What was distinctive about Jewish monotheism was its avoidance of physical representations of God and its often vehement and mocking critique of idol worship. What is more, Jewish monotheism (though it's strictness is a matter of some debate) for the most part avoided conceiving of Yahweh as a transcendent but impersonal deity or as a capricious and even mischievous anthropomorphic being prone to sally upon the earth in want of amusement.[60] Jewish monotheism could accommodate intermediaries and hypostatization such as wisdom, angels, spirits, astral entities, and the logos of Heraclitus, but without forfeiting the exclusiveness of devotion afforded to Yahweh. In Jewish tradition, exemplified by the Hebrew Bible and Jewish Hellenistic apologetic literature, the God of Israel is known for his supremacy over other pseudo-deities, his differentiation from creation and human beings, and the simplicity of his being. Jewish monotheism which espoused the transcendence and unity of God, a God who rewarded virtue, who interacted with the world through intermediaries, and was sovereign over the created realm probably constituted a key point of intellectual attraction for educated Gentiles.

Sixth, a further issue that drew positive attention to Judaism was the civil and economic benefits of being a Jew. According to Strabo, Judaism did not put heavy financial burdens upon its adherents.[61] Under Julius Caesar the Jewish people gained a number of privileges such as exemption from military service and having to participate in the cultus of Roman gods. Philo maintains that proselytes should receive the material benefits of joining themselves to the Jewish people.[62] Converts could also benefit from a number of effective Jewish charities including the practice of giving alms to the poor.[63] Indeed, Tacitus's polemics presuppose that Jewish communities looked after each other at the expense of wider society in general.[64] Vespasian refused to trust

---

[59] Augustine, *De Cons.* 1.22.30 (Stern, *GLAJJ* 1: §72b).
[60] Cf., e.g., Josephus, *Ag. Ap.* 2.74–76; Wis 14:11–15:19.
[61] Strabo, *Geog.* 16.2.36 (Stern, *GLAJJ* 1: §115).
[62] Philo, *Virt.* 103–104.
[63] Josephus, *Ag. Ap.* 2.283.
[64] Tacitus, *Hist.* 5.5.1–2 ("[A]mong themselves they are inflexibly honest and ever ready to shew compassion, though they regard the rest of mankind

the report of a Jewish deserter because he knew "how faithful the Jews were to one another."[65]

Seventh, the ethics of the Jewish people, in either ideal or practice, could have provided further grounds for the attractiveness of Judaism. No Jewish author divided the Torah into civil, ceremonial, and moral components; but the Torah as a whole had a certain moral character in so far as it laid out the charter for the life and behavior of the Jewish people individually and corporately. While the ethical and pious life was certainly not unknown among Greco-Roman authors, pagan religions did not ordinarily include a moral component other than honoring the gods and their messengers. The pagan deities were either amoral or immoral by their own example.[66] Judaism was a way of life that integrated religious devotion, private and public living, and ethical behavior into a single matrix. That could be accentuated further with some Jewish groups who had a particular eschatology that focused on righteousness and reward in light of a coming eschaton. Furthermore, Judaism arguably had answers to the ethical questions posed by Greco-Roman philosophers such as what is the good life and what is the purpose of human existence?

Eighth, a final element of attraction was perhaps the well defined social identity and group boundaries of Jewish communities. The Jews of the Diaspora were socially, politically, and religiously visible and maintained a distinctive sense of self-identity and group values. To persons with either no or limited loyalty to their cultural and geopolitical circumstances, Judaism could constitute an alluring option if one wanted the security of an identity that was concrete and yet flexible enough to exist and flourish in the Greco-Roman *polis*. Conversion to Judaism could allow those of low social status a degree of *magnanimity* by association with the Jewish people and bestow *nationality* through incorporation into the Judean nation.

How one went from attraction to association to incorporation into Judaism is a further matter for discussion. Several things could have precipitated this shift including political alliances, intermarriage, slavery, work-relations, philosophical engagement in the *agora* (market place),

---

with all the hatred of enemies").

[65] Josephus, *J.W.* 3.320.

[66] Which is very much in contrast to modernist post-Kantian conceptions of religion as reducible to ethics.

interaction at rhetorical schools, conversing at symposia (Greek drinks party), information given through Jewish literature, and the fact that synagogues were sometimes willing to receive inquirers. Networks of social relationships (political, business, patron-client) were probably crucial for any exposure to and transference into Judaism. Philip Harland notes that, "associations, synagogues, and congregations were small noncompulsory groups that could draw their membership from several possible social network connections within the polis . . . all could engage in at least some degree of external contacts, both positive and negative, with other individuals, benefactors, groups, or institutions in the civic context."[67] But if attraction to Judaism was a key mechanism through which pagans became adherents/sympathizers and finally proselytes, this very much assumes that converts themselves take the initiative, at least early on, in making moves towards Judaism.[68]

This propensity for attraction must be juxtaposed with several factors that facilitated not attraction, but revulsion or misunderstanding by outsiders towards the Jews and their religious practices. First, the Jewish failure to honor the gods of the pantheon could create the impression of impiety and atheism. Failure to embrace the imperial cult might indicate disloyalty to the ruling powers. Second, the separateness, insulation, and relative homogeneity of Jewish communities promoted anti-Jewish feelings among many non-Jews. The Jewish emphasis on purity and separation was orientated against non-Jews and gave rise to allegations of xenophobia. The degree of contact that Jews could have with non-Jews, especially concerning pagan social space and in proximity to unclean food, was sharply limited and led to many Jews separating entirely from Gentiles and refusing to eat with Gentiles at all.[69] The anti-Jewish riots of Alexandria and Antioch in the first century brought to the surface underlying suspicions of disloyalty and distrust in the Jewish people and whether their distinctive way of life and (varying degrees) of deliberate isolation from the surrounding culture was ultimately for the good of Greco-Roman society. Third, the rites and rituals of Judaism perplexed and displeased some Greco-Roman

---

[67] Philip A. Harland, *Associations, Synagogues, and Congregations: Claiming a Place in Ancient Mediterranean Society* (Minneapolis: Fortress, 2003), 211.

[68] Cf. Feldman, *Jew and Gentile in the Ancient World*, 322.

[69] Cf. Acts 10:28; 11:3; Tacitus, *Hist.* 5.5.2; *Jos. Asen.* 7:1; *Jub.* 22:16–17; Diodorus of Siculus, *Bibliotheca Historia* 34.1.2; Philostratus, *Vita Apollonii* 5.33.

authors. Obviously circumcision, as a rite of passage into the Jewish nation, was not a particularly attractive procedure for male pagans.[70] Abstinence from pork was a curiosity to many.[71] In some cases it seemed like the Jews' distinctiveness led to contempt from many of their intellectual contemporaries.

Overall, it has to be acknowledged that the Jewish interaction with the Greco-Roman world certainly did create factors that were conducive to fostering associations and relations with non-Jews resulting ultimately in conversions. But the potential for some to "drift towards Jewish ways" was also hindered by the same factors that gave the Jewish Diaspora its distinctive identity: Yahwism and separation from Gentiles. That in turn provided a setting for anti-Semitism to develop through caricature and misinformation of Jewish beliefs and practices and from further resentment against the particular freedoms and privileges bestowed upon them by certain rulers.

The complexity of Jewish life in the Roman cities of the Mediterranean meant that cultural influence was always a two-way affair resulting in potentially increased or diminished prospects for conversions to Judaism depending on the volume of traffic. On the one hand, cultural and social interaction with a host culture would provide more opportunities for positive encounters between Jews and Gentiles. In this scale of interaction there was ample opportunity for Jews to effectively embed Hellenism (understood as a sociocultural phenomenon) into their own frameworks and to couch Judaism in language and concepts favorable to Hellenists. Many Jews, like Philo, were effective bicultural communicators. On the other hand, this encounter with Hellenism could result in assimilation and a flattening out of Jewish distinctiveness leading, on the extreme scale, to apostasy. There again, resilience against the values and hegemony of the host culture could facilitate an emphasis on separation and lead to a predominating concern for maintaining the integrity of the Jewish *ethos* and *ethnos*. Some Jews on this scale could be limited in their ability to communicate across cultural boundaries.

Neither of these admittedly extreme paradigms of assimilation and separation seems particularly conducive to the deliberate missionizing of non-Jews. Nonetheless the extremes were navigated by many Jews

---

[70] Hence Philo's apology for the practice in *Spec. Leg.* 1.1–11.

[71] Cf. Juvenal, *Sat.* 14.98–99: "They see no difference between eating swine's flesh, from which their father abstained, and human flesh."

in the Diaspora in such a way as to facilitate proselytizing, although in many cases the initiative was most usually going to be with a non-Jewish observer. Hence the complexity of interaction among Jews and non-Jews is apparent on every level imaginable especially against the backdrop of Jewish apologetics and their reception of proselytes. Two authors who exemplify that complexity most of all are Josephus and Philo, and to them I now proceed.

JOSEPHUS

Joseph son of Mathias otherwise known as Flavius Josephus (ca. 37–100 C.E.) was a Judean aristocrat born into a priestly family. A one-time general for the Jews in Galilee during the Jewish war with Rome, he was captured by the Romans, successfully changed sides, became a valuable advisor, interpreter, and mediator for the Romans, and eventually entered the retinue of the Flavian emperors. His major literary works were written between 75–95 C.E. and contribute immensely to our understanding of first-century Judaism and also to Jewish views of Gentiles and accounts of proselytism. The cross-cultural challenges that Josephus has to address are reflected in the fact that his first work, *Jewish War,* was predominantly a defense of Roman hegemony to the Jews, while in *Against Apion* he provides a defense of the Jews to the Romans, and in *Antiquities* he seems to occasionally express a form of Jewish triumphalism.[72] He is a valuable source of information since he spent a significant amount of time in Judea, Galilee, and the Roman Diaspora. Moreover, he possessed an intimate knowledge of Jew-Gentile relations, which are written about from the geographical position of Rome and from the political point of view of a Roman sympathizer of Jewish origins. He is arguably our best source for a survey of Diasporan attitudes towards non-Jews and provides information about Gentile conversions outside of Palestine. At the same time, it is important to read Josephus critically as he was evidently aware of how inflammatory and deeply offensive accounts of Gentile conversion to Judaism were to some sophisticated Greek-reading Roman audiences. He arguably plays it down at some points or else attributes it to more radical elements

---

[72] Crossan, *Historical Jesus,* 94; Shaye J. D. Cohen, *Josephus in Galilee and Rome: His Vita and Development as a Historian* (Leiden: Brill, 1979), 240.

of Judaism. Josephus's sensitivity to this matter in fact appears to have fluctuated over the course of his literary career.

To begin with, the early chapters of *Antiquities* are a form of "rewritten Bible," and at several places Josephus's unique articulation of the narratives informs us of Jewish views of Gentile, and Gentile attachment to Jewish, practices. Two examples suffice to show the distinctive spin that Josephus applied to the biblical narratives. Feldman and Rokéah think that Josephus portrays Abraham as a Jewish missionary in Egypt. In *Ant.* 1.161–167 Abraham goes down to Egypt driven by word of their prosperity, but also to hear what the priests said about gods (περὶ θεῶν) so that, "if he found their doctrine more excellent than his own, to conform to it, or else to convert them (μετακοσμήσειν αὐτούς) to a better mind should his own beliefs prove superior."[73] Goodman argues that what Abraham taught was not monotheism but "arithmetic" (ἀριθμητικήν) and "astronomy" (ἀστρονομίαν).[74] Yet the fact that Abraham is depicted as disputing specifically with the priests is evidence of the religious dimension of his sojourn to Egypt. As well as that, mathematics and astronomy were not unreligious activities and were a key part of the worship of celestial deities and the formation of religious calendars.

In addition, in Solomon's dedication of the temple, as retold by Josephus in *Ant.* 8.116–117 (= 1 Kgs 8:41–43; 2 Chron 6:32–33), the remarks pertaining to Gentiles conspicuously omit the phrase "that all the peoples of the earth may know your name and fear you," and Josephus inserts a plea that the nations would know that "we are not inhumane by nature or unfriendly to those who are not of our country, but wish that all men equally should receive aid from Thee and enjoy thy blessings." This revision of the biblical text purposefully neglects to mention Gentiles coming to know and fear God and it furnishes instead Josephus's own propaganda that Jews are not Gentile-haters. Cohen[75] alleges that Josephus had numerous opportunities to emphasize the importance of Gentile adherence to Judaism but failed to do so in the

---

[73] *Ant.* 1.161; Gen 12:10–13:1; cf. Feldman, *Jew and Gentile in the Ancient World*, 320; Rokéah, "Ancient Jewish Proselytism," 213–14; depictions of Abraham in *Jubilees* 12; *Apocalypse of Abraham* 1–8; Philo, *Abr.* 60–88.

[74] *Ant.* 1.167; Goodman, *Mission and Conversion*, 89, n. 2; cf. Hayward, "Abraham as Proselytizer," 30–31.

[75] Cohen, "Respect for Judaism by Gentiles according to Josephus," 422.

case of the "God-fearers" among Pharaoh's servants,[76] Rahab's reverence to Israel's God,[77] and in the stories of Ruth[78] and Jonah.[79] In the *Antiquities*, then, Josephus does not deny the positive interactions of learned Jewish sages with pagans, but he seems to consciously fall short of anything that could be interpreted as praising pagan conversion to the Jewish way of life.

Josephus never denied that conversions took place and that many learned Greeks and Romans were attracted to Jewish ways. There are several descriptions of conversions and adherence to Judaism in Josephus's writings. He recounts how Nero's wife, Poppaea, convinced Nero to make a decision in favor of the Jewish delegation because "she was a God-worshipper" (θεοσεβὴς γὰρ ἦν).[80] It would be a significant occurrence if the Roman empress was an adherent to Jewish ways. Yet her attitude presented here may be indicative of no more than an act of piety or goodwill towards the Jews and their cultus. Mason suggests that Josephus is playing on a tradition of Roman aristocratic hostility to Poppaea[81] by contrasting her purported piety towards the Jews with the fact that she kept two priests from the Jewish delegation as hostages.[82] Alternatively, Poppaea may have kept the priests as tutors of some form to provide instruction in Jewish ways as Feldman argues.[83] Still, the plainest sense of the text is that Poppaea had some affinity for Judaism, even if it was limited to merely showing a friendly disposition towards the Jewish people rather than actually practicing its customs.[84] Such a benevolent disposition is not unreasonable considering that several other Roman noble women were Jewish sympathizers or adherents including Fulvia (the wife of the senator Saturninus),[85] Julia Severa (relative of the

[76]Exod 9:20 (LXX: ὁ φοβούμενος τὸ ῥῆμα κυρίου); Josephus, *Ant.* 2.305.

[77]Josh 2:9–11; Josephus, *Ant.* 5.11–12.

[78]*Ant.* 5.318–337.

[79]*Ant.* 9.208–214.

[80]*Ant.* 20.195; cf. *Life* 16.

[81]On animosity towards Poppaea's machinations, see Tacitus, *Ann.* 13.45; 14.1.60–64.

[82]Mason, "The *Contra Apionem* in Social and Literary Context," 27.

[83]Feldman, *Jew and Gentile in the Ancient World*, 351–52.

[84]Cf. Margaret H. Williams, " 'Θεοσεβὴς γὰρ ἦν' – The Jewish Tendencies of Poppaea Sabina," *JTS* 39 (1988): 97–111.

[85]*Ant.* 18.81–83; cf. Feldman, *Jew and Gentile in the Ancient World*, 310.

senator Lucius Servenius Cornutus),[86] and Flavia Domitilla who was banished from Rome by Domitian for "drifting into Jewish practices."[87] If Poppaea was favorably disposed towards the Jewish religion, there would not necessarily be any apparent contradiction between her civil religious duties and benevolence towards Jewish priests since Romans did not regard the respect and observance of multiple religions and their rites as an inconsistency of belief.

Josephus also provides some information about Jewish sympathizers and converts in Syria. He relates how the Gentile men in Damascus, after the routing of Cestius's forces, conspired to kill the Jewish population but had to keep it a secret from their wives, who had "become converts to the Jewish religion" (ὑπηγμένας τῇ Ἰουδαϊκῇ θρησκείᾳ).[88] Undoubtedly the notion that all/most of the wives of Damascus were Jewish sympathizers contains no small detail of exaggeration. Yet the popularity of Judaism among Gentile women outside of Palestine is confirmed by Acts[89] and by seven proselyte inscriptions from Rome, five of which pertain to females.[90] Josephus narrates how during the outbreak of the Jewish war the Jewish and Gentile inhabitants of cities in Syro-Palestine were divided into "two camps" (δύο στρατόπεδα) resulting in various massacres. In the towns and cities of Syria some militant factions had determined to "rid themselves of the Jews" but remained fearful of the "Judaizers" who lived in each city.[91] He further notes that calamity upon the Jewish community was avoided since these "judaizers" aroused the alarm and the Syrians "feared these mixed elements as much as resident aliens" (μεμιγμένον ὡς βεβαίως ἀλλόφυλον ἐφοβεῖτο). These judaizers are somehow mixed-into Jewish communities and their identity can be said to *function* rather like that of Jews living in a foreign city. In addition, we should note that Josephus was wholly against forced conversions of the type performed by Hasmonean rulers upon territories outside of Judea, the memory of which did not endear the Jews to the Syrians. This is illustrated by

---

[86] Frey, *CIJ* 2: §766.

[87] (τῶν Ἰουδαίων ἤδη ἐξοκέλλοντες), Dio Cassius, *Hist.* 67.14.1–3 (Stern, *GLAJJ* 2: §435).

[88] *J.W.* 2.560–561.

[89] Acts 13:50; 16:14; 17:4, 12.

[90] Frey, *CIJ* 1: §§21, 202, 256, 523, 576; cf. Leon, *The Jews of Ancient Rome*, 250–56.

[91] Josephus, *J.W.* 2.462–463.

his biographical account where he saved two Gentile dignitaries from being forcibly circumcised and his description of the commander of the Roman garrison in Herod's palace, Mitelius, who was captured.[92] The jewel in Josephus's crown of conversions to Judaism is the house of Adiabene.[93] Bracketed by Claudius's decision in favor of the Jews (*Ant.* 20.6–16) and the tumult of Theudas (*Ant.* 20.97) the events in the story may be dated ca. 44–46 C.E.[94] Izates adopted Jewish customs and beliefs when a Jewish merchant called Ananias visited the king's wives and "taught them to worship God after the manner of the Jewish tradition" (τὸν θεὸν σέβειν, ὡς Ἰουδαίοις). Concurrently, Queen Helena had "likewise been instructed by another Jew and had been brought over to their laws" (τοὺς ἐκείνων μετακεκομίσθαι νόμους).[95] Tannaitic sources portray Izates and Helena quite positively, reporting Helena as observing a Nazarite vow and donating golden vessels to the temple.[96] If the details of the conversion are historically correct in broad outline at least (and Neusner and Schiffman think that they are),[97] then this is perhaps the clearest evidence for Jewish missionary activity in Second Temple literature. J. C. Paget goes so far as to say that Ananias and Eleazar must have had some perception of themselves as Jewish missionaries.[98] However, several lines of evidence indicate that while conversions did take place, this was not the result of any precise

---

[92] *Life* 112–113, 149–154; *J.W.* 2.454.

[93] Josephus, *Ant.* 20.34–49. See also a rabbinic version of the conversion of Monbazus and Izates in *Bereshith Rabbah* 46.11. According to Lawrence H. Schiffman ("The Conversion of the Royal House of Adiabene in Josephus and Rabbinic Sources," in *Josephus, Judaism, and Christianity* [eds. Louis H. Feldman and Gohei Hata; Detroit: Wayne State University Press, 1987], 301–2), Josephus's account is more reliable than the haggadic narrative.

[94] Schiffman, "The Conversion of the Royal House of Adiabene," 294.

[95] Josephus, *Ant.* 20.34–35.

[96] *m. Nazir* 3.6; *t. Yoma* 3.3; *m. Yoma* 3.10; cf. *t. Sukk.* 1.1; cf. Schiffman, "The Conversion of the Royal House of Adiabene," 298–300.

[97] Josephus may have been acquainted personally with the Adiabenians as they had homes in Jerusalem, participated in the Jewish war, and when their princes were captured they were sent to Rome as hostages (*J.W.* 2.520; 5.474–475; 6.356–357). See Jacob Neusner, "The Conversion of Adiabene to Judaism: A New Perspective," *JBL* 83 (1964): 60; Schiffman, "The Conversion of the Royal House of Adiabene," 293–97.

[98] Paget, "Jewish Proselytism," 91; cf. Cohen, "Respect for Judaism by Gentiles according to Josephus," 424; Borgen, *Early Christianity and Hellenistic Judaism*, 54; McKnight, *A Light among the Gentiles*, 56.

form of missionary activity. First, the conversion may have been more politically motivated than Josephus reports. The Adiabenians may have wanted to foster an anti-Roman coalition in the region and in a post-Roman Palestine possibly to lay a claim to the Judean throne since they already ruled over Jewish subjects in the city of Nisibis.[99] Second, Josephus's inclusion of the story is apologetic and didactic. He clearly takes pride in the conversion of this royal family and presents them to his readers as righteous converts whom the Jews had accepted. That is all the more significant when we observe that, according to Cohen, almost all conversions in *Antiquities* are portrayed in negative terms as all the converts suffer unhappy consequences—all except Izates! The reason for the exception is that the story concerns the propagation of Judaism outside of the Roman Empire and Roman sentiment would be less affronted by a successful conversion of a royal household outside of its imperial jurisdiction.[100] In any case, the chief virtue of Izates is his trust in God alone, which is a lesson that can be applied to all Gentiles regardless of which part of a religious continuum towards Judaism that they are on.[101] Third, it appears that Ananias, for political reasons, did not wish Izates to be circumcised but remain a God-worshipper (τὸ θεῖον σέβειν). Ananias was evidently satisfied with adherence rather than conversion for Izates. It took the figure of Eleazar to urge the king to be circumcised, thereby bringing his affiliation with Judaism to a deeper level of commitment.[102] This underscores that some Jews were quite aware that explicit proselytizing was politically dangerous in Hellenistic culture, while more zealous Jews were dissatisfied with any attachment to Judaism by Gentiles less than circumcision and full commitment to the Jewish way of life laid out in the Torah. Fourth, Goodman and McKnight are correct in their observation that there is no suggestion that Ananias or Eleazar traveled abroad specifically for the purpose of mission.[103] Ananias was a merchant, and Eleazar wished to pay his respects to the king. It does appear that they were quite willing to discuss

---

[99] Neusner, "The Conversion of Adiabene to Judaism," 63–66; Feldman, *Jew and Gentile in the Ancient World*, 330.

[100] Cohen, "Respect for Judaism by Gentiles according to Josephus," 424–25.

[101] Schiffman, "The Conversion of the Royal House of Adiabene," 308; Donaldson, *Judaism and the Gentiles*, 337–38.

[102] Josephus, *Ant.* 20.43–47.

[103] McKnight, *A Light among the Gentiles*, 56; Goodman, *Mission and Conversion*, 84.

and explain Judaism to others who were interested in Judaism (esp. with women!) and happily instructed those who wished to adopt such beliefs. What can be said is that both individuals were quite eager to see Izates drawn into a closer relationship to Judaism and they willingly commended that course of action to him. What we can say in the end about the story of the conversion of Helena and Izates, is that some Jews were willing to guide foreigners into conversion. But even so, as Paul Bowers states, we should caution against "the frequent tendency ... to construct from this one example [i.e., Ananias and Eleazar] a complete typology of the proselyte effort."[104]

Josephus, writing in response to the accusation that Jews are hateful towards outsiders,[105] frequently commends the Jewish law as exemplary for all humankind, noting that Jews largely accept outsiders into their midst. In one occurrence he recounts how in Moses' day there were Greeks who "revere our customs (τιμῶντες ἔθη) because they are not able to contradict them."[106] According to Josephus, the speech of Nicolaus of Damascus emphasizes at length the benefits of law-devout Jews for Roman society. God delights in being honored and delights in those who permit him to be honored. The openness of the Jewish practices is accentuated: "Nor do we make a secret of the precepts that we use as guides in religion and in human relations; we give every seventh day over to the study of our customs and laws ... Now our customs are excellent in themselves, if one examines them carefully" which arguably functions as an invitation to attend exposition of the law on the Sabbath.[107]

The spread of Jewish practices is reiterated by Josephus in another narrative set in Antioch at the end of the Jewish War: "Moreover, they were constantly attracting (προσαγόμενοι) to their religious ceremonies (ταῖς θρησκείαις) multitudes of Greeks, and some of these they had in some measures incorporated (μοῖραν) themselves."[108] The Jews

---

[104] Paul Bowers, "Paul and Religious Propaganda in the First Century," *NovT* 22 (1980): 321.

[105] Cf., e.g., Tacitus (*Hist.* 5.5.1), "towards every other people they feel only hate and enmity"; cf. Apollonius Molon who charged Jews that they do not admit anyone who disagrees with them which Josephus cites in *Ag. Ap.* 2.145, 148; Juvenal (*Sat.* 14.100–101 [Stern, *GLAJJ* 2: §301]) states that Jewish converts learn to despise Roman customs.

[106] Josephus, *Ant.* 3.217.

[107] Josephus, *Ant.* 16.43–44 (Nicolaus's speech 16.31–57).

[108] Josephus, *J.W.* 7.45.

were blamed for a fire in the city and a leading instigator of a pogrom against them was an apostate Jew named Antiochus. Josephus juxtaposes this Antiochus with the many Greeks who had come to be associated with the Jewish community in Antioch. It is hard to determine whether the Greeks became converts or sympathizers to Judaism.[109] On the one hand the word "incorporated" (μοῖραν) suggests more than emulation of certain rituals but of participation in the Jewish community itself. Yet the phrase "in some measures" (τρόπῳ τινί) makes this incorporation partial or selective rather than total. The account documents attraction, not mission *per se,* although the reference to "incorporated" may signify that some pagans eventually converted fully. Donaldson is correct that Josephus is probably speaking of the group as a whole rather than individuals within it who would very probably include a mixture of persons who sympathized (what we've been calling adherents) and others who finally became proselytes (what we've been calling converts). In either case, we have an instance of Greeks participating in the socioreligious life of the Jewish community in Antioch. In addition, we can ask where the initiative came from for this incorporation. The LCL translation by Thackery is somewhat misleading because the participle προσαγόμενοι means "leading" not "attracting" (cf. Gen 48:9 [LXX]; Matt 18:24; Luke 9:41; Acts 12:6; 16:20).[110] Yet at the same time there is a reflexive element in the middle voice of the participle, and some degree of self-involvement is implied by incorporating *themselves* since the middle voice emphasizes the subject's participation in the action and not merely their being acted upon.[111] Some Antiochene Jews were willing to lead Greeks into socioreligious participation with the Jewish community, and many Greeks took the initiative to adopt Jewish customs and integrate themselves into the Jewish community there.

It is in the propaganda piece *Against Apion* that Josephus's most concerted effort to produce evidence of Hellenistic acceptance of Judaism is found. He rhetorically appeals to Pythagoras, Anaxagoras, Plato, and the Stoics as admirers of the Jewish laws, who held similar views to the

---

[109] Contrast Feldman, *Jew and Gentile in the Ancient World,* 350 and Cohen, "Respect for Judaism by Gentiles," 417.

[110] BDAG, 875–76.

[111] Cf. Daniel B. Wallace, *Greek Grammar beyond the Basics* (Grand Rapids, Mich.: Zondervan, 1996), 415–17; Stanley E. Porter, *Idioms of the Greek New Testament* (2d ed.; Sheffield: Sheffield Academic Press, 1994), 66–67.

Jewish people concerning the nature of God.[112] The purpose here, much like in Philo, is to show the philosophical convergence between Greek philosophy and Jewish monotheism. Drawing from Theophrastus and Herodotus, Josephus states that Jewish practices have been adopted by other nations surrounding Palestine indicating further the utility and attractiveness of the Jewish way of life.[113] Josephus enjoys and laments the fact that many Greeks "have agreed to adopt our laws (εἰς τοὺς ἡμετέρους νόμους συνέβησαν εἰσελθεῖν); some of whom have remained faithful while others, lacking the necessary endurance, have again seceded."[114] In context this statement serves to show that the Jewish people do not despise aliens or outsiders of their community. Proof of that is the Jewish willingness to share their customs with others. The adoption of Jewish laws by Greeks could imply no more than imitation of a few specific Jewish precepts like ethical monotheism and the avoidance of adultery; it might not necessarily require full adherence to the Jewish way of life. However, the reference to Greeks entering "into" (εἰς) Jewish laws and "remaining faithful" (ἐμμένω) as contrasted to those who have "seceded" (ἀφίστημι) gives the impression of initiation followed by continuance or apostasy. This pattern is perhaps more indicative of proselytes than adherents. Once more though, the "who," "how," and "why" of Gentile conversions eludes us.

Whereas proselytism is in view in the quotation above, elsewhere in *Against Apion* garnering adherents is more or less the goal of the Jewish interface with the Greco-Roman world. Towards the end of *Against Apion* Josephus states:

> The masses have long since shown a keen desire to adopt our religious observances (ζῆλος γέγονεν ἐκ μακροῦ τῆς ἡμετέρας εὐσεβείας); and there is not one city, Greek or barbarian, nor a single nation, to which our custom of abstaining from work on the seventh day has not spread, and where the fasts and the lighting of lamps and many of our prohibitions in the matter of food are not observed.[115]

It should be observed that Josephus is not talking about proselytes, nor does he mention circumcision. As he goes on to say, Greeks "imitate" (μιμεῖσθαι) the Jews in many respects (kindness, charity, devoted

---

[112] Josephus, *Ag. Ap.* 1.162–165; 2.168, 255–257.
[113] Josephus, *Ag. Ap.* 1.167–171.
[114] Josephus, *Ag. Ap.* 2.123.
[115] Josephus, *Ag. Ap.* 2.282.

labor, endurance), but they do not necessarily become Jews as a result of this. Josephus adds, with no sense of hyperbolic restraint, that "as God permeated the universe, so that the Law found its way *among all humankind*" (διὰ πάντων ἀνθρώπων).[116] This renders the law as something that is ubiquitous among the various regions, cities, and lands of the Roman world. Law, however, remains localized around the Jewish communities spread through the world. In any case, Josephus does not distinguish here the types of assent that range from respect, imitation, partial adherence, and full observance.

For all of his efforts to show the openness of the Jewish people to outsiders, Josephus does not (and probably cannot) avoid the fact of Jewish separation, both social and intellectual, from the Hellenistic world. Nonetheless, Josephus states that there is "a gracious welcome" to "all who desire to come and live under the same laws with us (ὅσοι μὲν γὰρ θέλουσιν ὑπὸ τοὺς αὐτοὺς ἡμῖν νόμους ζῆν ὑπελθόντες) . . . holding that it is not family ties alone which constitutes relationship, but agreement in the principles of conduct"; Josephus can also add: "On the other hand, it was not his pleasure that casual visitors should be admitted to the intimacies of our daily life" (τοὺς δ᾽ ἐκ παρέργου προσιόντας ἀναμίγνυσθαι τῇ συνηθείᾳ οὐκ ἠθέλησεν).[117] This means that there were limits beyond which Jewish amicability would not extend. Similarly he cites Plato as an example that "it is hazardous to divulge the truth about God to the ignorant mob" and regards Plato as like Moses with his proscription against mixing fables with theology.[118] That provides a Hellenistic counter-part to Jewish practices of separation and Josephus, apologetically driven as he is, endeavors to show outsider interest in Jewish rites and beliefs, but he does not shirk from the reality that Judaism did have conscious boundaries in terms of full inclusion into its religious communities.

Overall, Josephus's perspective is best summarized in his own words: "We, on the contrary, while we have no desire to emulate the customs of others (τὰ μὲν τῶν ἄλλων ζηλοῦν οὐκ ἀξιοῦμεν), yet gladly welcome any who wish to share our own (τοὺς μέντοι μετέχειν τῶν ἡμετέρων βουλομένους ἡδέως δεχόμεθα). That, I think, may be

---

[116] Josephus, *Ag. Ap.* 2.284.
[117] Josephus, *Ag. Ap.* 2.210.
[118] Josephus, *Ag. Ap.* 2.224, 255–257.

taken as a proof of both our humanity and magnanimity."[119] The Jewish people are more appropriately understood, then, as open to outsiders coming into Judaism, but not necessarily active in recruiting them. Part of the problem with much of the discussion over this subject is precisely that the differentiation between openness, on the one hand, and activity, on the other is not properly made.[120] Ultimately, Josephus is not that interested in the ideology or social engineering behind conversion, but focuses instead on the compatibility and commensurability of the Jewish way of life with the highest ideals of Greek philosophy and its philosophers. Josephus is fully aware that Jewish triumphalism, messianism, apocalyptic fervor, and proselytism create social and religious tensions, and he downplays it where necessary (e.g., in his report of Solomon's speech at the dedication of the temple in *Ant.* 8.117–118, and Josephus transfers messianic prophecies to Vespasian in *J.W.* 6.312–313; 3.400–408). He provides many glowing accounts of non-Jews sympathizing with Jewish ways and positively portrays conversions to Judaism (unless they are forced). The story of Izates's conversion remains determinative for identifying Josephus's own perspective and whether he saw this event as exceptional or something that he hoped readers themselves would imitate. The positive portrayal of Jewish adherents and/or converts in *Antiquities* is ratcheted up in *Against Apion* as Josephus's *apologia* for the Jewish people makes sympathy and imitation central to his argument. I would surmise that Josephus would be quite contented for large numbers of Greeks to adopt Jewish ways in whole or part, but like Philo (yet with less intensity and complexity) he regards virtuous Gentiles and noble rulers as having their own path to "a true and befitting conception of God."[121]

PHILO

The Alexandrian Jew Philo (20 B.C.E.–50 C.E.) came from the upper echelons of the Jewish community of Egypt and was thoroughly schooled in both the Jewish Scriptures and Hellenistic philosophy. His

---

[119] Josephus, *Ag. Ap.* 2.261.

[120] Cf., e.g., Hvalvik, *The Struggle for Scripture and Covenant*, 316.

[121] Josephus, *Ag. Ap.* 2.255. See the summary of Josephus in Donaldson, *Judaism and the Gentiles*, 357–61.

literary output was vast and the chief goal of his literary endeavors appears to be to show that Moses attained the highest summit of philosophical reflection.[122] Philo was not concerned with proper views of missionary theology and practice, but with the relationship of Israel to the Greek world and the philosophical coherence (and attractiveness) of Judaism to outsiders. The enigma of Philo is trying to understand how two strands of thought (Jewish particularism and philosophical universalism) are constantly invoked and interwoven within his writings and what significance this has for views of Gentiles, sympathizers, proselytes, and proselytism. Donaldson writes:

> Thus, depending on which of Philo's two poses function as the primary point of reference, one ends up with two quite different portraits of Gentile inclusion. How is one to correlate the figure of the proselyte, for whom Moses makes provision on the literal surface of his "most excellent" law (*Moses* 2.12), with that of the "one who sees God," to whom Moses's writings are addressed at the level of "the hidden and inward meaning" (*Abraham* 147)? Are they the same in Philo's conception? If so, are his "proselytes" really just ethical monotheists, living a life committed to virtue and the vision of the one God, and thus becoming part of "Israel" in the etymological sense but not adopting those practices that would turn them into Jews? Or does he assume that those who seek to "see God" become part not only of "Israel" in an abstract sense but also of "the Jews" in a very real sense?[123]

According to Philo the law has universal significance for non-Jews. He alleged that it can attract (ἐπάγεται) and influence (συνεπιστρέθει), "barbarians, Greeks, dwellers on the mainland and islands, of nations of the east and the west, of Europe and Asia, of the whole inhabited world from end to end."[124] The translation of the Septuagint transpired, Philo thought, because it was shameful that only one half of the human race could know the law. Ptolemy II Philadelphus, who had affection for the Jewish law, sponsored the translation of the Jewish Scriptures from Chaldean into Greek on the island of Pharos. This event was celebrated in Philo's time every year with a feast on the island, and was attended by both Jews and "multitudes" of others who honor the "light of that version first shone out."[125] Philo also held out

---

[122] Philo, *Op. Mundi* 8; cf. *Quod Omn. Prob* 160.

[123] Donaldson, *Judaism and the Gentiles*, 222–23.

[124] Philo, *Vit. Mos.* 2.20.

[125] Philo, *Vit. Mos.* 2.26–42; cf. Josephus, *Ag. Ap.* 2.279–295.

hope that "each nation would abandon its peculiar ways, and, throwing overboard their ancestral customs, turn to honoring our laws alone."[126] The term "particularistic universalism," as coined by Borgen, may be an adequate term to describe how the *Jewish* law omits a *universal* effect.[127] Philo's account is, however, highly romanticized in its extolling of the magnificence of the law and we can question if the ideal matched the reality. After all, the Septuagint's primary function was to be the scriptures of Hellenistic Jews and only secondarily could it intend to bring Judaism to the attention of Greeks.[128] Those Gentiles who admire the law have Philo's approval and admiration, but they still remain Gentiles and do not enter Israel in the ethnic sense. A day will come, Philo believes, when their partial observance becomes total, but that is projected to the future and is not achieved by any missionary effort.

Philo, like Josephus, also draws attention to the Jewish openness to outsiders. In *Legatio ad Gaium* Petronius is portrayed as seemingly aware of the Jewish act of accepting outsiders who "pay homage" to the law: "they welcome them no less than their own countrymen."[129] Borgen thinks this refers specifically to proselytes but it is impossible to specify.[130] The mystics who conceal their teachings to a circle of three or four are vehemently denounced by Philo. Instead, such doctrines should be circulated in the marketplace so as to extend security, happiness, and virtue to all people. Those whose actions serve the common good are exhorted to "walk in daylight through the midst of the market-place, ready to converse with crowded gatherings (πολυανθρώποις ὁμίλογοις), to let the clear sunlight shine upon their own life."[131] Furthermore, Philo writes "that we should follow its [nature's] intentions and display (προτιθέναι) in public all that is profitable and necessary for the benefit

---

[126] Philo, *Vit. Mos.* 2.43–44.

[127] Borgen, "Proselytes, Conquest, and Mission," 59.

[128] Goodman, *Mission and Conversion*, 57–58; cf. Victor Tcherikover, "Jewish Apologetic Literature Reconsidered," *Eos* 48 (1956): 169–93. On possible citations of the Jewish Scriptures by pagan authors see Feldman, *Jew and Gentile in the Ancient World*, 312. Nock (*Conversion*, 79) writes: "Certainly there is no indication of substantial knowledge of the Septuagint except as heard by those who frequented synagogues or were concerned to write polemical treatises against Christianity: as a book it was bulky, expensive and inaccessible."

[129] *Leg. Gai.* 210–211.

[130] Borgen, "Proselytes, Conquest, and Mission," 62.

[131] Philo, *Spec. Leg.* 1.319–321 (denoting the law in particular, 324).

of those who are worthy to use it?"[132] This sounds like an injunction to the public propagation of Torah, though not necessarily "the method of missionaries."[133] Dickson concludes from this: "The fact that Philo is so adamant that Judaism must be proclaimed in the market-place ought to be taken as evidence of his own missionary activity or at least of a missionary ideal which found some historical expression in Alexandria."[134] Yet as to whether this actually occurred or simply remained Philo's cherished ideal of the public Jewish philosopher-orator cannot be known. The Sabbath, Philo explains, is supremely for the public exposition of Moses: "So each seventh day there stand wide open in every city thousands of schools of good sense . . . But among the vast number of particular truths and principles there studied, there stand out practically high above the others two main heads: one of duty to God as shewn by piety and holiness, one of duty to men as shewn by humanity and justice."[135] It may be true, as Georgi remarks, that synagogues operated as centers of Jewish propaganda.[136] The synagogues, with their prayers, hymn-singing, interpretation of Scripture, and ethical admonition, were more like a philosophical assembly than the usual pagan altar involving sacrifice and libations.[137] However, the effectiveness of synagogues as centers of Jewish apologetics and propaganda would be contingent upon Gentile curiosity being sufficiently aroused by their operation and a willingness on their part to attend a Jewish religious assembly. Furthermore, Philo thinks of teaching only the initiated as opposed to the superstitious that are proud and lacking in holiness. Indeed, he exhorts his readers not to reveal certain "mysteries" to the uninitiated.[138]

A distinguishing feature of Philo is his consistently positive attitude towards proselytes.[139] Converts are those who have rejected idols,

---

[132] Philo, *Spec. Leg.* 1.323.

[133] Feldman, *Jew and Gentile in the Ancient World*, 318.

[134] Dickson, *Mission-Commitment in Ancient Judaism*, 38.

[135] Philo, *Spec. Leg.* 2.62–63. For Torah instruction on the Sabbath, cf. Philo, *Leg. Gai.* 156–157, 312–313; *Som.* 2.127; *Vit. Mos.* 2.216; *Spec. Leg.* 2.62–63; *Omn. Prob. Lib.* 81–82; *Vit. Cont.* 30–33; Josephus, *Ant.* 16.43–44; *Ag. Ap.* 2.175; Mark 1:21–22; Luke 4:16–29; Acts 13:42; 15:21; 17:2; 18:4.

[136] Georgi, *The Opponents of Paul in Second Corinthians*, 84.

[137] Hengel and Schwemer, *Paul between Damascus and Antioch*, 61–62.

[138] Philo, *Cher.* 42, 48; *Sacr.* 60.

[139] Philo, *Spec. Leg.* 1.51–53; 1.309; 2.117–119; 4.176–178; *Som.* 1.60–62; 2.273; *Virt.* 102–104, 108, 180, 214, 218–219; *Praem. Poen.* 152; *Vit.*

forsaken their country and customs, become lovers of truth, servants of the true and living God, and left behind family to join a new "commonwealth" (πολιτεία).[140] Importantly, proselytes are to be granted the same rights as native Jews, and are superior to apostates.[141] Proselytes even have a place in heaven.[142] To get a complete picture of Philo's attitude towards proselytes we have to point out some of his negative remarks about certain types of converts. Philo argues, based on Deut 23:7–8, that Egyptians who wish to "convert" (μεταλλάξασθαι) are not to be admitted to the "Jewish community" (ἰουδαίων πολιτείαν) until the third generation.[143] He also thinks of hereditary Jews as being superior to those who convert for spurious reasons.[144] Overall though, Philo is very positive towards proselytes, and he regards proselytes and faithful Jews as models for the kind of piety and worship that is the goal of life according to the commandments of the Decalogue.

A significant designation in Philo is that of Israel who "sees God" (ὁρῶν θεόν).[145] Jacob Neusner thinks that for Philo, "Israel" is essentially a network of philosophical tenets, a certain perception of God, indicating that Israel is primarily a philosophical category rather than a social entity.[146] Ellen Birnbaum goes further, helpfully suggesting that "seeing God represents the height of human happiness and that, in and of itself, seeing God may be considered universal since anyone—regardless of birth—may pursue this quest or goal."[147] With the exception of Legatio, Philo is careful to distinguish Israel from the Jewish people. Birnbaum says: "Accordingly, 'Israel' is not a clearly recognizable social group but instead may be similar to what we speak of today as an 'intellectual elite.'"[148] The result is that "Israel" in Philonic thought represents all respected philosophers, or philosophically minded people, regardless

---

Mos. 1.147; Leg. Gai. 210–211; Quaest. in Ex. 2.2; and see also 2 Bar. 41:1–5; 42:4–5.

[140] Philo, Spec. Leg. 1.51–53.

[141] Philo, Spec. Leg. 1.52–57; Virt. 104, 108.

[142] Philo, Praem. Poen. 152.

[143] Philo, Virt. 108; on his derogatory view of the Egyptians see, Vit. Mos. 2.193–197; Decal. 80; Vit. Cont. 8–10.

[144] Philo, Vit. Mos. 1.147.

[145] Philo, Migr. Abr. 113–114; Conf. Ling. 56; Her. 78.

[146] Jacob Neusner, Judaism and Its Social Metaphors: Israel in the History of Jewish Thought (Cambridge: Cambridge University Press, 1989), 221.

[147] Birnbaum, The Place of Judaism in Philo's Thought, 11.

[148] Birnbaum, The Place of Judaism in Philo's Thought, 12.

as to whether they are Jews or not.[149] Although one joins the race of
the Jews by adopting certain customs, one strives to belong to Israel by
philosophical reflection.[150] This signifies some kind of universal outlook,
importantly, one that is not attained through any conversion experience.

Philo's thinking contains a mixture of universalistic and exclusivis-
tic traits. On the universal side there is hope that some Gentiles would
eventually be saved through ceasing their iniquity.[151] Philo asserts the
possibility of a moral and philosophical life without conversion to Judaism.[152] God is the Father, Creator and Savior of all humankind.[153] The
vocation of Israel is to be a prophet and priest for the salvation of the
whole world.[154] Philo can also admonish against making offensive remarks against other religious traditions.[155] This stands in contradistinc-
tion to exclusivist notions in Philo's writings. Although Philo implies
that the law and philosophy represent two paths to the same ultimate
ends, virtue and enlightenment, elsewhere he states that reason alone
cannot ascend to God and God provides prophecy so that humans
might grasp that which the mind cannot of itself reach.[156] Abraham
was the first one to have seen God and is the prototype of all proselytes.[157] Like Abraham, the pagans who live in the exile of idolatry
and ignorance come home in Judaism.[158] When given to writing about
eschatological themes he echoes Num 24:7 and Philo looks forward
to the domination of the world by the Jews, but it will only happen if
they are faithful to their laws.[159] Philo can also denounce acculturated
Jews who apostatize completely.[160] He can offer long and vivid lists that
catalog Gentile immorality and idolatry.[161] In yet another instance he

---

[149] Birnbaum, *The Place of Judaism in Philo's Thought*, 115–16.

[150] Birnbaum, *The Place of Judaism in Philo's Thought*, 212–13.

[151] Philo, *Spec. Leg.* 2.12–17.

[152] Philo, *Poster. C.* 21; *Spec. Leg.* 2.44–48; *Quod Omn. Prob.* 74.

[153] Philo, *Op. Mundi*, 72, 78, 169.

[154] Philo, *Spec. Leg.* 1.97, 168, 190; 2.163; *Vit. Mos.* 1.149–152; *Leg. Gai.*
306; cf. McKnight, *A Light among the Gentiles*, 39.

[155] Philo, *Spec. Leg.* 1.53.

[156] Philo, *Virt.* 65; *Leg. Gai.* 4–6; *Vit. Mos.* 2.6 (see Donaldson, *Judaism
and the Gentiles*, 275).

[157] Philo, *Virt.* 215–219.

[158] Philo, *Spec. Leg.* 4.177–178.

[159] Philo, *Praem. Poen.* 93–97, 162–170; *Vit. Mos.* 1.290.

[160] Philo, *Vit. Mos.* 1.31; *Virt.* 182; *Conf. Ling.* 2; cf. 3 Macc 7:10–16.

[161] Cf., e.g., Philo, *Sacr.* 32.

can conceive of the destruction of Gentiles who fail to convert and of proselytes who apostatize.[162] This shows that notions of salvation, specifically the "who" and "how," are not neatly and clearly drawn up in his writings. Overall, one would think that Philo is more inclined to see a positive place in an eschatological future for the virtuous and philosophically minded pagan, like the "righteous men who follow nature and her ordinances."[163]

In summary, Philo demonstrates an openness to Gentiles who wish to join Judaism, find wisdom, denounce idols, and follow the law. Philo seems to emphasize the welcoming of converts, while not necessarily seeking them out.[164] The statements on proselytes reflect a mix of social complexities about conversion and ideals of the noble proselyte as well. However, one cannot extrapolate from these writings a missionary movement or discern deliberate proselytizing practices. As McKnight concludes, "almost nothing can be inferred from Philo about a missionary movement among Gentiles. His own obvious integration, however, tends to suggest Gentile conversions."[165]

Apologetic-Propagandistic Literature

A significant number of Jewish writings written in Greek, such as the *Sibylline Oracles, Epistle of Aristeas, Joseph and Aseneth, Tobit,* and works by Eupolemos, Demetrius, and Josephus's *Against Apion,* among others, have been regarded as part of the missionary literature of Diaspora Judaism.[166] However, Victor Tcherikover, in his landmark study, argued that Hellenistic Jewish propaganda was meant primarily for Jewish readers, not Gentile readers.[167] According to Tcherikover, in the Ptolemaic period numerous works such as Aristeas, Artapanos, and Aristobolus were written to convince Jews living in Hellenistic society

---

[162] Philo, *Spec. Leg.* 1.54–55.

[163] Philo, *Spec. Leg.* 2.42.

[164] Cf., e.g., Philo, *Leg. Gai.* 210–211; *Spec. Leg.* 1.51–53; 2.118–119; *Virt.* 102–104, 108.

[165] McKnight, *A Light among the Gentiles,* 40.

[166] See for example, Peter Dalbert, *Die Theologie der hellenistisch-jüdischen Missionsliteratur unter Ausschluss von Philo und Josephus* (Hamburg: Herbert Reich, 1954).

[167] Tcherikover, "Jewish Apologetic Literature Reconsidered," 170–93.

amidst Jewish acculturation and apostasy that they could still cling to Judaism since it stood on equal grounds with Hellenism. In response to the sporadic anti-Semitism of the early Roman period, Jews could take consolation in the antiquity of their religion and the immorality and folly of pagan cults. Tcherikover does not deny that certain documents from the Roman period such as Philo's *Flaccus* and *Gaius* were directed towards Roman authorities; likewise Josephus's *Against Apion* and selections from *Antiquities* possess a tacit apologetic function. Yet he thinks we should guard against making these exceptions into a corpus of Jewish Hellenistic missionary literature. He concludes:

> Our examination of the so-called "Apologetic literature" led us to the conclusion that this literature was directed inwards and not outwards and it would be an exaggeration to say that its purpose was solely that of propagating the Jewish religion among the Gentiles.[168]

To that can be added further arguments about the physical production of books, rates of literacy, and the extent to which Greek was spoken in the provinces. Tcherikover maintains that widespread Jewish propaganda literature was practically impossible since there was no mass production of documents for widespread dissemination. In other words, we should not think of this literature as "tracts" designed to facilitate conversion. To that I would add that literacy rates among the general population, according to most estimates, were probably somewhere between 10–15 percent (and even less for women). We should not presume that all men and women in antiquity were bilingual and therefore spoke Greek or Latin in addition to their own indigenous language. Greek was a "prestige" language and was spoken by cultural and literary elites and not by the masses. In which case, the number of persons who could have even read this literature would have been relatively small.

Tcherikover's thesis has been somewhat controversial. On the one hand, McKnight and Goodman have largely accepted Tcherikover's argument and have even tried to reinforce it.[169] Alternatively, there has been a vocal minority of scholars who have resisted Tcherikover's con-

---

[168] Tcherikover, "Jewish Apologetic Literature Reconsidered," 183–84; cf. Smith ("The Gentiles in Judaism 125 BCE–CE 66," 200–201): "But the abysmal intellectual level of most of these works practically proves that their authors were preaching to believers."

[169] McKnight, *A Light among the Gentiles*, 57–60; Goodman, *Mission and Conversion*, 65–67, 77–79.

clusions. Against Tcherikover, Feldman thinks, for one, that literacy was more widespread than he allows and Feldman goes so far as to draw a direct correspondence between the increase in literacy rates and the number of conversions to Judaism between 250 B.C.E. to 100 C.E.[170] Additionally, within the Pseudepigrapha and the Apocrypha, it is possible to detect "missionary motives," though Feldman candidly admits that they were also "needed by Jews to heighten their self-esteem and to define self-identity."[171] Barclay questions the notion that Jewish works did not receive Gentile attention. Alexander Polyhistor (first century B.C.E.), for instance, was able to draw upon a variety of Jewish texts: "Demetrius, Eupolemus, Artapanus, Malchus/Cleodemus, Philo the epic poet, and Ezekiel the Tragedian."[172] It is worth perusing several Jewish texts to see if Tcherikover's thesis that the Jewish apologetic-propagandistic literature was written primarily for insiders remains viable.

Over and against Tcherikover, Paget asserts that wisdom literature offers evidence of missionary consciousness as it possesses "an inbuilt kerygmatic character" in urging people to become disciples of wisdom.[173] The Wisdom of Solomon constitutes a good place to test whether that thesis is correct. On Paget's side, we could point out that the Wisdom of Solomon (12:2–18) evokes the theme of God's punishment and grace for the Gentiles and many of its exhortations could appeal to any one with a concern for virtuous living. Yet much of this document presupposes a prior knowledge of Israel's sacred traditions evidenced by the references to Enoch, Joseph, and Sodom in the Wisdom of Solomon.[174] As Tcherikover noted, critiques of idolatry and paganism, often put in vituperative language and rancorous polemics, would be convincing probably only to Jews with a thorough commitment to monotheism and who already possessed a tradition of derision towards idols (e.g., Isa 44:9–20; Wis 13:1–18).[175] In which case, large segments of the Wisdom of Solomon are more likely to confirm Jewish prejudices

---

[170] Feldman, *Jew and Gentile in the Ancient World*, 306–7.

[171] Feldman, *Jew and Gentile in the Ancient World*, 314.

[172] John M. G. Barclay, "Apologetics in the Jewish Diaspora," in *Jews in the Hellenistic and Roman Cities* (ed. John R. Bartlett (London: Routledge, 2002), 142; cf. Feldman, *Jew and Gentile in the Ancient World*, 312–13.

[173] Paget, "Jewish Proselytism," 85.

[174] Wis 4:10; 10:13; 19:13; see also Sirach 44–50 with the inventory of Israel's heroes of the past.

[175] Tcherikover, "Jewish Apologetic Literature Reconsidered," 181–82.

against pagan worship than to convince non-Jewish readers of the inherent virtue of Israel's imageless worship. Somewhat more reserved in his assertions is Hans Conzelmann who thinks that the polemic against paganism in Wisdom of Solomon demonstrates the dialectic tension inherent in Jewish thought—that of denouncing idolatry and of winning over Gentiles—but even that may be granting too much.[176] We have to remember that although the introduction of Wisdom of Solomon is addressed to "you rulers of the earth" (Wis 1:1–2; 6:9–11), it is unlikely that the author really thought this document would be read by kings of the Gentile nations. More likely, the introduction comprises a literary device with one king supposedly exhorting others.[177] Furthermore, there is nothing in Wisdom that declares that righteousness and virtue are the exclusive property of the circumcised or attained through initiation into Judaism. At most, Wisdom of Solomon is advocating "ethical monotheism" rather than conversion to Judaism and joining Israel.[178]

Another piece of Jewish wisdom literature, *Tobit*, exhibits a particular hope for the eschatological pilgrimage of the nations to come and worship Israel's God.[179] Such a hope is projected well into the future and is made subservient to a larger theme of national restoration consisting of a return from exile, the rebuilding of Jerusalem, the reconstruction of the temple, and a renewal of covenant faithfulness. In which case, the orientation of *Tobit* is perhaps optimistic for the future of the Gentiles, but the apparent universalism presupposes the particularism of Israel's election. In the interim Israel has the vocation of acknowledging God before the nations, but that is not necessarily tantamount to converting Gentiles into Jews.[180] Concurrent with the prophetic vision for the salvation of the Gentiles is also the need for separation from them by not eating their food and by strenuously avoiding intermarriage.[181] Part of Tobit's piety involves giving alms to the "orphans and widows and

---

[176] Hans Conzelmann, *Gentiles–Jews–Christians: Polemics and Apologetics in the Greco-Roman Era* (trans. M. Eugene Boring; Minneapolis: Fortress, 1992 [1981]), 175.

[177] *Pace* George W. E. Nickelsburg (*Jewish Literature between the Bible and the Mishnah: A Historical and Literary Introduction* [London: SCM, 1981], 184) who thinks the exhortation to royalty is genuine.

[178] Donaldson, *Judaism and the Gentiles*, 65–68.

[179] Tob 13:11–14; 14:5–7.

[180] Tob 13:3–4.

[181] Tob 1:11; 4:12–13.

to the converts who had attached themselves to Israel."[182] Given the Persian setting, the "convert" (προσηλύτος) is not a resident alien, but a full proselyte to the Jewish way of life. Once more, nothing is said about the "who" and "how" of proselytism and for what end a proselyte is made. The only "missionary" activity of dispersed Israelites in this regard is passive, remaining faithful to God in a foreign land in the hope that God will restore the fortunes of faithful Israelites (like Tobit) and eventually have mercy on a repentant Israel. The author acknowledges that "none of the nations has understanding" but also believes that "the Lord himself will give them good counsel."[183] Participation in salvation, while indelibly connected to Israel, is something bestowed sovereignly and directly by the Lord. Thus, Tobit offers a picture of universal salvation (at least in ethnic scope), but without forfeiting the privileges and boundaries of Israel's election even in a pagan context.

Another text that has been regarded as part of the Diaspora missionary literature is *Joseph and Aseneth* (ca. 100 B.C.E.–115 C.E.),[184] a Hellenistic romance depicting the conversion of Aseneth from paganism and her marriage to Joseph. Aseneth represents the proselyte par excellence who abandons her idols,[185] confesses her sin and appeals for mercy,[186] is accepted by God as indicated by an angelic visit,[187] and marries Joseph.[188] She is blessed by God through the failure of Pharaoh's son to capture her,[189] and she is enrolled in the "book of the living."[190] Aseneth's conversion is described in terms of new creation, renewal, and vivification.[191] Significantly, on two occasions it is reported that Aseneth's conversion will bring blessings to other Gentiles and her "name shall be City of Refuge, because in you many nations will take refuge with the Lord God."[192] She is the prototype and symbolic

---

[182] Tob 1:8.

[183] Tob 4:19.

[184] Randall D. Chesnutt (*From Death to Life: Conversion in Joseph and Aseneth* [Sheffield: Sheffield Academic Press, 1995], 80–85), while acknowledging the uncertainties, suggests a date before 38 B.C.E.

[185] *Jos. Asen.* 9.2; 10:12–13; 11:4–5; 12:12; 13:11.

[186] *Jos. Asen.* 11:3–14, 16–18; 11:19–13:12; 21:10–21.

[187] *Jos. Asen.* 14:1–17:10.

[188] *Jos. Asen.* 19:1–21:9.

[189] *Jos. Asen.* 24:1–29:6.

[190] *Jos. Asen.* 15:3–4.

[191] *Jos. Asen.* 8:9; 15:5, 12; 12:1–2; 20:7.

[192] *Jos. Asen.* 15:7; cf. 17:4–6.

representative of all proselytes and all pagans who are incorporated into Israel.[193] Segal perceives that the narrative in *Joseph and Aseneth* "is meant to be the model of proselytism in the Hellenistic world."[194] Consequently, a missionary purpose is often assumed for it, as Craig Evans comments:

> [An] evangelistic and apologetic thrust does seem to be intended. The conversion of Aseneth, the virtues of Joseph, and the gallantry of Joseph's brothers in defense of the Egyptian king are surely meant to garner admiring sympathy, to deflect criticism aroused by the Jewish presence in Egypt, and *to attract proselytes*.[195]

Several elements, however, seem to count against this missionary hypothesis. The tale presupposes familiarity with the story of Joseph, the patriarchal narratives, and attempts to solve to the question of how a righteous man like Joseph could marry an Egyptian like Aseneth (Gen 41:45), something that would be a specifically Jewish concern.[196] The answer is that God revealed himself, somewhat mystically, to Aseneth and she became a proselyte. Aseneth is described as already being in appearance like a Hebrew woman when the author says that she, "had nothing similar to the virgins of the Egyptians, but she was in every respect similar to the daughters of the Hebrews."[197] Joseph does not attempt to convert Aseneth. Instead, in their first meeting he repels her because "it is not fitting for a man who worships God who will bless with his mouth the living God . . . to kiss a strange woman who will bless with her mouth

---

[193] *Jos. Asen.* 16:16; 19:5.

[194] Segal, "The Cost of Proselytism and Conversion," 349.

[195] Craig A. Evans, "Scripture-Based Stories in the Pseudepigrapha," in *Justification and Variegated Nomism: Volume 1—The Complexities of Second Temple Judaism* (eds. D. A. Carson, Peter T. O'Brien and Mark A. Seifrid; Grand Rapids, Mich.: Baker 2001), 63 (italics added); Feldman, *Jew and Gentile in the Ancient World*, 316; see similar proponents cited in McKnight, *A Light among the Gentiles*, 140, nn. 49, 51; Chesnutt, *From Death to Life*, 257, n. 1; and Schürer, *History of the Jewish People in the Age of Jesus Christ*, 3.1.546–50. In particular Nickelsburg (*Jewish Literature between the Bible and the Mishnah*, 262–63) argues for a purposed Gentile readership.

[196] Christopher Burchard, "Joseph and Aseneth," in *OTP* (ed. James H. Charlesworth; 2 vols.; ABRL; New York: Doubleday, 1985), 2.197; Goodman, *Mission and Conversion*, 79; Chesnutt, *From Death to Life*, 258; Donaldson, *Judaism and the Gentiles*, 142.

[197] *Jos. Asen.* 1:5.

dead and dumb idols."[198] Her conversion is a divine act in which Joseph has no part. There is no zealous proclamation of monotheism or Torah by Joseph. There is no reference to baptism, circumcision, or sacrifices either. While a Torah-centered piety is perhaps eclipsed or even deliberately effaced in the story,[199] the boundaries between Jew and Gentile are still maintained, especially the obstacles to intimate interaction posed by idolatry and the unwillingness of Jews to consent to intermarriage with pagans. When Aseneth does convert, however, she becomes the model proselyte par excellence in that she destroys her household idols and turns in prayer to the God of the Hebrews.[200] It is only after her conversion that she professes to have heard things about the mercy of the God of Israel and that he is the living God who grants forgiveness.[201] Ultimately what drives Aseneth's conversion is not a belief in the intellectual superiority of Judaism, but her desire to marry the handsome Joseph with whom she is infatuated. Christopher Burchard adds: "Judaism is not depicted as mission-minded in Joseph and Aseneth. Proselytes are welcomed, not sought, and conversion is not an easy affair."[202] A careful reading of *Joseph and Aseneth*, then, leads to the conclusion that it is not concerned with missionary activity towards Gentiles; instead, it addresses the problem of maintaining ethical and ethnological integrity in Hellenistic society and how this dilemma relates to the incorporation of proselytes by marriage into the Jewish community.

The *Epistle of Aristeas* (ca. second century B.C.E.) purportedly gives a Gentile account of the translation of the Septuagint. Ptolemy II Philadelphus is informed by the court librarian that his mammoth library lacks a copy of the Jewish law, which requires a translation. Subsequently a request is sent to Eleazar the high priest in Jerusalem for a team of translators to complete the task.[203] The delegates arrive in Egypt and during a banquet they are quizzed by the king on matters of philosophical and political substance in which the Jewish contingent

---

[198] *Jos. Asen.* 8:5.

[199] Donaldson, *Judaism and the Gentiles*, 149.

[200] *Jos. Asen.* 13:8–15.

[201] *Jos. Asen.* 11:10–11.

[202] Burchard, "Joseph and Aseneth," 2.196–97; cf. Chesnutt, *From Death to Life*, 261–62; McKnight, *A Light among the Gentiles*, 60–62; Riesner, "A Pre-Christian Jewish Mission," 227; Schnabel, *Early Christian Mission*, 1.145–46; Donaldson, *Judaism and the Gentiles*, 151.

[203] *Ep. Arist.* 9–12, 28–40.

distinguish themselves before the king.[204] The translation team then begins their task and, with attention to detail, completes it after seventy-two days.[205] The translation is read to the Jews of Alexandria who ratify it as authentic.[206] The translators return to Judea and the epistle closes with an epilogue by Aristeas to Philocrates.[207]

Some argue that *Aristeas* is geared towards Gentile readers.[208] The designated addressee, Philocrates, is described as "favorably inclined toward the piety and disposition of those who live by the sacred Law."[209] The purpose of the exercise is not only translation, but interpretation of the Jewish laws for Gentiles.[210] Of interest is the section on Eleazar's answer to a question concerning the law posed by Aristeas and his companions, which includes a defense of the law and an allegorizing of its precepts dealing with the uncleanness of certain animals, a critique of polytheism, the logic of monotheism, divine instructions for justice, and an apology of the Jewish practice of separation from non-Jews. The section concludes with Aristeas's aim to "expound to you the solemnity and characteristic outlook of the Law."[211]

In addition, the actions and interactions of the lead characters tell us something about how some Jews would ideally like to relate to Gentile peoples. The Jewish translators are depicted as pious, learned, and committed to Jewish separation while indulging Gentiles in dialogue. King Ptolemy is exceptionally accommodating towards the Jewish people, particularly in emancipating Jewish slaves (through divine providence), but in a number of other ways too.[212] His benevolence towards the visitors is evident in his preferential treatment in not making them wait for an audience,[213] and in that he allows the translators to offer prayers instead of his pagan priests[214] and thanks God for the law.[215]

---

[204] *Ep. Arist.* 172–300.

[205] *Ep. Arist.* 301–307.

[206] *Ep. Arist.* 308–311.

[207] *Ep. Arist.* 319–322.

[208] Cf., e.g., Schürer, *History of the Jewish People in the Age of Jesus Christ*, 3.1.679; Feldman, *Jew and Gentile in the Ancient World*, 315–16.

[209] *Ep. Arist.* 5.

[210] *Ep. Arist.* 15.

[211] *Ep. Arist.* 128–171 (171).

[212] *Ep. Arist.* 16–27.

[213] *Ep. Arist.* 174–176.

[214] *Ep. Arist.* 184–186.

[215] *Ep. Arist.* 177.

Aristeas also touts the superiority of the Jewish scribes over their pagan counterparts at the king's symposium. Notably, all the various answers to the king's question espouse a theocentric framework for a pious and just monarch.[216] When reading the finished product the king marvels at the genius of the law-giver, Moses.[217]

In light of the exposition of the law and the favorable rapport between Jews and Gentiles, it still remains more probable that *Aristeas* commends the Jewish faith for Jews.[218] The materials from *Aristeas* cited above could equally be addressed to Jews with the purpose of convincing them of the superiority of their own traditions compared to Hellenistic ones. This is evidenced by the device of using Gentile adulation of learned Jews similar to Nebuchadnezzar and Cyrus in the book of Daniel. A degree of pluralism is apparent in so far as that the Gentiles worship the same God: "These people worship God the overseer and creator of all, whom all men worship including ourselves, O King, except that we have a different name. Their name for him is Zeus and Jove."[219] The qualification being that only Jews worship the one true God and other people worship the gods of their hands or venerate mere animals.[220] In a sense the Jews become, religiously speaking, the first among equals. Even so, there is little reason in converting Gentiles if they are already monotheists, albeit, under a different guise. If Gentiles are in mind at all the purpose is education not proselytizing, thus a desired outcome may be adherents not converts.[221] Barclay claims that we do not have to choose between a Jewish and Gentile readership if it is the case that the Jewish community from which *Aristeas* emerged included Gentile adherents and sympathizers.[222] We cannot discount that possibility but we are faced with evidence that suggests that the implied readers are more probably Jewish with specifically Jewish concerns. The

---

[216] *Ep. Arist.* 187–300 (esp. 201–202, 295–296).

[217] *Ep. Arist.* 312–314.

[218] Goodman, *Mission and Conversion*, 79; Chrys C. Caragounis ("Aristeas, Epistle of," in *DNTB* [eds. Stanley E. Porter and Craig A. Evans; Downers Grove, Ill.: InterVarsity 2000], 117) writes: "*Aristeas* was not written for Greek readers: its simplistic narrative and historical blunders could not but alienate them and thus defeat its purpose. It was written for Jewish consumption outside Palestine, in particular Alexandria."

[219] *Ep. Arist.* 16; cf. Josephus, *Ant.* 12.22.

[220] *Ep. Arist.* 132–138.

[221] See Collins, "A Symbol of Otherness," 166.

[222] Barclay, *Jews in the Mediterranean Diaspora*, 148.

document also seems to be partly fixated on the need to validate the Septuagint, a distinctly Jewish concern. *Aristeas* also contains stringent and forceful reminders of separation of Jews from Gentiles, even if that separation is understood to be for the purpose of preserving a pure philosophical monotheism rather than maintaining Israel's election, the offense that this creates for outsiders is recognized but never entirely removed.[223] A further element apparent in *Aristeas* is the intent to defend the efforts of the Jewish upper class in Alexandria who wished to engage Hellenistic culture in a positive way, and to also reformulate the conviction of Israel's election with the corollary of being separated by God but without completely withdrawing from Greek society.[224] To conclude, then, a dual readership of Gentiles and Jews is conceivable,[225] but proselytism is hardly intended.[226] In fact, *Aristeas* gives the impression that ethical monotheism by educated Greeks is the most that one can or should expect from them. We can speculate of *Aristeas's* potentially positive impact upon Gentiles, but we cannot derive from this any explicit intent by the author for it to do so.

The Jewish redaction of *Sibylline Oracles* Book 3 (160–50 B.C.E.) is another document offered as evidence of Jewish missionary efforts in literary form.[227] A specific concern of this document is the end times and Israel's relationship to the nations in the interim. The Jews are praised as a race of righteous people,[228] they are guides to the blind,[229] and there is an exhortation for the Gentiles to abandon polytheism and to worship at the temple in Jerusalem.[230] There is an expectation that all people will kneel before God at the defeat of Egypt,[231] the islands and

---

[223] *Ep. Arist.* 139, 142.

[224] Schnabel, *Early Christian Mission*, 1.142.

[225] Schürer, *History of the Jewish People in the Age of Jesus Christ*, 3.1.679; Conzelmann, *Gentiles–Jews–Christians,* 173; Paget, "Jewish Proselytism," 83.

[226] Cf. Collins, "A Symbol of Otherness," 166; Segal, "The Cost of Proselytism and Conversion," 349; Schnabel, *Early Christian Mission*, 1.140–42; Donaldson, *Judaism and the Gentiles*, 116.

[227] Nickelsburg, *Jewish Literature between the Bible and the Mishnah*, 165; Segal, "The Cost of Proselytism and Conversion," 348–49; Feldman, *Jew and Gentile in the Ancient World*, 314; Conzelmann, *Gentiles–Jews–Christians,* 227; Paget, "Jewish Proselytism," 83–84.

[228] *Sib. Or.* 3:219.

[229] *Sib. Or.* 3:195.

[230] *Sib. Or.* 3:5–10, 547–579, 624–634, 732–740; 4:162–167.

[231] *Sib. Or.* 3:615–617.

cities of the world will be converted to the God of Israel,[232] Gentiles will embark on a pilgrimage to Jerusalem,[233] and Greeks will "ponder the law of the Most High God."[234] The Jewish Sibyl admonishes pagans to avoid sexual immorality and idolatry and calls for the law to be accepted by all nations.[235] The Torah given at Sinai is a great joy ($\chi\acute{\alpha}\rho\mu\alpha$) for all people, but she predicts disasters on the nations that do not recognize the one true God and his law.[236] The Sibyl is not necessarily advocating the proselytizing of the pagan nations en masse, but of partial observance of the Jewish laws and/or respect for its way of life in order to avoid cataclysmic misfortunes.[237] The author does not demand the demise of Greek culture and looks forward to the time when Jews and Gentiles are joined in the worship of the one God.[238] Yet there is no suggestion that salvation has anything to do with the Gentiles until the final days.[239] Before that time it is a matter of the nations giving respect where respect is due. Nock contends, "there is no evidence that the Judaizing redaction of the Sibylline oracles and of certain Orphic texts exercised any influence outside Judaism and Christianity."[240]

In light of the analysis of all these texts above, Tcherikover, with qualification, appears to be correct that the intended audience for these texts was Jewish. These documents are too ambiguous, too focused on strictly Jewish concerns, too hostile to Gentiles at some points, and lacking formal invitations to conversion for them to qualify as lucid evidence of missionary literature. That said, it would be wholly presumptuous to deny that this type of literature sometimes found its way into the hands of Gentiles. Indirectly, it could be used to give an appositive account of Jewish belief and encourage Gentile respect for or veneration of Jewish customs. In theory such documents could be used to defend the Jews

---

[232] *Sib. Or.* 3:710–723.

[233] *Sib. Or.* 3:716–723.

[234] *Sib. Or.* 3:719.

[235] *Sib. Or.* 3:195.

[236] *Sib. Or.* 3:583, 770.

[237] Contra Feldman (*Jew and Gentile* 314 n. 320) who cites *Sib. Or.* 3:547–549 and 4:162–167 as evidence that the Sibyl wanted to persuade Gentiles to become proselytes.

[238] Nickelsburg, *Jewish Literature between the Bible and the Mishnah*, 165.

[239] Collins, "A Symbol of Otherness," 165–66; Goodman, *Mission and Conversion*, 80; Schnabel, *Early Christian Mission*, 1.143.

[240] Nock, *Conversion*, 79.

against certain allegations or to promote Judaism among Gentiles.[241] In some instances such as Josephus's *Against Apion* this purpose is extraordinarily explicit. That is because Josephus argues for the antiquity of Judaism, he attempts to refute allegations that the Jewish people are xenophobes, and he demonstrates the conformity of the Jewish religion to the highest ideals of Greek culture. This is still far from urging Gentiles to become Jews by renouncing paganism and taking upon themselves the yoke of Torah including the requirement to be circumcised. Collins writes that such literature has "little interest in proselytizing, but shows a desire to share and be accepted in the more philosophically sophisticated strata of Hellenistic culture."[242] Goodman similarly thinks that such literature, at best, represents a partial mission to win Gentile adherents.[243] John Barclay objects to such views on the grounds that the difference between sympathizers and proselytes was one of *degree*, not of *kind*. Respect for Judaism was a continuum which evinced a range of attachments and relations to Jewish belief, practice, and community. Any hard and fast distinction between literature that is designed to win sympathizers and literature that is designed to win converts is artificial, as the effect of such literature would be contingent upon the specific situation of a Gentile.[244] Barclay is correct in terms of *effect*, but the issue is one of *literary purpose* and *authorial intent*. Given the *apparent* role of circumcision as the demarcating line between sympathizers and proselytes, it is surely strange that we do not find any known exhortation for Gentiles to be circumcised and to become Jews. It is precisely because of Hellenistic revulsion towards the practice that such authors may well have avoided the subject, eminently practical but hardly fitting if one's overarching purpose is to solicit proselytes. In documents where Gentiles are circumcised (e.g., Esther and Judith[245]) it is hardly prescriptive, but resounds notes of Jewish triumphalism over paganism and the attraction

---

[241] Cf. Feldman, *Jew and Gentile in the Ancient World*, 321.

[242] Collins, "A Symbol of Otherness," 169.

[243] Goodman, *Mission and Conversion*, 88.

[244] Barclay, "Apologetics in the Jewish Diaspora," 146–48; cf. Paget, "Jewish Proselytism," 79.

[245] Donaldson (*Judaism and the Gentiles*, 61) says of Jdt 14:10: "But while the world projected by the book of Judith is one in which Gentile converts have an established place, there is no indication that such converts are to be actively sought or encouraged. Israel's role is a passive one; moved by what they have seen of God's care for Israel, Gentiles turn to God and seek to join God's people."

of Gentiles to an Israel blessed by God. Perhaps the authors of apologetic works may have been aware that any sympathizers won over might take a fuller step of commitment towards Judaism by undergoing circumcision. Yet such an observation is moving further and further away from the intentionality of the texts: literature which was *indirectly* addressed to Gentiles may have *indirectly* led them to become proselytes.

To summarize, the issue of who read Jewish apologetic literature and what effect it had on Gentiles remains open. Yet any broad description of Jewish apologetic works as *Missionsschriften* is misleading, because, as Tcherikover suggests, that literature was intended primarily for internal consumption.[246] This conclusion has been reaffirmed by L. Michael White who supposes that "most apologetic literature was really addressed to insiders who were looking toward that margin with the larger society as the arena of acculturation and self-definition."[247] While admittedly such works could in theory have facilitated the conversions of Gentiles, either from reading or hearing such documents, or through oral persuasion where Jewish speakers use the arguments found in these texts, we have no examples of such conversions occurring in this way. Nor do the documents themselves indicate such happenings.

Greek and Latin Literature

Among Greco-Roman authors there are several instances where passing reference is made to possible proselytizing activity by Jews among Gentiles. Horace wrote that poets, like the Jews, "will compel you to make one of our throng," which is a fancy way of saying that they will make you join our club.[248] Feldman argued that this is an allusion to the "zeal of Jewish missionary activity as if it were proverbial."[249] Yet

---

[246] The internal nature of apologetics is underscored by Tertullian (*Test.* 1), "no one comes to our writings for guidance unless he is already a Christian." Cf. Nock, *Conversion*, 192.

[247] L. Michael White, "Visualizing the 'Real' World of Acts 16: Toward Construction of a Social Index," in *The Social World of the First Christians: Essays in Honor of Wayne A. Meeks* (eds. L. Michael White and O. Larry Yarbrough; Philadelphia: Fortress, 1995), 259.

[248] Horace, *Satirae* 1.4.142–143 (Stern, *GLAJJ* 1: §127).

[249] Feldman, *Jew and Gentile in the Ancient World*, 299; cf. Stern, *GLAJJ* 1: §323.

such a perspective is more often assumed than argued.[250] John Nolland has pointed out that Horace is drawing a comparison between the powers of poets who can collectively change people's minds with the political clout of Jewish groups who in military-like fashion seek to get their way. Similarly, Cicero (*Flac.* 66) refers to a demonstration by a Jewish crowd who were trying to prejudice a judicial outcome. The primary point of Horace's remarks at the end of his satire is the aggressive stance of a group to defend its rights and way of life over and against the rest of society. Neither the context nor content pertains to conversions.[251]

From Seneca, via Augustine, the following statement is recorded: "The customs of this accursed race have gained such influence that they are now received throughout the entire world. The vanquished have given laws to their victors."[252] Based on this text Paget thinks that it does "at least imply proselytic activity, of whatever sort,"[253] and Stern regarded it as being written "at the height of the Jewish proselytizing movement."[254] This perspective reads too much into what Seneca describes because sympathizing and conversion are both possibilities here. Alternatively, the primary point is not so much proselytizing, but Seneca's derision of foreign cults and their influence (to whatever degree and by whatever means) among the Roman people.[255] Overall, Seneca is lamenting that the Jews at least know their own rituals whereas Romans perform their native rituals ignorant of their meaning. Yet this text does imply the spread of Torah observance among the Roman people in both passive ("received throughout the entire world") and active ("given laws to their victors") forms. Seneca clearly holds the Jews culpable for this process and scorns them for it, but the precise "customs" and the extent to which the laws have been received is not determined, and there remains the

[250] Cf., e.g., Georgi, *The Opponents of Paul in Second Corinthians*, 97; Feldman, *Jew and Gentile in the Ancient World*, 299, 302; Leon, *The Jews of Ancient Rome*, 250.

[251] John Nolland, "Proselytism or Politics in Horace *Satires* 1,4,138–43," *VC* 33 (1979): 347–55; cf. Collins, "A Symbol of Otherness," 171 n. 26; Cohen, "Was Judaism in Antiquity a Missionary Religion?" 17; Goodman, *Mission and Conversion*, 64; Paget, "Jewish Proselytism," 74; Barnett, "Jewish Mission," 273; Donaldson, *Judaism and the Gentiles*, 368–69.

[252] Seneca, *De Superstitione* cited in Augustine, *Civ. D.* 6.11.

[253] Paget, "Jewish Proselytism," 87.

[254] Stern, *Greek and Latin Authors on Jews and Judaism*, 1.429.

[255] See Levinskaya, *The Book of Acts in Its Diaspora Setting*, 28.

problem (once more) of our inability to differentiate between activities that induce sympathy, respect, partial adherence, and full conversion. In any case, Seneca would disparage any Roman citizen adopting customs that could be confused with Jewish observances, which is why he gave up vegetarianism earlier in his life during the reign of Tiberius.[256]

The Roman politician turned historian, Tacitus, who lived during the late first and early second century C.E., made several comments about the Jewish people in his *Histories* and *Annals*. Tacitus was no Judeophile, and in many ways his bitter remarks about the Jews are typical of Roman cultural elitest animosity towards Jewish communities. In Book Five of his *Histories*, Tacitus discusses Titus's siege of Jerusalem and provides some details of the religion of the Jewish people as a background. He observes chiefly the Jews' separation from outsiders, their communal homogeneity, and their religious distinctiveness. To that he adds: "They adopted circumcision to distinguish themselves from other peoples by this difference. Those who are converted to their ways follow the same practice, and the earliest lesson they receive is to despise the gods, to disown their country, and to regard their parents, children and brothers as of little account."[257] These converts (*transgressi*) adopted the "same practices" and these practices involve not only circumcision but sending tribute to Jerusalem, separating themselves from outsiders, a refusal to intermarry, renouncing their ancestral religion, disowning their citizenship, and reneging on reciprocal expectations of kinship. When it comes to initiative in conversion, on the one hand, the converts "follow" (*usurpant*) Jewish customs, which might suggest their own active role in crossing over. But on the other side, the converts are formally instructed in the matter by receiving lessons, which is more indicative of recruitment. What can we say about this? Donaldson is probably correct: "[I]f Jews were engaged in aggressive proselytizing activity, one would expect that Tacitus would have pounced on the fact, holding it up as further evidence of Jewish opposition to everything that a traditional Roman held dear. The picture that emerges is more of one where the primary initiative lay with Gentiles. Jews may have been willing to instruct those who sought them out, but seeking was the first step."[258]

---

[256] Seneca, *Ep. Mor.* 108.22 (Stern, *GLAJJ* 1: §189).
[257] Tactius, *Hist.* 5.5.2.
[258] Donaldson, *Judaism and the Gentiles*, 395.

The Roman writer Juvenal who wrote his *Satirae* in the early second century (ca. 130 C.E.) often had derogatory things to say about Jews, Judaism, and conversion to Judaism. In chapter fourteen of his *Satirae* he lambastes the bad effects that parents have upon their children. One example that he gives of this is that of the father who fears the Sabbath and the son who inevitably takes to circumcision.

> Some who have had a father who reveres the Sabbath, worship nothing but the clouds, and the divinity of the heavens, and see no difference between eating swine's flesh, from which their father abstained, and that of man; and in time they take to circumcision. Having been wont to flout the laws of Rome, they learn and practice and revere the Jewish law, and all that Moses handed down in his secret tome, forbidding to point out the way to any not worshipping the same rites, and conducting none but the circumcised to the desired foundation. For all which the father was to blame, who gave up every seventh day to idleness, keeping it apart from all the concerns of life.[259]

We should take into account that this passage says nothing about how such adherence to Jewish customs began by the father and what motivates or encourages the son to continue on in becoming a circumcised proselyte. What is genuinely interesting is that Juvenal does mention what was probably the standard way of becoming a proselyte: it begins by initially observing some of the commandments like keeping the Sabbath, abstinence from consumption of pork, belief in one invisible God, study of the Jewish law, a change in attitude towards their own nation and customs, and then finally full conversion typified by Juvenal as including circumcision and an emphasis on altruism limited towards the Jewish community. Conversion is staged: what the father adheres to the son eventually converts to. Yet this does not occur via the active recruitment of the synagogue but transpires "in time" and in any case it is the father who is blamed, not Jewish missionaries.[260] Even though there is a lack of precision in the designations, in the short text from Juvenal is a story of a generational shift from "adherence" to "conversion." The picture that emerges here is that conversions indeed happened, but they are a slow and drawn out process resulting from a gradual course of social interaction and through social networks that link a family to

---

[259] Juvenal, *Sat.* 14.96–106 (Stern, *GLAJJ* 2: §301).
[260] Riesner, "A Pre-Christian Jewish Mission," 230; Donaldson, *Judaism and the Gentiles*, 409.

a synagogue, as opposed to the result of an evangelistic encounter with Jewish teachers. All that can be said at this point is that some Romans followed Jewish customs, some even as far as being circumcised, but without mention of missionary activity or active recruitment. Suetonius provides some additional information about Roman edicts and imperial actions against converts and conversion during the reign of Domitian at the end of the first century. In one section he writes:

> Besides other taxes, that on the Jews were levied with the utmost vigour, and those were prosecuted without publicly acknowledging that faith yet lived as Jews, as well as those who concealed their origin and did not pay the tribute levied upon their people. I recall being present in my youth when the person of a man ninety years old was examined before the procurator and a very crowded court to see whether he was circumcised.[261]

Here Suetonius narrates how the *fiscus Iudaicus* was applied to those who did not publicly acknowledge their faith yet, he says, "lived as Jews" (*Iudaicam viverent vitam*) as well as those "who concealed their origin and did not pay the tribute levied upon their people."[262] This first group could be either proselytes[263] or adherents,[264] and it is hard to determine which one it might be. It depends if the inspection of circumcision carried out upon the ninety year old man was meant as an example of those who followed Jewish ways or those who had tried to conceal their identity as typical of someone liable to pay the tax but was trying to avoid it. Most likely, the first group consists of those who outwardly lived a Jewish way of life but were not formally professing or officially recognized as Jewish, that is, sympathizers or adherents. This group could claim to avoid paying the tax on the grounds that they were neither ethnically Jewish, nor formal converts to Judaism. In fact, they were very probably sympathizers not proselytes since proselytes were obligated to pay the temple tax and thus the *fiscus Iudaicus* which evidently removes the ambiguity of their status as "taxable." The second group appears to consist of those who were ethnically Jewish but had attempted to conceal their identity, most probably by ceasing Jewish practices, in order to avoid

---

[261] Suetonius, *Domitian* 12.2 (Stern, *GLAJJ* 2: §320).

[262] Suetonius, *Domitian* 12.2.

[263] Cf. Cohen, *The Beginnings of Jewishness*, 42–43.

[264] Cf. Feldman, *Jew and Gentile in the Ancient World*, 347; McKnight, *A Light among the Gentiles*, 74.

having to pay the tax. This group could be said to be trying to separate their ethnic identity from their religious practices so as to avoid incurring a financial liability; a move that would have a serious impact in the subsequent definition of Jewish identity by Jewish communities as well as for the parting of the ways between Christianity and Judaism in the coming centuries.[265] They sought to avoid paying the tax by claiming that, although ethnically Jewish, they are not practicing. In summary, it appears that the tax was levied upon a strange mix of people including sympathizers and apostates![266] Those who imitated Jewish customs and even those who had come to deny their (religious) Jewishness were seen as categorically alike when it came to taxation.

Suetonius refers to the execution of the Roman consul Flavius Clemens during Domitian's reign, which is attested also by Dio Cassius.[267] The specific charges resulting in Flavius Clemens's death and the banishment of his wife were a charge of atheism and drifting into Jewish ways. Dio Cassius writes:

> And the same year Domitian slew, along with many others, Flavius Clemens the consul, although he was a cousin and had to wife Flavia Domitilla,[268] who was also a relative of the emperor. The charge brought against them both was that of atheism, a charge on which many others who drifted into Jewish ways (ἐς τὰ τῶν Ἰουδαίων ἤθη ἐξοκέλλοντες) were condemned. Some of these were put to death, and the rest were at least deprived of their property, Domitilla was merely banished to Pandateria.[269]

---

[265] Cf. Mikael Tellbe, "The Temple Tax as Pre-70 CE Identity Marker," in *The Formation of the Early Church* (ed. Jostein Ådna; WUNT 183; Tübingen: Mohr/Siebeck, 2005), 19–44.

[266] In view of this fact, I disagree with Goodman (*Mission and Conversion*, 122–23) who thinks that the first group comprises of those Jews who gave up the public identification of their religion by hiding their Jewish practices or by asserting that they had nothing to do with Judaism, yet this makes the first and second group practically indistinguishable from each other. This text from Suetonius indicates not merely a more rigorous enforcement of those who were liable to pay the tax (i.e., proselytes and Jews), but an expansion of the taxable population so as to include Jewish sympathizers and Jewish apostates. See also Donaldson *Judaism and the Gentiles*, 403–4.

[267] Suetonius, *Domitian*, 15.1; Dio Cassius, *Hist.* 67.14.1–3 (Stern, *GLAJJ* 2: §435).

[268] According to Eusebius (*Hist. Eccl.* 3.18.3) Domitilla was banished due to her "testimony of Christ."

[269] Dio Cassius, *Hist.* 67.14.1–2 (Stern, *GLAJJ* 2: §435).

The charge of atheism was commonly leveled at Jews and Christians and stemmed from perceptions of an impious neglect of the Roman pantheon.[270] The legal grounds behind the charges may have been aimed at eliminating proselytizing in Rome, which provides reasonable evidence that pagans were converting to Judaism and in significant numbers to alarm the authorities. It appears that adherence to Judaism had penetrated the highest levels of the social strata of imperial Rome which gave further cause for concern to the Emperor as Flavius's sons were Domitian's heir designates. Dio Cassius also reports that Nerva released all who were on trial for "impiety" (*maiestas*, ἀσέβεια) and reversed Domitian's policy of permitting Roman citizens "to accuse anybody of *maiestas* or of adopting the Jewish mode of life."[271] Alternatively, Domitian's aims were perhaps less concerned with cultural purity and hegemony, as they might simply have been an example of his reign of terror and his attempt to remove rivals and competitors under the guise of maintaining the integrity of Roman life and religion. What it meant to have "drifted into Jewish ways" seems ambiguous at best, but it probably denotes a variety of postures in relation to Judaism ranging from adherence to full conversion or even excessive fraternizing with Jewish groups. In both accounts taken from the time of Domitian (concerning the expansion of the *fiscus Iudaicus* and the execution of Flavius Clemens) we can say that sympathizing and conversions were indeed taking place in Rome in the late first century, and in the aftermath of the war in Judea, this was seen as virtual treachery by some authorities.[272] Once more it is the "how" and "who" and the "why" of conversion that eludes interpreters, and it is those elements that determine whether we are dealing with the attraction of Gentiles to Judaism or more overt missional activity by Jewish teachers.

Another perplexing issue revolves around two expulsions of Jews from Rome, which may relate to proselytizing activities by Jews in the city. The first expulsion of 139 B.C.E. is known from Valerius Maximus in *de Superstitionibus* and is preserved through two Byzantine epitomists, Paris and Nepotianus, both of whom wrote around the fourth-fifth century C.E. In both accounts *the praetor peregrinus*, the magistrate

---

[270] Cf., e.g., Josephus, *Ag. Ap.* 2.148; *Mart. Pol.* 9.2.

[271] Dio Cassius, *Hist.* 68.1.2 (Stern, *GLAJJ* 2: §436).

[272] On proselytism in Rome in particular see, McKnight, *A Light among the Gentiles*, 73–74.

overseeing disputes involving foreigners, banished the Jews from Rome because they were trying to "transmit" (*tradere*) their sacred rites among the Romans (Nepotianus) or "infect" (*inficere*) Roman customs with the cult of Jupiter Sabazius (Paris).[273] Feldman soberly admits that it is not clear whether Jews were trying to convert pagans or whether they simply sought to spread Jewish customs among Romans in trying to win sympathizers, or even wanted permission to practice their rites in public; although he thinks it does denote some kind of aggressive missionary activity.[274] For many scholars this event seems to imply Jewish efforts to proselytize.[275] Schürer even suggests that part of the retinue of Simon Maccabee's visit to Rome instigated the propaganda campaign and proselytizing.[276] If the delegation arrived in 142 B.C.E. they are unlikely to have remained for three years until expelled for proselytizing.[277] Goodman notices too that Valerius Maximus himself lived a century after the event, and the event is cited five centuries later by two writers who themselves differ on the details such as to whether the Jews were banished from Rome for erecting private altars in public places (Nepotianus) or if they were ordered to return home for syncretism involving the Sabazius cult[278] (Paris). For these reasons, the textual witness to the account is suspect. Instead of proselytizing, Goodman posits an attempt of Jewish sympathizers to introduce new cults into public places without permission. Jews themselves would be unlikely to erect such altars.[279] Thus the imperial ban may have been on account of the publicizing of a foreign cult without permission. Alternatively, Gruen locates the expulsion in the circumstance of "Roman public relations" which

---

[273] Stern, *GLAJJ* 1: §§147a, 147b.

[274] Feldman, *Jew and Gentile in the Ancient World*, 301.

[275] McKnight, *A Light among the Gentiles*, 73; Cohen, "Was Judaism in Antiquity a Missionary Religion?" 18; Paget, "Jewish Proselytism," 87; Rokéah, "Ancient Jewish Proselytism," 209.

[276] Schürer, *History of the Jewish People in the Age of Jesus Christ*, 1.197 n. 19.

[277] Gruen, *Diaspora*, 17.

[278] Sabazius was a Phrygian god identified with Dionysus. However, it may have resulted as a mistaken identification of the word *Sabazi* with σαβαώθ (cf. Hengel, *Judaism and Hellenism*, 1.263; Stern, *GLAJJ* 1: §359). Then again, identification of the Jewish God with Dionysus is attested in pagan literature: Tacitus, *Hist.* 5.5 (Stern, *GLAJJ* 2: §281); Plutarch, *Conv.* 6.1 (Stern, *GLAJJ* 1: §258).

[279] Goodman, *Mission and Conversion*, 82–83; cf. Levinskaya, *The Book of Acts in Its Diaspora Setting*, 29–30; Riesner, "A Pre-Christian Jewish Mission," 231; and Gruen (*Diaspora*, 17) who disagrees.

attempted to maintain the national image in response to the influx of Near Eastern rites into Rome. Over the previous twenty years there had been three expulsions of Greek philosophers from Rome, illustrating Roman tenacity in defending its heritage from foreign influence.[280] Thus, while proselytism is certainly one factor or explanation worth entertaining, it is not the only one, and it is wise to take into account the complex religiopolitical context of Rome at the time when attempting to understand the context and cause for the expulsion. It would seem, however, that there is evidently an element of Jewish initiative here in causing disturbances through the dissemination of their particular religious practices, but this should not be over emphasized as the chief objection seems to be the spread of foreign religions among the Roman populace. The precise degree and means of dissemination is not stated, yet it testifies to Jewish groups who felt confident enough to live out their rites and beliefs in the public sphere of Roman society.[281]

Regarding the 19 C.E. expulsion during Tiberius's reign, the event is preserved in four different accounts: Dio Cassius, Josephus, Tacitus, and Suetonius.[282]

As the Jews flocked to Rome in great numbers and were converting (μεθιστάντων) many of the natives to their ways, he [Tiberius] banished most of them.[283]

There was a certain Jew, a complete scoundrel, who had fled his own country because he was accused of transgressing certain laws and feared punishment on this account. Just at this time he was resident in Rome and played the part of an interpreter of the Mosaic law and its wisdom (ἐξηγεῖσθαι σοφίαν νόμων τῶν Μωυσέως). He enlisted three confederates not a whit better in character than himself; and when Fulvia, a woman of high rank who had become a Jewish proselyte (προσεληλυθυῖαν), began to meet with them regularly, they urged her to send purple and gold to the temple in Jerusalem. They, however, took the gifts and used them for their own personal expenses, for it was this that had been their intention in asking for the gifts from the start. Saturninus, the husband of Fulvia, at the instigation of his wife, duly reported this to Tiberius, whose friend he

---

[280] Gruen, *Diaspora*, 18–19.
[281] Donaldson, *Judaism and the Gentiles*, 378.
[282] There is a possible allusion to the same episode by Seneca (*Ep. Mor.* 108.22 [Stern, *GLAJJ* 1: §189]) who talks about the introduction of foreign rites that stirred up trouble.
[283] Dio Cassius, *Hist.* 57.18.5a (Stern, *GLAJJ* 2: §419).

was, whereupon the latter ordered the whole Jewish community (πᾶν τὸ Ἰουδαϊκὸν) to leave Rome. The consuls drafted four thousand of these Jews for military service and sent them to the island of Sardinia; but they penalized a good many of them, who refused to serve for fear of breaking the Jewish law. And so because of the wickedness of four men the Jews were banished from the city.[284]

Another debate dealt with the proscription of the Egyptian and Jewish rites (*sacris Aegyptiis Iudaicisque pellendis*), and a senatorial edict directed that four thousand descendants of enfranchised slaves, tainted with that superstition (*superstitione infecta*) and suitable in point of age, were to be shipped to Sardinia and there employed in suppressing brigandage: "if they succumbed to the pestilential climate, it was a cheap loss." The rest had orders to leave Italy, unless they had renounced their impious ceremonial by a given date.[285]

He abolished cults, especially the Egyptian and the Jewish rites, compelling all who were addicted to such superstitions to burn religious vestments and all their paraphernalia (*Externas caerimonias, Aegyptios Iudaicosque ritus compescuit, coactis qui superstitione ea tenebantur religiosas vestes cum instrumento omni comburere*). Those of the Jews who were of military age he [Tiberius] assigned to provinces of less healthy climate, ostensibly to serve in the army; the others of the same race or similar beliefs (*reliquos gentis eiusdem vel similia sectantes*) be banished from the city, on pain of slavery for life if they did not obey.[286]

The accounts diverge on several fronts. According to Josephus and Suetonius, all the Jews were expelled, but in Dio Cassius it is only many of them. Josephus and Suetonius also agree that the edict came from Tiberius, whereas Tacitus states that it derived from the senate. Different reasons for the expulsion are given. For Dio Cassius it is proselytization, according to Josephus it was due to four iniquitous Jewish con-artists, while Tacitus and Suetonius offer no substantial reason. Georgi's claim that Josephus deliberately suppresses the reference to missionary activity, like Goodman's contention that Josephus would have tried to justify it if he knew about it, are arguments from silence.[287] It should be noted

[284] Josephus, *Ant.* 18.81–84.
[285] Tacitus, *Ann.* 2.85.4 (Stern, *GLAJJ* 2: §284).
[286] Suetonius, *Tiberius* 36 (Stern, *GLAJJ* 2: §306).
[287] Georgi, *The Opponents of Paul in Second Corinthians*, 95; Goodman, *Mission and Conversion*, 83.

that all four of the accounts have a religious dimension, which is particularly explicit in Dio Cassius.[288] Josephus reports the Jewish shyster as "expounding" (ἐξηγεῖσθαι) the law and influencing a Roman noble woman Fulvia. Tacitus discusses those "infected with the superstition" (*superstitione infecta*) and Suetonius refers to those of the "same race" (*gentis eiusdem*) and with "similar beliefs" (*similia sectantes*) showing that the expulsion affected born Jews and Jewish sympathizers alike. Taken together with Dio Cassius's account, this may well be indicative of mission activity in Rome.[289] Nevertheless, Dio Cassius's account remains problematic. First, the text is known only from the seventh-century Christian writer John of Antioch, so its veracity is questionable. Second, Dio Cassius's remark is in the context of his discussion of Claudius's anti-Jewish measures in 41 C.E., which grew out of an increase in the Jewish population in Rome with the result being a ban against Jewish public gatherings.[290] It remains possible that Dio Cassius is retrojecting events from Claudius's reign onto Tiberius's as he assumed the expulsion was for the same reason.[291] Third, according to Tacitus and Suetonius, Egyptian cults were also abolished, yet it would be strange to assume that the Egyptian cults were expelled for missionary activity too. Expulsions of these kinds were usually meant to protect Roman culture and virtue from pollution by foreign cults whether they are those of Dionysus, Sabazius, Bacchanalia, or Judaism.[292] In any case, it was the growth of Judaism that was the problem in Rome, and

---

[288] Gruen (*Diaspora*, 31–34) thinks that the expulsion resulted from an official Tiberian policy against the Jewish religion, prompted by public suspicions that Germanicus's death (Tiberius's heir, cf. Tacitus, *Ann.* 2.85) was due to black magic, therefore, reprisal was to expel all foreign practices from Rome. This is however sheer speculation.

[289] McKnight, *A Light among the Gentiles*, 73–74; Cohen, "Was Judaism in Antiquity a Missionary Religion?" 18; Feldman, "Was Judaism a Missionary Religion in Ancient Times?" 31–32; idem, *Jew and Gentile in the Ancient World*, 303; Goodman, *Mission and Conversion*, 83, 144; Paget, "Jewish Proselytism," 88–90; Rokéah, "Ancient Jewish Proselytism," 209–10; Borgen, "Proselytes, Conquest, and Mission," 66; Grabbe, *Judaism from Cyrus to Hadrian*, 398, 423.

[290] Dio Cassius, *Hist.* 60.6.6 (Stern, *GLAJJ* 2: §422).

[291] Goodman, *Mission and Conversion*, 144; Riesner, "A Pre-Christian Jewish Mission," 232.

[292] Levinskaya, *The Book of Acts in Its Diaspora Setting*, 31–32; cf. Fredriksen, "Judaism, the Circumcision of Gentiles, and Apocalyptic Hope," 538–39; Schnabel, *Early Christian Mission*, 1.161.

Tiberius acted, from whatever motivation, to expel them. Part of the growth was no doubt Jewish immigration, high birth rates, but also some degree of attraction of Romans to Jewish ways. It may well have been the scandalous fact of Roman citizens imitating, sympathizing with, and finally converting to Judaism that brought a whole host of anti-Jewish feelings to the surface and warranted (in Roman imperial minds) the expulsion.

Inscriptions from Rome provide little evidence of proselytism. Of the 500 or so Jewish inscriptions in Rome only seven refer to proselytes.[293] Thus, the evidence does not necessitate a conclusion of widespread proselytizing by Jews in the city of Rome. What can be said is that some Roman authors knew of a tendency among their own countrymen to practice Jewish customs and in some instances assume Jewish identity; they scorned those who Judaized and those who encouraged them.

---

[293] See Leon, *The Jews of Ancient Rome*, 254–56; Figueras, "Epigraphic Evidence for Proselytism in Ancient Judaism," 198–201.

Chapter Five

Evidence from the New Testament and Early Christian Literature

One of the most neglected pieces of evidence for Jewish proselytizing activity in the Second Temple period is the wider body of early Christian literature. Matthew 23:15 comes up for routine discussion, but Acts, the Pauline epistles, the Johannine corpus, the Catholic Epistles, Apostolic Fathers, and Apologists are habitually glossed over in most studies. Yet early Christian sources arguably contain the clearest and most widely attested imprints of Jewish missionary work. This can be seen in two principal areas: (1) Jewish Christian proselytizers who urged Gentiles to be circumcised in addition to having faith in Jesus as the Messiah, and (2) competition between Jews and Christians for Gentile converts and sympathizers.[1]

---

[1] Several scholars have tried to enlist Rom 2:17–24 (on being guides to the blind see Isa 42:7; *1 Enoch* 105:1; *Sib. Or.* 3:194–195; Josephus, *Ag. Ap.* 2.291–295) as evidence for Jewish missionary work in the Diaspora. Lloyd Gaston (*Paul and the Torah* [Vancouver, B.C.: University of British Columbia Press, 1987], 146) identifies the Jewish teacher in the diatribe with Jewish missionaries trying to make proselytes from Gentiles; Stanley Stowers (*A Rereading of Romans: Justice, Jews, Gentiles* [New Haven, Conn.: Yale University Press, 1994], 151–53) detects Jewish teachers who endeavor to make righteous Gentiles by teaching them to observe certain elements of the law; John Gager (*Reinventing Paul* [Oxford: Oxford University Press, 2000], 115) perceives an imaginary debate between "Paul and a nameless Jewish competitor for Gentile followers." Even though this passage presumes the didactic function of Jewish teachers we need to keep in mind: (1) The purpose of 2:17–24 is to highlight the universal sinfulness of humankind as affecting the Jewish people and to show that mere possession of the law does not guarantee divine favor; (2) as a diatribe the passage is hyperbolic and rhetorical and we should not envisage all Jews in Rome as either temple robbers or hypocritical pedagogues; (3) there is no active recruitment of Gentiles attributed to this imaginary Jewish teacher;

AN EARLY JEWISH CHRISTIAN MISSION TO GENTILES

The most controversial and divisive topic in the early church up to ca. 50 C.E. was over Jewish Christian attitudes to the inclusion of Gentiles in the church. "Jewish Christianity" is a slippery term and in one sense can be used to describe the entire Christian movement at least before 70 C.E.[2] More specifically, Jewish Christianity was typified by a continued hope that Israel may yet respond to the message of Jesus and remained committed to the distinctive practices that characterized the Jewish way of life, namely, circumcision, food laws, and Sabbath keeping. Contrary to the opinion of some scholars, there is no evidence that Jewish Christianity was ever opposed to a Gentile mission, only the terms of the entrance of Gentiles into the church was disputed.[3]

The existence of Gentiles who had come to have faith in Jesus meant that Jewish Christians were faced with the problem of integrating non- or semi-law observant persons into association with law-observant Jewish Christians. That brought to the surface several contentious issues, such as the continuing validity of the Mosaic dispensation in the messianic age and whether or not Torah observance should be imposed on Gentiles who expressed faith in Jesus. The two burning questions for the first fifty years of early Christianity were, Who had to obey the law? and How much of the law?, and these questions were answered differently by various groups in the early church. In Luke's telling, it appears that a group a Greek-speaking Jewish Christians first accepted Gentiles into their association without requiring them to become proselytes to Judaism (Acts 11:19–21). Perhaps the abandonment of circumcision for Gentile converts to faith in Jesus was pragmatic with a theological rationale for this decision only being provided later.[4] Nonetheless, Paul's

---

(4) McKnight (*A Light among the Gentiles*, 105) rightly cautions that consciousness of possessing universal truth would not necessarily lead to a universal dispensing of this truth. It is the nationalistic privilege of the Jewish people as custodians of God's law over and against the lawlessness of the pagan masses that is the central matter in Rom 2:17–24.

[2] See James Carleton Paget, "Jewish Christianity," in *Cambridge History of Ancient Judaism* (ed. W. D. Davies; 3 vols.; Cambridge: CUP, 2002), 3.731–75.

[3] See Bird, *Jesus and the Origins of the Gentile Mission*, 53.

[4] Jörg Frey, "Paul's Jewish Identity," in *Jewish Identity in the Greco-Roman World* (eds. J. Frey, D. R. Schwartz, and S. Gripentrog; AJEC 71, Leiden: Brill, 2007), 311; Crossley, *Why Christianity Happened*, 166.

various missionary endeavors, at least in their mature form, advocated a policy of non-Torah observance by Gentiles as the central platform of his mission with intense theological reflection made in support of that conviction in his letters (especially in Romans and Galatians). Paul was influenced in this view probably by a range of factors including his conversion-experience, traditions received from Hellenistic Jewish Christians in Damascus and Antioch, pragmatic experience in his evangelistic activities, and by passages from Isaiah that refer to an eschatological pilgrimage of Gentiles to Zion in which Gentiles coming to Jerusalem in the last days to worship the God of Israel do not immediately convert to Judaism.[5]

However, the Pauline non-Torah observance principle for Gentiles, although it would eventually become the proto-orthodox position, was neither uniformly accepted nor uncontested in the early church. It appears that there was a Jewish Christian mission underway in the Diaspora that competed with Paul for converts (Phil 1:15–18) and at times formed a loose block of opposition against him. In fact, Acts 15:1–5 and Gal 6:12 clearly demonstrate that Jewish Christian elements were active in trying to proselytize Christian Gentiles. Paul experienced opposition in Antioch from "false brothers" (Gal 2:4), "those of the circumcision" and "certain men from James" (Gal 2:11–12, cf. Acts 15:1), the "agitators" and "trouble-makers" in Galatia (Gal 5:10, 12), the "super-apostles" in Corinth (2 Cor 11:5; 12:11),[6] the "dogs" and "mutilators" mentioned in Philippians (Phil 3:2), and the persons who "cause divisions" that Paul warns the Romans to be wary of (Rom 16:17–18). In some cases this opposition intended to protect the integrity of Jewish Christians as Jews and prevent either their apostasy from Judaism or to prevent them from excessively fraternizing with Gentiles (e.g., Gal 2:11–14). On other occasions the activities of certain Jewish Christian delegates clearly had the purpose of trying to proselytize Paul's Gentile converts and intended to bring them into a closer relationship with the Jerusalem church in particular and the Jewish religion in general.

---

[5] John Barclay (*Jews in the Mediterranean Diaspora*, 395) states that Paul's proselytizing activities make him "[a]n anomalous Diaspora Jew."

[6] It needs to be acknowledged that the issues in Corinth do not seem to reflect matters pertaining to proselytism, but to Paul's apostolic status and the collection for Jerusalem. The opponents of Paul here represent an alternative apostolic group of messengers who are well crafted in philosophy and rhetoric.

Since F. C. Baur, the existence of a counter-Pauline mission has been posited to account for this opposition. There was a loose network of Jewish Christians that Paul's Gentile converts encountered and these Jewish Christians mandated at least partial Torah-observance for Gentile believers. The clearest example of this is obviously Galatians where one learns that certain persons, probably connected to the Jerusalem church in some way, were urging the Galatians to be circumcised, and Paul regarded this as a departure from his gospel, an attempt to find righteousness through the law, and a fall from grace (Gal 5:1–12). This theory readily explains the diversity in the early Christian mission as there were groups of Christians who maintained that the arrival of the Messiah had not eroded the architecture of the Mosaic covenant. In their perspective, the dispensation of Moses was completed or perfected by the coming of Messiah, not negated by it. Consequently, a Gentile must become a Jew in order to become a "Christian." For at least one wing of the primitive Christian movement, faith in Jesus did not eclipse the basic demands of the Mosaic dispensation in relation to the conversion of Gentiles.

At the same time we have to keep in mind that there was some degree of cross-fertilization between the two missions (Law-free and Proselytizing), as Barnabas belonged to both the Jerusalem church and also to the Hellenistic Christian mission to the Gentiles.[7] Also, in 1 Cor 15:11, Paul assumes that the Corinthians could have heard the same gospel from Peter or James, and in Gal 1:6–9, 2:1–10 the different "gospel" diverges from the one that he and the Jerusalem pillars agreed on. The resolution to this inner-church conflict was made at the Jerusalem council where, according to Luke, James cited Amos 9:11 to the effect that Gentiles were participants in the restoration of David's tent and the remnant of Israel (Acts 15:13–18), and the apostolic decree only required that Gentile converts abstain from practices associated with paganism and refrain from acts that offended Jewish scruples (Acts 15:24–29).

The Jewish Christian proselytizers are arguably the clearest example of Jewish missionary activity in the Second Temple period.[8] While these

---

[7] Hahn, *Mission*, 81.

[8] Some might object to this line of argumentation and say that the Christian proselytizers (sometimes erroneously called "judaizers") were "Jewish Christians" and not "Jews," therefore, they cannot be counted as evidence for Jewish missionary activity. The problem is that this distinction between "Jew" and "Christian" did not exist prior to 70 C.E. All Christianity, in some form or other, is "Jewish Christianity" as "Christianity" was essentially a Jewish

Jewish Christians may not have represented a unified "party" in the early church, they evidently sought out Gentiles and attempted to socialize them into Israel through the ritual of circumcision. In our earlier definition of conversion, we said that its identifying marker was circumcision. Thus, by advocating the necessity of circumcision, the Jewish Christian proselytizers were undertaking a form of missionary activity that attempted to bring Christian Gentiles to full conversion. Other Christian missionaries like Paul had succeeded in bringing Gentiles to the point of ideological and ethical transformation and partial integration into the church through repentance, faith, and baptism. Yet the proselytizers required circumcision as the rite of passage for membership in the people of God who would be saved at the eschaton.

Whereas the Jewish Christian proselytizers can legitimately be regarded as a form of Jewish missionary activity albeit with a messianic bent, this cannot be said of Paul and like-minded associates. The ethnocentric nomism[9] of Paul's opponents stands in contrast to the non-Torah message of Paul's gospel that accepts Gentiles as Gentiles and makes them full members of the church of God entirely without law observance. Given the Jewish nature of the early Christian Gentile missions it is tempting to regard them too as evidence for Jewish missionary activity. However, in the absence of circumcision as a requisite for membership in the church and for salvation in the future age, such missionary activity cannot be called Jewish if we think of circumcision as the *sine qua non* of conversion to Judaism.[10] In sociological terms, the

---

messianic sect. Even Paul with his sectarian notion of self-identity considered himself an "in-Christ" Jew not a non-Jew. Given their centrifugal movement away from Palestine, their focus on Gentiles (or Christian Gentiles), and their insistence on circumcision, these Jewish Christian proselytizers meet the criteria to be considered a form of Jewish missionary activity.

[9] On "ethnocentric nomism" see Michael F. Bird, *The Saving Righteousness of God: Studies on Paul, Justification and the New Perspective* (Milton Keynes, U.K.: Paternoster, 2007), 117–18 where I define this as the view that "Jewish identity is the locus of salvation (hence ethnocentric) and that one must perform the law so as to enter the Jewish constituency and be vindicated at the eschaton (hence nomistic)."

[10] That said, several scholars (Francis Watson, *Paul, Judaism and the Gentiles* [Cambridge: Cambridge University Press, 1986], 28–38; and those listed in Terence L. Donaldson, *Paul and the Gentiles: Remapping the Apostle's Convictional World* [Minneapolis: Fortress, 1997], 313 n.75) argue that Paul's Torah-free Gentile mission was a subsequent development in Paul's thinking

difference between Paul and the Jewish Christian proselytizers is that Paul regards Gentile "adherents" as full "initiates" with a legitimized "Christian" identity wholly apart from Jewish covenantal markers, whereas the Jewish Christian proselytizers are urging a full transference from "adherent" to "initiate" through incremental additions of Torah observance of which the most significant was circumcision. In the words of Frey:

> In the Jewish diaspora there was also the question how and to what extent gentiles could enter Israel. Paul does not accept the "God-fearers" pattern of a reduced form of membership and obligations. Instead, in analogy to the Jewish "proselyte pattern," they should be regarded as full members of the community without any reservation just as they were granted full salvation in Christ. If such a full membership is possible without circumcision and without the obligation to observe the law, there is a *redefinition of the requirements* for the Gentiles to be included in the benefits of the promise or a "reconfiguration" of basically Jewish convictions and categories.[11]

Quite expectedly, much of the discussion above focuses on Galatians where Paul was combating those who wanted to impose circumcision on his Gentile converts. Yet, were Paul's opponents in Galatia Jewish Christians or non-Christian Jews? Mark Nanos has recently argued that in Galatians the false teachers who are encroaching upon the Galatians are Jews or possibly proselytes who are part of the Jewish communities of Galatia. These "influencers" (as he calls them) have begun urging the Galatian Christians to be circumcised in order to resolve their anomalous status in relation to the synagogue (are they "in" or "out"?) and so avoid the stigma of their uncertain attachment to Judaism in the eyes of pagan authorities. These non-Christian observers are not against Christ or Paul's gospel, it is simply not their concern. Thus, the letter is part of an intra-Jewish debate whereby Paul offers an ironic rebuke to the Galatians to avoid circumcision which subverts the value of Christ for Gentiles. Nanos writes:

> This reevaluation of the evidence suggests that the Galatian influencers were not believers in Jesus Christ, nor was their message good news of

---

and that his initial missionary work included preaching circumcision (e.g., Gal 5:11). If that is the case, then the early Paul would constitute evidence for Jewish missionary activity.

[11] Frey, "Paul's Jewish Identity," 314–15 (italics original); cf. Donaldson, *Paul and the Gentiles*, 215–48; Blaschke, *Beschneidung*, 395 n. 110.

Christ. Their concerns did not arise from an inter-Christian opposition to Paul or his supposed Law-free gospel, and they did not arrive suddenly from outside Galatia . . . Rather, I suggest that the influencers represented Jewish communities in Galatia that were concerned about the integration of these particular Gentiles, who were, through their involvement in the (still Jewish) Jesus subgroups, an integral part of the larger Jewish communities at this time.[12]

The merit of Nanos's proposal is that any Jewish Christian group who had a proselytizing conviction when it came to the means of Gentile recruitment may have been warmly supported in their activities by local synagogues in Galatia (even if their messianic orientation was itself suspect). In that case, a hard and fast distinction between Jewish and Jewish Christian proselytizing efforts cannot be held too rigidly. Yet on the whole, contra Nanos, it is hard to characterize the influencers or false teachers troubling the Galatians as non-Christian Jews since Paul would not characterize their message as "another gospel" (Gal 1:6–9), and the purpose of the proselytizing efforts of the intruders is to avoid persecution on account of the cross (Gal 6:12), something that is again unlikely to be true of non-Christian Jews.[13]

Paul's letter to the Galatians undoubtedly touches upon explosive issues related to Gentile observance of the Mosaic law and whether or not Gentiles need to be circumcised. Arguments of this nature and with similar pathos could be expected to be found among Jews living in Rome, Alexandria, or Adiabene over what to do with Gentile sympathizers and how close a connection with Judaism they need to have in order to be acceptable to God. Yet in Galatians the entire debate over circumcision is framed in light of particular stances on eschatology, Christology, pneumatology, and hermeneutical approaches to Scripture. The contours of the debate possess an intra-Christian character. While the content and context of the tension is influenced quite evidently by Jewish halakic concerns, ultimately this tension is resolved by Paul in light of convictions connected to faith in Jesus as Lord and Messiah for Jews and Gentiles. It is far more likely, then, that the agitators in

---

[12] Mark D. Nanos, *The Irony of Galatians: Paul's Letter in First-Century Context* (Minneapolis: Fortress, 2002), 317.

[13] For further criticism of Nanos see Michael F. Bird and Preston M. Sprinkle, "Jewish Interpretation of Paul in the Last Thirty Years," *CBR* 6 (2008): 365–69.

Galatia are Jewish Christians, although we might want to keep an open mind as to how the intruders relate to non-Jesus-believing Jews in the Galatian synagogues.

MISSIONARY COMPETITION BETWEEN JEWS AND CHRISTIANS

Further proof of Jewish missionary activity derives from evidence of competition between Jews and Christians for Gentile converts. Whereas I believe that Galatians reflects a competing mission for Gentiles *within* Jewish Christianity (i.e., Paul versus the proselytizers), more fertile soil for locating a competing Jewish mission is to be found in the situation and environment represented by Paul's letter to the Colossians. Irrespective of whether or not Paul did write Colossians, this letter represents a real socioreligious setting as opposed to a fictitious one fabricated by an author from the Pauline school. This is probable given the concrete rather than generalized formulation of the Colossian "philosophy," and is verified further by the fact that the sum of the teaching does not correspond to any known doctrinal aberration discussed by Christians in the first and second centuries. Indeed, it is the nature, origin, and source of the philosophy that is the most perplexing aspect of Colossians itself. If the Colossian "philosophy" has its roots in a Jewish setting, then it may represent the propaganda efforts of a Jewish group in the Lycus valley by whom the Christians in Colossae are being influenced. This is the perspective I intend to argue below.[14]

Colossae was one of the smaller cities of the Lycus Valley, along with Laodicea and Hierapolis, located in the interior of Asia Minor. Colossae was once a densely populated and wealthy city according to Xenophon, and later Strabo described Colossae as a πόλισμα or small city.[15] There was a sizable Jewish population in the Lycus Valley.[16] Antiochus the Great settled some two thousand Jews into the regions of Lydia

---

[14] See further Michael F. Bird, *Colossians and Philemon* (New Covenant Commentary Series; Eugene, Ore.: Wipf & Stock, 2009).

[15] Xenophon, *Anabasis*, 1.2.6; Strabo, *Geog.* 12.8.13.

[16] A number of Jewish sacrcophagi in Hierapolis have been collected together by Walter Ameling, *Inscriptiones Judaicae Orientis: II Kleinasien* (TSAJ 99; Tübingen: Mohr/Siebeck, 2004), 398–440 which indicate a sizeable, but largely undocumentable, Jewish presence in the Lycus Valley.

and Phrygia and Philo refers to the large population of Jews in every city of Asia Minor.[17] Laodicea in particular was a collection point for payment of the temple tax by Jews living in the region, and in 62 B.C.E. Flaccus attempted to seize the collection that, according to Cicero, consisted of twenty pounds of gold.[18] If the temple tax was a half-shekel or two drachmae, that could represent a collection from Jewish males numbering as many as 10,000, though a slightly lower figure might be more cautious.[19] Like other Anatolian cities, Colossians probably had a substantial Jewish population (possibly between 1,000–2,000 persons) and at least one synagogue or prayer house.

The nature and substance of the "Colossian philosophy" remains disputed. To begin with, Morna D. Hooker is somewhat correct to argue that there were not in fact any false teachers or any Colossian "error" that Paul was confronting *within the church*; rather, the problem was "a situation in which young Christians are under pressure to conform to the beliefs and practices of their pagan and Jewish neighbors."[20] This means that we have to look outside the church for ideological influences besetting the Colossian assembly. But what exactly is the nature of this "philosophy"? A plethora of options have been proposed, including Gnosticism, Essenism, Stoicism, Pythagoreanism, Jewish mysticism, Platonism, Cynicism, syncretism, and others. My contention is that the Colossian philosophy represents a form of Jewish Mysticism that is indebted somewhat to Hellenistic philosophy but remains Jewish nonetheless. This Jewish "philosophy" probably exudes from the propaganda efforts of a synagogue somewhere in the vicinity of the Lycus Valley.[21]

---

[17]Josephus, *Ant.* 12.147–153; Philo, *Leg. Gai.* 245.

[18]Cicero, *Pro Flacco* 28.68.

[19]Cf. Trebilco, *Jewish Communities in Asia Minor*, 13–14; Feldman, *Jew and Gentile in the Ancient World*, 69–74.

[20]Morna D. Hooker, "Were There False Teachers in Colossae?" in *From Adam to Christ* (Cambridge: CUP, 1990), 134. I would depart from Hooker by positing a definite external doctrinal threat to the theological integrity of the Colossian congregation from a group in the Lycus Valley at least from the viewpoint of Paul and his co-workers.

[21]In this regard I am particularly influenced by N. T. Wright, *The Epistles of Paul to the Colossians and to Philemon* (TNTC; Grand Rapids, Mich.: Eerdmans, 1986), 23–30; Thomas J. Sappington, *Revelation and Redemption at Colossae* (JSNTSup 53; Sheffield: JSOT Press, 1991), 15–24, 151–70; Christian Stettler, "The Opponents at Colossae," in *Paul and His Opponents* (ed. Stanley E. Porter; Leiden: Brill, 2005), 167–200; James D. G. Dunn, "The Colossian

That the "philosophy" that Paul opposes is both Jewish and the result of missionary activity is indicated by several elements within the epistle. First, the warning in Col 2:4, "in order that no one might deceive you with persuasive speech," suggests that someone or some group is trying to persuade the Colossians at one level or other. That influence is emphasized at a number of points by Paul's injunction against the Colossians letting τὶς or μηδείς ("anyone" or "no one") regard them as condemned and disqualified or render them seducible (Col 2:8, 16, 18). Moreover, the contents of the epistle implies that adherence to certain elements of the Torah is the desired end state of the Colossian teachers who are pressuring the Colossian Christians by using language related to deviance and outsider status because of their failure to observe certain customs. Second, in Col 2:8, Paul warns, "watch out that no one takes you captive through philosophy and vain deceit according to the traditions of men, according to the elemental principles of this world, and not according to Christ." Here "philosophy" (φιλοσοφία) could be a reference to Hellenistic philosophy like Platonism, Stoicism, or Cynicism. While rabbinic Judaism could use "philosophy" and "philosopher" as references to Gentile philosophical schools, Judaism could also be described as a philosophy in apologetic literature.[22] Josephus describes the various Jewish sects as philosophies,[23] and he can even refer to the Jewish religion as a form of national philosophy.[24] Philo represents Judaism as achieving the highest ideals of Hellenistic philosophy.[25] In principle, then, "philosophy" could conceivably represent the self-designation of a propagandist Jewish group. This is reinforced by the observation that in Colossians the "traditions" that Paul objects to being imposed on the Colossian Christians are addressed in much the same way that other New Testament authors respond to the "traditions" of Jewish *halakah*.[26] In addition, there may be deliberate pun on words in Col 2:8 where συλαγωγεῖν ("to take captive") is close in sound

---

Philosophy: A Confident Jewish Apologia," *Bib* 76 (1995): 153–81; Ian Smith, *Heavenly Perspective: A Study of the Apostle Paul's Response to a Jewish Mystical Movement in Colossae* (LNTS 326; London: Continuum, 2006).

[22] 4 Macc 5:22; *Ep. Arist.* 30–31.

[23] *J.W.* 2.119, 166; *Ant.* 18.11, 25.

[24] *Ant.* 1.18; 16.398; *Ag. Ap.* 1.181; 2.47.

[25] Cf. *Op. Mundi* 8, 128; *Migr. Abr.* 34; *Som.* 1.226; 2.244; *Vit. Mos.* 2.2; *Spec. Leg.* 1.32, 37; 3.185–191; *Leg. Gai.* 156, 245, 318.

[26] Mark 7:3–13/Matt 15:2–6; Gal 1:14.

to συναγωγή ("synagogue") meaning that the Colossians are not to become captive to the philosophy of the local synagogue.[27] Third, there is the injunction in Col 2:16–17, "Therefore, then, do not let anyone condemn you in matters pertaining to food and drink or in festivals, or new moons, or sabbaths." The triadic formula of festivals, new moons, and Sabbaths occurs in the Septuagint and represents the commandments of the Torah.[28] The prohibition of food probably signifies a call to observe the Jewish food laws of *kashrut,* and the reference to avoiding drink probably means avoiding libations in honor of pagan gods (see Rom 14:21). Thus the prohibition is about avoiding defilement through both impurity and idolatry, which are specific Jewish concerns. We can note, also, that Paul's reference to these practices as a "shadow of the things to come, but the substance belongs to Christ" (Col 2:17) is very similar to how the writer to the Hebrews relates the Old Testament to the coming of Christ (Heb 10:1), where the former becomes obsolete in light of Christ's sacrificial death and exaltation. Fourth, the reference to circumcision and ethnic identity in Col 2:11–13 and 3:11 underscores the Jewish nature of the threat to the Christians in Colossae. Paul contrasts the effectiveness of circumcision with a "circumcision not by human hands" undertaken in Christ and marked out by baptism. Such a baptism enables one to put off the body of flesh and to experience God's vivifying power. What is more, the renewing power associated with Christ breaks down ethnic barriers so that there is no longer, "Greek and Jew, circumcised and uncircumcised, barbarian, Scythian, slave and free; but Christ is all and for all." In this argument, circumcision is replaced by Christ as the single most important determinative factor for the soteriological state and social identity of the Colossians. The end of the letter also emphasizes the limited support that Paul has received from "the ones being from circumcision" (οἱ ὄντες ἐκ περιτομῆς), which was a designation identical to that of Paul's opponents in Antioch (Gal 2:12). That would suggest, again, a Jewish target for the polemics.

What is more, there are a number of large similarities between how the philosophy in Colossians and how the proselytizers in Galatia are perceived and engaged by Paul. The philosophy is touted as an oppressive spiritual force in much the same way that Paul regards the law in Galatians as likened to hostile spiritual powers (see Col 2:8, 14–15; Gal

[27] Wright, *Colossians and Philemon,* 100.

[28] Hos 2:13; Ezek 45:17; 1 Chron 23:31; 2 Chron 2:3; 31:3; *Jub.* 1:14.

4:9–11). In Colossians as in Galatians, the erroneous beliefs required Paul to shore up the integrity of Gentile Christian identity without the need to take on law observance (Col 3:11; Gal 3:28). In Colossians as in Galatians, Paul also exhorts that one does not require Torah to facilitate righteous living (Col 2:20–23; 3:1–17; Gal 5:13–15). In Colossians as in Galatians, freedom from the Colossian philosophy and from the proselytizers is indebted to dying with Christ and being baptized into Christ (Col 2:12; 3:3; Gal 3:26–27). Colossians and Galatians both refer to the freedom of the Christian from circumcision and festivals (Col 2:11–12, 16; Gal 4:10; 5:2; 6:12–15). In light of the above survey of Colossians, it seems that Paul is evidently negating the value of Jewish boundary markers and lessening the social and religious function of the law as it stands as a threat to the integrity of Christian Gentiles and involves a devaluing of the preeminence of Christ.

In addition to exhibiting some elements of Jewish belief and practice it also appears that the Colossian philosophy had Hellenistic rudiments and perhaps even some form of Jewish mystical traditions attached to it as well. The Hellenistic form of the philosophy is exemplified by reference to the πλήρωμα ("fullness") which was important in later hyper-Hellenistic Gnostic systems of belief (Col 1:19; 2:9–10). The content of Col 1:12, 21–22; 2:13 and 3:11 clearly presupposes Jewish distinctives of covenantal identity but are accompanied by elements apparent in Col 2:8–10, 15, 18, 20, and 23 that require a Hellenistic orientation. The mention of "the elemental forces of the cosmos" (τὰ στοιχεῖα τοῦ κόσμου) in Col 2:8, 20 could signify the cosmological makeup of a number of philosophical and pagan systems as they relate to forces and powers of an otherworldly realm. Similarly, the "rulers" (ἀρχή) and "authorities" (ἐξουσία) in Col 1:16, 2:10, 15 designate comparable forces oppressing the Colossians, from which Christ's death frees them. The mention of θρησκεία τῶν ἀγγέλων could denote an objective genitive as "worship of angels" or a subjective genitive of "worship by angels."[29] The latter is perhaps preferred on the grounds that the visions referred to in Col 2:18 are based on knowledge, which enables the teachers to enter into visions and join the state of angelic worship in heaven.[30]

There are two primary ways of dealing with these parallels that include Jewish and Hellenistic/Mystical components. One option is to

---

[29] Cf. discussion in Arnold, *The Colossian Syncretism*, 90–95.
[30] Stettler, "Opponents at Colossae," 184–88.

regard the letter to the Colossians as a syncretistic religious phenomenon including Jewish and Hellenistic elements;[31] the other option is to see in Colossians the response of Paul to a set of teachings and practices enmeshed in Judaism but expressed in the idiom of Hellenistic religions and influenced by Jewish mystical traditions. We have no concerted evidence for a Jewish or Jewish Christian syncretism in Asia Minor in the first century. At any rate, a Jewish/pagan syncretism would be most unlikely to leave the Jewish identity markers, circumcision and Sabbath-keeping, intact. From what is known of pagan revulsion towards the practice of circumcision, circumcision would be among the first things to be excised and allegorized in most forms of hyper-Hellenized Judaism as demonstrated by Gnosticism (which I tentatively suspect grew out of Judaism)[32] and by the strict allegorical interpreters of the law (like those known to Philo).[33] Paul Trebilco states: "No evidence has arisen from this study to suggest that Judaism in Asia Minor was syncretistic or had been compromised by paganism."[34]

Thus, I regard the second option, that the letter to the Colossians is Paul's response to Jewish teaching expressed in Hellenistic idioms, as eminently more plausible. I identify in the Colossian philosophy evidence of certain teachers who are commending to the Colossian Christians a mystical way that is clearly Judaism, but that is communicated in language, imagery, and metaphors indebted to the indigenous philosophical context of mid first-century Asia Minor. James Dunn asserts:

> The main proponents of the Colossian "philosophy," therefore, almost certainly have to be understood as belonging to one of the Colossian synagogues. If indeed there were Jews in Colossae confident of their religion (2:4, 8), above all in the access it gave them to worship of heaven (2:18)

---

[31] As argued with some rigor by Arnold, *The Colossian Syncretism*, 150–55, 234–41. I disagree with Arnold on a number of fronts. (1) I think that the "philosophy" was external to the Colossian church rather than within it as Arnold supposes. (2) I am not convinced by his contention of syncretistic Jewish practices in Asia Minor which depends mostly on his claims about Jewish use of the magical papyri and Jewish influence on the *Theos Hypsistos* cult. (3) Arnold does not differentiate between syncretism and acculturation which are two related but separate things.

[32] Cf. Carl B. Smith, *No Longer Jews: The Search for Gnostic Origins* (Peabody, Mass.: Hendrickson, 2004).

[33] Cf. Philo, *Migr. Abr.* 92.

[34] Trebilco, *Jewish Communities of Asia Minor*, 142.

through faithfulness to what were tradition (Jewish) observances (2:16, 21–23), then we should not be surprised if they professed such claims in dialogue and debate with other Colossians. And if there then grew up in their midst a new version of their own teaching, proclaiming the Jewish Messiah and the fulfillment of ancient Jewish hopes (note again particularly 1:12 and 3:12), then, again, it would hardly be a surprise if some of the more outspoken and self-confident members of the synagogues spoke dismissively of the beliefs, devotions, and praxis of the new movement as compared with their own.[35]

A circle of Jewish teachers, rabbis, orators, rhetoricians steeped in Jewish mystical tradition and Hellenistic thought, and who have come into contact with Christians in Colossae, provides an appropriate background to the Colossian philosophy and explains the sociorhetorical dynamics of the letter.[36] This, I believe, accounts for the Jewish character of the philosophy as well as the Hellenistic terminology in which it is expressed. The philosophy, as it is written about in the letter to the Colossians, arguably represents an attempt by one or more Jewish individuals to recruit Christian Gentiles to a form of Jewish belief and practice through a highly contextualized missionary approach. If this reconstruction of the situation behind Colossians is correct, then it arguably represents one of the best indications we have for Jewish missionary activity.

I would add as well that the Pauline mission in the book of Acts competes against both paganism and Judaism with violent results often ensuing for the Lukan Paul and his coworkers. Whether we take Luke's account as historical or not matters little. The narrative either depicts or imagines Jewish and Christian competition over Gentiles, and the debates that develop are rhetorically powerful on the textual level precisely because they may resonate with real debates known to the real readers of Acts. The Johannine writings are arguably set against a backdrop of intra-Jewish debate over confession of Jesus as the Messiah, the experience of expulsion from synagogues probably in Asia Minor, and divisions occasioned by docetic secessionists. At the same time there are hints that competition for Gentile converts was at least an ancillary issue given certain textual indications in the Johannine corpus where

---

[35] James D. G. Dunn, *The Epistles to the Colossians and to Philemon* (NIGTC; Grand Rapids, Mich.: Eerdmans, 1996), 34.

[36] Cf. Stettler, "Opponents at Colossae," 193.

there is hope for the Gentiles to believe in Jesus amidst persecution and/or resistance from Jewish communities (John 7:35; 12:20; Rev 2:9; 15:4; 22:2).[37] The Epistle to the Hebrews appears to be set against a backdrop where the recipients are experiencing the temptation to return to Judaism and abandon Christianity. For Christians experiencing persecution by governing authorities, conversion to Judaism was a safe and attractive option given its status as a *religio licita* (tolerated religion).

Several scholars, while denying a first-century Jewish mission to Gentiles, nonetheless posit more active measures in the second century in response to Christian successes among Gentiles.[38] In the early second century further competition is possibly detectable in the Apostolic Fathers and Justin. Reidar Hvalvik has argued that such rivalry between Jews and Christians is echoed in the *Epistle of Barnabas* and the source of hostility was over missionary competition for Gentile converts.[39] In fact, the author of *Barnabas* even goes so far as to warn Christians against adopting Jewish laws since God "revealed all these things to us beforehand, that we should not rush forward as rash acceptors of their laws."[40] Ignatius warned against "living in accord with Judaism" and "Judaizing."[41] Justin knew of Christians who had adopted Judaism and "gone over to the polity of the law" and "have for some reason switched (μεταβαίνω) and joined the legal community, now denying that he is the Christ."[42] The second century *Apocalypse of Peter* (ca. 132–35 C.E.) suggests that sometime around the Bar Kochba revolt, Jewish Christians were forsaking Jesus as Christ and following an apparently false Messiah until they changed their minds and were themselves martyred.[43] Eusebius refers to a letter of Serapion of Antioch (end of the second century) to a certain Domnus who lapsed from the faith during a time of persecution in favor of a Jewish form of worship.[44] The fourth-century Council of Laodicea forbade Christians from keeping Jewish feasts and

---

[37] On which, see Hvalvik, *The Struggle for Scripture and Covenant*, 295, and the response by Riesner, "A Pre-Christian Jewish Mission?" 235.

[38] Cf., e.g., Goodman, *Mission and Conversion*, 129–53.

[39] Hvalvik, *The Struggle for Scripture and Covenant*, 319.

[40] *Barn.* 3.6.

[41] Ignatius, *Magn.* 8.1; 10.3.

[42] Justin, *Dial. Tryph.* 47.4.

[43] *Apoc. Pet.* 2.8–13; cf. Justin, *1 Apol.* 31.6; *Dial. Tryph.* 16; Eusebius, *Hist. Eccl.* 4.6.2.

[44] Eusebius, *Hist. Eccl.* 6.12.

the Sabbath, most likely because defection to Judaism by Christians remained a theoretical or real threat in the minds of ecclesial authorities. Similarly, the Theodosian code also attempted to curtail Christian conversion to Judaism.[45] While evidence for outright competition between Christians and Jews for Gentile converts is scant, one would expect that the emergence of such a situation would be inevitable given that many if not most Gentile converts to Christianity came from God-fearer or proselyte ranks, and Christian communities were established in cities with a sizable Jewish constituency (e.g., Antioch, Ephesus, and Rome) where interaction and friction between the two groups amidst a larger pagan population was inevitable.

CONCLUSION

In summary, the New Testament and later Christian literature provide a window into two types of missionary activity undertaken by Jewish individuals and groups: (1) Jewish Christians who were attempting to supplant or correct Paul's gospel by bringing his churches into closer association with the Jerusalem church and also with the national religion of Judea; and (2) a counter-Christian Jewish mission where Jewish groups were stirred into missionary work in order to stave off further successes by Christian workers. Strictly speaking, neither group here was attempting to convert ranks of pagans, but was usually building on what they saw as the prior and partial conversion of individuals already. Jewish Christians who were no doubt appreciative of the fact that Paul had turned Gentiles "to God from idols" (1 Thess 1:9) intended, nonetheless, to complete their conversion with circumcision. Similarly, counter-punching Jewish missionary efforts may have wanted to see former Gentile God-fearers or proselytes return to the synagogue. Consequently they tried to present a religious alternative to the Christian sect where returnees to Judaism could enjoy legal recognition in Roman cities and a greater claim to historical antiquity.[46]

---

[45] *Codex Theodosianus* 16.8.19, 22, 26.

[46] We might say that "Gentiles for Jesus" was countered with "Gentiles for Judaism."

CHAPTER SIX

CONCLUSION

Did Jews proselytize Gentiles? Undoubtedly so, according to the results of this investigation. Several Jewish groups and individuals actively facilitated the conversion of Gentiles to a form of Judaism and even incorporated them into Jewish communities. We have found evidence from Jewish Christian proselytizers who are still part of common Judaism (pp. 134–40), a case of very energetic Jewish propaganda in Colossae in the 60s C.E. (pp. 140–48), good reason to suspect that Jews in Rome were perhaps unusually active in recruiting converts (pp. 121–32), and evidence gleamed from Josephus's account of the royal family of Adiabene about two Jewish figures who were pleased to promote Judaism to a foreign king (pp. 97–99). In light of this, Alan Segal is correct when he writes:

> One may question whether Jews actively sought out proselytes in an aggressive way or whether they just developed a philosophical interest in the attractiveness of Jewish services and life-styles. But the undeniable truth appears to be that they did come, in sufficient numbers to cause anxiety in the pagan world.[1]

Was Second Temple Judaism, in its diversity, a missionary religion? The evidence presented above seems to vindicate the growing consensus that the Judaism of the period was not by and large a missionary religion.[2] What evidence does exist for it is either ambiguous (like what happened to trigger the expulsions of Jews from Rome), spasmodic (like the activity of Jewish Christian proselytizers), or exceptional (like Ananias and Eleazar in Adiabene). There is no evidence for an organized

---

[1] Segal, "The Cost of Proselytism and Conversion," 346.
[2] Cohen, "Adolf Harnack's 'The Mission and Expansion of Judaism,'" 166–67.

campaign or a widely held ethos that endeavored to recruit Gentiles to Judaism via the process of proselytizing.

But this conclusion must be qualified considerably. First, as we have seen, it depends entirely on how one defines mission and conversion. Labels of "missionary" or "non-missionary" are potentially anachronistic, freighted, and misleading if they presuppose equivalence with modern missionary religions.[3] Second, in the Second Temple period, different Jewish communities and individuals had wide-ranging views on the fate of the Gentiles, the role of the synagogue in a pagan city, and the means and necessity of Gentiles entering into Israel. Some groups were more interested in proselytes than others. This generated a constellation of views and practices towards Gentiles. What pagans saw in Judaism would depend entirely on what they saw of it, and that would vary from Alexandria to Antioch, from Gaul to Galilee.

There were indeed conscious attempts to give pagans a positive disposition to Judaism, to defend Judaism against criticism, to demonstrate the parity of the Jewish way of life with Hellenism, and a willingness to receive incomers. There was also great pride in the number of Gentiles who imitated or adopted the Jewish way of life. But we still have not discovered anything that might go under the aegis of mission as it was defined in chapter two. For the Jewish people, in general, there was a pervasive consciousness that they had a divinely given role vis-à-vis the nations, but there was a tension within Judaism itself as to what that vocation precisely consisted of. In no case did it erupt into aggressive mission activity. In some instances it appears that it meant sharing monotheism and the way of Torah with outsiders, urging philosophical respect for the divine law, looking forward to the subjugation of the nations, and for others still it meant proselytizing sympathizers. The diverse patterns of universalism that typified Second Temple Judaism led to a variety of attempts to interface with surrounding culture and to different attitudes about how to relate to Gentiles. When this "universalism" is in some sense outward looking and concerned with recruitment, then we observe two predominant types of activity in Judaism geared towards Gentiles: (1) The willingness to assist non-Jews in abandoning the immorality and idolatry of paganism and discover the coherence of "ethical monotheism"; or (2) to actively encourage God-fearers (i.e., adherents and associates) to take the full step into

---

[3] Cf. Hvalvik, *Struggle for Scripture and Covenant*, 279.

becoming proselytes.[4] *Neither action can strictly be termed "mission."* In the first instance, there is no reference to circumcision, which is the *sine qua non* of conversion for males (females is an entirely different and more complicated matter as we've seen). Meanwhile, in the second instance it is more akin to socializing, since the necessary ethical and theological shifts have already occurred at least for sympathizers. In all but a few isolated cases is there any intention to persuade rank pagans to become bona fide Jews.

Second Temple Judaism did attract proselytes and facilitate the conversion of Gentiles that wanted to convert to Judaism, but it was not *self-consciously missionary* since the role of Israel, the Torah, and the synagogue was never directed unequivocally towards Gentile recruitment. Jewish Hellenistic literature, above all Philo and Josephus, defend the philosophical reasonableness of Judaism and emphasize at length the willingness of Jewish communities to receive converts. Even so, a philosophical apology for Judaism has more benefit for insiders than for outsiders, and a willingness to receive is not equivalent to active recruitment. It was the fact of conversions to Judaism and not the method of conversion that infuriated Greek and Latin authors who saw adherence to the Jewish way of life and conversion to Judaism as a betrayal of their own rites, religion, and customs. It seems, then, that efforts to turn pagans into God-fearers or God-fearers into proselytes were spasmodic and opportunistic or else at the initiative of the Gentile.

What is more, Gentile adherence and conversion to Judaism created a number of issues and controversies for Jewish communities. The perceived level of ideal Gentile adherence and assimilation to Jewish communities remained widely disputed. Conversion was usually a slow and drawn-out affair, even taking a generation to finalize. I do not doubt that virtually every Jewish group thought that being initiated into the commonwealth of Israel and living under the Torah was good and desirable for Gentiles, whether it was politically expedient was another matter. It is important that Josephus's story of the conversion of the house of Adiabene occurs in a territory outside the realm of the Roman Empire and thus without any anti-Roman implications. Thus, conversion understood as initiation into Judaism and integration into a Jewish community was not the only option for Gentile sympathizers. It could be the case that for some Jews, the participation of Gentiles in

---

[4]Cf. Goodman, *Mission and Conversion*; Barnett, "Jewish Mission," 280.

the synagogue as sympathizers/adherents, their reverence for Israel and her traditions, and a partial obedience to the Torah could have been deemed sufficient of itself. But that raises the question, sufficient for what? Not all Jewish teachers would have necessarily thought that God-fearers had fulfilled "everything that God expected of them as Gentiles."[5]

On some accounts, it was deemed socially expedient for Gentiles to observe select Jewish customs without going through the torturous and towering process of circumcision. In this way, God would be glorified in their praise, Jews could respect virtuous pagans, and God would bless the Gentile for his or her limited devotion. Thus, if one operates in largely non-sectarian, non-eschatological, and philosophical categories, then adherence (as opposed to full conversion) is a perfectly plausible praxis to pursue for Gentile guests. But the opposite holds when partial participation in the Jewish religion is not deemed sufficient to actualize Gentile salvation. If one believes in the exclusiveness of Israel's worship, the efficacy of its covenants, in Israel's eventual domination of the world with the destruction of her enemies where, "no Gentile has a share in the age to come" and there is "no ransom for Gentiles,"[6] then only full proselytizing suffices. Hence, in a national-covenantal-eschatological scheme, conversion by circumcision is necessary in order to join the Israel who will be vindicated over and against the pagan nations. Moreover, this approach attempts to safeguard the incursion of Hellenism into Judaism, so as to preserve Israel's ethics, ethos, and ethnicity. Therefore, the tension in Judaism as evinced in pluriform attitudes towards Gentiles revolved around conflicting national, eschatological, and soteriological convictions.

We are finally in a position now to comment on the relationship between Jewish proselytizing activities and the emergence of the early Christian missions to the Gentiles.

First, the origins of the Christian Gentile missions and subsequent intra-Christian disputes about the admission of Gentiles into the church are all explicable within a Jewish framework. The universalism of the Christian missions to Jews and Gentiles is rooted in reading and reflection of Israel's sacred traditions. Particularly influential was the Isaianic paradigm which emphasized God's concern to reach the world through a restored Israel and how in the final days the Gentiles would begin to worship God without necessarily becoming proselytes or resident

---

[5] Donaldson, *Judaism and the Gentiles*, 481.
[6] *t. Sanh.* 13.2; *Mekilta Exodus.* 21.30.

aliens (e.g., Isa 2:2–4; 42:6; 49:6; 54:1–11; 55:1–5; 56:3–8; 60:1–16; 66:19–21).[7] In addition, disputes about the necessity of circumcising sympathizers and the limits of fraternizing with Gentiles are simply the appearance of day-to-day Jewish issues in Christian texts. The Pauline mission and its proselytizing counter-mission by Jewish Christians, was arguably about how this tension concerning the incorporation of the Gentiles into the church was fought out in early Christianity. Paul's narration and argument in Gal 1–2 and Luke's account of the Jerusalem council in Acts 15:1–5 could well include subjects *analogous* to what Eleazar and Ananias could have disputed over with regards to the obligations placed upon King Izates regarding his conversion as recorded by Josephus (*Ant.* 20.34–49) if the two had ever met. Likewise, Philo's argument for the acceptance of incomers (i.e., proselytes) at several points is at a piece with Luke's narrative defense of Gentile inclusion in Christian communities as equals in Acts 10–15. In many ways all of these debates can be situated within a "common Judaism."

Second, there emerged a broad but distinctive Christian viewpoint that was distinguishable from Jewish perspectives when it came to conversionist attitudes towards the Gentiles. An obvious point is that of *Christology* as beliefs about the risen and exalted Messiah were pressed in the aid of universalism via particularism, namely, that salvation comes to the world but through Israel and Israel's Messiah. To illustrate that point, the Matthean Jesus is sent only to the lost sheep of the house of Israel (Matt 10:5b–6; 15:24) and yet after the resurrection he commands his followers to make disciples of all nations (Matt 28:19–20). In the Johannine narrative, salvation is clearly from the Jews (John 4:22), and yet Jesus is also the savior of the world (John 4:42). The Johannine Jesus possesses a mission to Israel (John 1:13, 31) and leaves his disciples to testify to him before others (John 10:16; 12:20–23; 15:27; 20:21, 31). Likewise, in the letter to the Romans, Paul affirms the priority of the Jews over the Greeks (Rom 1:16), but he also sees Christ as a servant of the Jews as means of confirming God's promises made to the patriarchs about the Gentiles (Rom 15:8–9). Another characteristic Christian element is the drawing together of *eschatology* and *pneumatology*. The

---

[7] Cf. Graham Davies, "The Destiny of the Nations in the Book of Isaiah," in *The Book of Isaiah* (ed. J. Vermeylen; Leiden: Brill, 1989), 93–120; Donaldson, *Paul and the Gentiles*, 69–74; Schnabel, *Early Christian Mission*, 1.78–86; Bird, "A Light to the Nations," 122–31.

coming of the "end of ages" upon Christians (e.g., 1 Cor 10:11) and the pouring out of the Spirit upon all flesh (e.g., Acts 2:17) implied that the moment for the Gentiles to enter into God's salvific provision had finally come and the proof of this was the partaking of the Holy Spirit by persons without distinction. To that we can add also a particular *ecclesiology* whereby the followers of Jesus have become the elect of the final days with the corollary of the necessity of Jews and pagans entering into this new religious association if they are to experience true salvation. This election could be construed in various ways vis-à-vis Israel—remnant theology, supersession, or a renewal movement—depending on how one viewed Israel's rejection of the Messiah and his followers.

From a phenomenal viewpoint, then, the distinctive elements leading to the Christian mission were its religious devotion directed towards an exalted messianic figure who is regarded as the savior of Jews and Gentiles, a particular eschatological schema that incorporates the nations into salvation, shared religious experiences that transcend ethnic lines, and a re-reading of Israel's scriptures in light of those convictions. Of course this distinctiveness is characteristic rather than entirely unique as other groups and figures hold analogous beliefs. In the Dead Sea Scrolls, Enochic writings, and Philo you find various savior figures that relate to both Israel and the world, particular eschatological scenarios envisaging deliverance, groups regarding themselves as unique possessors of God's Spirit and God's Wisdom, a self-definition of their group as the elect, and also rancorous polemics against their coreligionists for not adopting their own viewpoint. Yet the genuine uniqueness of the early church as a missionary movement emerges because there is something that does ultimately set it apart from other Jewish groups. The difference is what I label "inclusive sectarianism." By "sectarian" I mean, as per most definitions, an ideological disposition that places a group in opposition to the values and meta-narratives of its environment. By "inclusive" I mean, paradoxically, a perspective that is ultimately affirming of others outside of the group. The Christian missions succeeded in incorporating persons of mixed ethnic identity, social class, economic position, and gender into their midst among the "church of God." According to the second-century apologist Aristides, Christians were a "Third Race" set apart from Jews and Greeks.[8] That meant that a break with Jewish communities was both inevitable and

---

[8] *Apologia* 2.

probably early as this cosmopolitan vision depreciated elements of Torah, Temple, Territory, and Election—pillars of Judaism—in such a way that could no longer be sustained within "common Judaism." Paul and other Christians established independent Jesus-believing communities in a response to Jewish rejection of their message. That rejection was subsequently followed by a rethinking of their relationship to Judaism itself, and competition for recruits among Jews, proselytes, sympathizers, and pagans ensued accordingly. For Helmut Koester, early Christians like Paul were trying to "accomplish the impossible." That was "to establish a new Israel on a foundation that could include both Jews and Gentiles."[9] That is not to say that all Christian communities in the first two centuries were equally sectarian (we could put Luke on one end of the spectrum and John the Seer on the other), nor did they have the same missional ethos or the same missional platforms in mind (the Antiochene church in Acts may have differed from that in Jerusalem on some matters early on), nor is it to imply that Christians had no negative views of outsiders and pagans (Paul forbade intermarriage with pagans [2 Cor 6:14] and the John the Seer warns of acculturation and assimilation in the letters to the seven churches [Rev 2:1–3:22]), nor does it demand that a breach with Judaism took place instantaneously and universally (instead it was a gradual and complex process usually driven by local pressures). The universalism that accompanied the birth of the Christian movement (detectable in the Jesus tradition, the Jerusalem church, and in Paul's letters), could not be sustained even within the gamut of a diverse and broad Judaism.[10] This resulted in breaches with various Jewish communities in Palestine and the Diaspora and that seems to have intensified Christian missionary efforts rather than stifling it.

Third, it is probably best to say that the early Christian mission to Gentiles represents a transformation of Jewish perspectives regarding the inclusion of the Gentiles in the salvation of God. While the early Christian missions have clear antecedents in Jewish interpretive traditions and are indebted to intra-Jewish debates about pagans, proselytism, and "God-fearers," four main differences emerge. (1) Taken as

---

[9] Helmut Koester, "Strugnell and Supersessionism: Historical Mistakes Haunt the Relationship of Christianity and Judaism," *BAR* 21 (1995): 26–27.

[10] Cf. Bird, "The Early Christians, the Historical Jesus, and the Salvation of the Gentiles" on the continuities and discontinuities between Jesus and the early Christian missionaries.

a whole the early Christian movement took Gentile proselytes and adherents who were on the periphery of Jewish communities and made them full and equal members in their own associations, to the point of eventually leading to a Gentile majority church in the post-70 C.E. era. (2) The spasmodic efforts at the recruitment of outsiders became more methodical and deliberate in primitive Christianity, as evidenced by the emergence of the offices of apostle and evangelist. (3) Christian missionary efforts *often* became centrifugal as opposed to centripetal and so shifted the initiative from the Gentile investigator to Christian leaders who, with the support and collaboration of others, made the formal declaration of its beliefs evident to outsiders.[11] (4) Primitive Christianity was *gradually* disengaged from the ethnocentric markers and territorial allegiance inherent within Judaism. For instance, circumcision seems to have given way to baptism, dietary laws were superseded by prayers over food, and the nexus between Lord and Land was redrawn around non-territorial, heavenly, and even platonic reinterpretations of Jewish traditions about land and inheritance. That is not to say that all Christian communities expressed all of these convictions at the same way and at the same time—that is most unlikely—but the emergence of the Christian missions stands within a Jewish milieu but ultimately exceeds it in the ways described above. Notably the degree and intensity levels of commitment required for conversion to Christianity were not essentially different from that required by conversion to Judaism. Instead, the mechanism for expressing that commitment in Christianity was redrawn around a new set of symbolic identifiers (e.g., faith in Christ, baptism, binitarian worship, eucharist, etc.) that required less drastic and more subtle changes in a convert's disposition towards his or her cultural environment than compared to what Judaism usually required for conversion.

Where exactly did this transformation come from? A. T. Kraabel writes, "without a Jewish mission it will be necessary to find another explanation for the early, energetic and pervasive mission of the new religion. Is it one of the *nova* of Christianity which derive from the message of Jesus himself?"[12] But that is another study in itself.

---

[11] On the origins of this shift see Bird, *Jesus and the Gentiles*, 162–68; idem, "Mission as an Apocalyptic Event," 133.

[12] Kraabel, "Immigrants, Exiles, Expatriates, and Missionaries," 85; cf. Goodman, *Mission and Conversion*, 90.

APPENDIX

SOURCE BOOK ON GENTILE CONVERSIONS AND JEWISH MISSIONARY ACTIVITY

This study has focused on the array of attitudes and actions on the part of Jews in Palestine and the Greco-Roman Diaspora that led to Gentile adherence to Judaism and even to full conversion to Judaism. During the course of this study recurring reference has been made to several particular ancient texts that have proven to be significant (and debated) for multiple subject areas. This appendix is by no means an exhaustive collection of these texts, but it aims more modestly at providing a short anthology of the most pertinent literary data in their original languages with English translations. The appendix is intended to be a quick reference to the most frequently discussed and disputed texts in scholarly literature concerning the extent and nature of Jewish missionary activity in the Greco-Roman world. Those looking for more exhaustive collections of texts detailing information about proselytes, Gentile adherence to Jewish customs, Jewish/Gentile relations, and Jewish Hellenistic propaganda literature should consult, besides the primary sources themselves,[1] works including J. B. Frey (ed.), *Corpus inscriptionum judaicarum* (2 vols.; New York: Ktav Publishing, 1975); Menahem Stern (ed.), *Greek and Latin Authors on Jews and Judaism: Edited with Introductions, Translations and Commentary* (3 vols.; Jerusalem: Israel Academy of Sciences and Humanities, 1974–1984); Harry J. Leon, *The Jews of Ancient Rome* (Peabody, Mass.: Hendrickson, 1995); Margaret H. Williams (ed.), *The Jews among the Greeks and Romans: A Diasporan Sourcebook* (London: Duckworth, 1998); Irina Levinskaya, *The Book of Acts in Its First Century Setting 5: The Book of Acts in Its Diaspora Setting*

---

[1] The most accessible primary sources with bilingual translations are those in the Loeb Classical Library series published by Harvard University Press.

(Carlisle: Paternoster, 1996); Louis H. Feldman and Meyer Reinhold (eds.), *Jewish Life and Thought among Greeks and Romans: Primary Readings* (Minneapolis: Fortress, 1996). Notable also is Terence Donaldson's *Judaism and the Gentiles: Jewish Patterns of Universalism (to 135 CE)* (Waco, Tex.: Baylor University Press, 2007) which lists many of the key texts about Jewish views of Gentiles and instances of proselytism in English translations with an excellent commentary after each text. The texts in this appendix include:

1. Jewish Novellas
   a. Esther 8:17
   b. Judith 14:10
   c. *Joseph and Aseneth* 15:1–8

2. The Dead Sea Scrolls
   a. 4Q174 1:3–5
   b. CD 14:5–6

3. Josephus
   a. *Jewish War* 2.454
   b. *Jewish War* 2.461–463
   c. *Antiquities* 20.34–35, 38–46.
   d. *Against Apion* 2.123
   e. *Against Apion* 2.210
   f. *Against Apion* 2.261
   g. *Against Apion* 2.282
   h. *Life* 112–113

4. Philo
   a. *Virtues* 102–104
   b. *Virtues* 179
   c. *Questions in Exodus* 2.2
   d. *Special Laws* 1.320–323

5. New Testament
   a. Matthew 23:15
   b. Acts 15:1–5

6. Pagan Authors
   a. Horace, *Sermones* 1.4.139–143
   b. Seneca, *De Superstitione* cited in Augustine, *Ciy of God* 6.11
   c. Epictetus, *Dissertationes* 2.9.20
   d. Tacitus, *Histories* 5.5
   e. Juvenal, *Saturae* 15.96–106
   f. Suetonius, *Domitian* 12.2

7. Inscriptions
   a. God-Fearer at Deliler, Lydia
   b. God-Fearer at Miletus
   c. Proselyte at Sebaste
   d. Proselyte at Rome
   e. Palestinian Proselyte Ossuary
8. Rabbinic Literature
   a. Mishnah, *Pesahim* 8.8
   b. Babylonian Talmud, *Niddah* 13b
   c. Babylonian Talmud, *Shabbath* 145b–6a

1. JEWISH NOVELLAS

a. Esther 8:17

וּבְכָל־מְדִינָה וּמְדִינָה
וּבְכָל־עִיר וָעִיר מְקוֹם אֲשֶׁר
דְּבַר־הַמֶּלֶךְ וְדָתוֹ מַגִּיעַ
שִׂמְחָה וְשָׂשׂוֹן לַיְּהוּדִים
מִשְׁתֶּה וְיוֹם טוֹב וְרַבִּים
מֵעַמֵּי הָאָרֶץ מִתְיַהֲדִים
כִּי־נָפַל פַּחַד־הַיְּהוּדִים
עֲלֵיהֶם׃

κατὰ πόλιν καὶ χώραν οὗ ἂν ἐξετέθη τὸ πρόσταγμα οὗ ἂν
ἐξετέθη τὸ ἔκθεμα χαρὰ καὶ εὐφροσύνη τοῖς Ιουδαίοις κώθων
καὶ εὐφροσύνη καὶ πολλοὶ τῶν ἐθνῶν περιετέμοντο καὶ
ιουδάιζον διὰ τὸν φόβον τῶν Ιουδαίων

In every province and in every city, wherever the king's command and his
edict came, there was gladness and joy among the Jews, a festival and a
holiday. Furthermore, many of the peoples of the country professed to be
Jews, because the fear of the Jews had fallen upon them (NRSV).

b. Judith 14:10

ἰδὼν δὲ Αχιωρ πάντα ὅσα ἐποίησεν ὁ θεὸς τοῦ Ισραηλ
ἐπίστευσεν τῷ θεῷ σφόδρα καὶ περιετέμετο τὴν σάρκα τῆς
ἀκροβυστίας αὐτοῦ καὶ προσετέθη εἰς τὸν οἶκον Ισραηλ ἕως
τῆς ἡμέρας ταύτης

When Achior saw all that the God of Israel had done, he believed firmly in God. So he was circumcised, and joined the house of Israel, remaining so to this day (NRSV).

c. *Joseph and Aseneth* 15:1–8

Καὶ ἦλθε πρὸς τὸν ἄνθρωπον καὶ ἰδὼν αὐτὴν ὁ ἄνθρωπος λέγει αὐτῇ· ἆρον δὴ τὸ θέριστρον ἀπὸ τῆς κεφαλῆς σου, διότι εἶ παρθένος ἁγνὴ σήμερον καὶ ἡ κεφαλή σού ἐστιν ὡς ἀνδρὸς νεανίσκου. Καὶ ἦρεν αὐτὸ ἐκ τῆς κεφαλῆς αὐτῆς. Καὶ εἶπεν αὐτῇ ὁ ἄνθρωπος· θάρσει, Ἀσενέθ, ἰδοὺ γὰρ ἤκουσε κύριος τῶν ῥημάτων τῆς ἐξομολογήσεώς σου. Θάρσει, Ἀσενέθ, ἰδοὺ ἐγράφη τὸ ὄνομά σου ἐν βίβλῳ ζωῆς καὶ οὐκ ἐξαλειφθήσεται εἰς τὸν αἰῶνα. Ἰδοὺ ἀπὸ τῆς σήμερον ἀνακαινισθήσῃ καὶ ἀναπλασθήσῃ καὶ ἀναζωοποιηθήσῃ καὶ φάγῃ ἄρτον ζωῆς καὶ πίεσαι ποτήριον ἀθανασίας καὶ χρισθήσῃ χρίσματι τῆς ἀφθαρσίας. Θάρσει, Ἀσενέθ, ἰδοὺ δέδωκέν σε κύριος τῷ Ἰωσὴφ εἰς νύμφην καὶ αὐτὸς ἔσται σου νυμφίος. Καὶ οὐκέτι κληθήσει Ἀσενέθ, ἀλλ᾽ ἔσται τὸ ὄνομά σου πόλις καταφυγῆς, διότι ἐν σοὶ καταφεύξονται ἔθνη πολλὰ καὶ ὑπὸ τὰς πτέρυγάς σου σκεπασθήσονται λαοὶ πολλοί, καὶ ἐν τῷ τείχει σου φυλαχθήσονται οἱ προσκείμενοι τῷ θεῷ διὰ μετανοίας. Διότι ἡ μετάνοιά ἐστι θυγάτηρ τοῦ ὑψίστου καὶ αὕτη παρακαλεῖ τὸν ὕψιστον ὑπὲρ σοῦ πᾶσαν ὥραν καὶ ὑπὲρ πάντων τῶν μετανοούντων, ἐπειδὴ πατήρ ἐστι τῆς μετανοίας καὶ αὕτη ἐστὶ μήτηρ παρθένων καὶ πᾶσαν ὥραν περὶ τῶν μετανοούντων ἐρωτᾷ αὐτόν, διότι τοῖς ἀγαπῶσιν αὐτὴν ἡτοίμασε νυμφῶνα οὐράνιον, καὶ αὕτη διακονήσει αὐτοῖς εἰς τὸν αἰῶνα χρόνον. Καὶ ἔστιν ἡ μετάνοια καλὴ σφόδρα παρθένος καθαρὰ καὶ ἁγνὴ καὶ πρᾶος καὶ ὁ θεὸς ὁ ὕψιστος ἀγαπᾷ αὐτὴν καὶ πάντες οἱ ἄγγελοι αἰδοῦνται αὐτήν.

And she went to the man into her first chamber and stood before him. And the man said to her, "Remove the veil from your head, and for what purpose did you do this? For you are a chaste virgin today, and your head is like that of a young man." And Aseneth removed the veil from her head. And the man said to her, "Courage, Aseneth, chaste virgin. Behold, I have heard all the words of your confession and your prayer. Behold I have also seen the humiliation and the affliction of the seven days of your want (of food). Behold, from your tears and these ashes, plenty of mud has formed before your face. Courage, Aseneth, chaste virgin. For behold, your name was written in the book of the living in heaven; in the beginning of the book, as the very first of all, your name was written by my finger, and it will not be erased forever. Behold, from today, you will be renewed and formed anew and made alive again, and you will eat blessed bread of life, and drink a blessed cup of immortality, and anoint yourself with blessed ointment of incorruptibility. Courage, Aseneth, chaste virgin. Behold, I have given you today to Joseph for a bride, and he himself will be your bridegroom for ever (and) ever. And your name shall no longer be called Aseneth, but your name shall be City of Refuge, because in you many nations will take refuge with the Lord God, the Most High and under your wings many peoples trusting in the Lord God will be sheltered, and behind your walls will be guarded those who attach themselves to the Most High God in the name of Repentance. For Repentance is in the heavens, an exceedingly beautiful and good daughter of the Most High. And she herself entreats the Most High God for you at all times and for all who repent in the name of the Most High God, because he is (the) father of Repentance. And she herself is guardian of all virgins, and loves you very much, and is beseeching the Most High for you at all times and for all who repent she prepared a place of rest in the heavens. And she will renew all who repent, and wait on them herself for ever (and) ever. And Repentance is exceedingly beautiful, a virgin pure and laughing always, and she is gentle and meek. And, therefore, the Most High Father loves her, and all the angels stand in awe of her. And I, too, love her exceedingly, because she is also my sister. And because she loves you virgins, I love you, too" (*OTP*).

2. THE DEAD SEA SCROLLS

a. 4Q174 frg. 1, II, 3–5

מקדש אדני כ]וננו ידיכה `--` [
יהוה ימלוך עו לם ועד הואה הבית
אשר לו א יבוא שמה
עד]עֹולם ו עמֹוני ומואבי `--` [
וממזר ובן נכר וגר עד עולם כיא קדושי
שם
עולם תמיד עליו יראה[`--`]הֹ[ ] י
ולוא ישמוהו עוד זרים כאשר השמו
בראישונה

[Moses: "A temple of] the Lord are you to prepare with your hands; the Lord will reign forever and ever" (Exod 15:17). This passage describes the temple that no [man with a] permanent [fleshly defect] shall enter, nor Ammonite, Moabite, bastard, foreigner or alien, forevermore. Surely His holiness shall be rev[eal]ed there; eternal glory shall ever be apparent there. Strangers shall not again defile it, as they formerly defiled (Wise, Abegg, Cook).

b. CD 14:3–6

[ ] וס רך מושב כל
המחנות יפקדו כלם
בשמותיהם הכ הנים ל
ראשונה
ו הלוים שנים ובני
ישראל שלשתם והגר רביע
ויכתבו בש מו תיהם
איש אחר אחיהו
הכהנים לראשונה והלוים
שנים ובני ישראל
שלושתם והגר רביע
וכן ישבו וכן ישאלו לכל
והכהן אשר י פקד

The rule for those who live in all the camps. All shall be mustered by their names: the priests first, the Levites second, the children of Israel third, the proselyte fourth. In the same order they shall sit, and in the same order they will inquire of all (Wise, Abegg, Cook).

3. JOSEPHUS

a. *Jewish War* 2.454

οἱ μὲν οὖν οὕτως ὠμῶς ἀπεσφάγησαν ἅπαντες πλὴν Μετιλίου
τοῦτον γὰρ ἱκετεύσαντα καὶ μέχρι περιτομῆς ἰουδαΐσειν
ὑποσχόμενον διέσωσαν μόνον τὸ δὲ πάθος Ῥωμαίοις μὲν ἦν
κοῦφον ἐκ γὰρ ἀπλέτου δυνάμεως ἀπαναλώθησαν ὀλίγοι
Ἰουδαίων δὲ προοίμιον ἁλώσεως ἔδοξεν.

And in this way all these men were savagely murdered, except Metilius; for when he searched for mercy, and promised that he would Judaize to the point of circumcision, they left him alone alive. This setback to the Romans was insignificant, there being no more than a few killed out of an immense army; but this still appeared to be a forecast to the Judean's own destruction (author's trans.).

b. *Jewish War* 2.461–463

Οὐ μὴν οἱ Σύροι τῶν Ἰουδαίων ἔλαττον πλῆθος ἀνήρουν ἀλλὰ καὶ αὐτοὶ τοὺς ἐν ταῖς πόλεσιν λαμβανομένους ἀπέσφαττον οὐ μόνον κατὰ μῖσος ὡς πρότερον ἀλλ᾽ ἤδη καὶ τὸν ἐφ᾽ ἑαυτοῖς κίνδυνον φθάνοντες δεινὴ δὲ ὅλην τὴν Συρίαν ἐπεῖχεν ταραχή καὶ πᾶσα πόλις εἰς δύο διῄρητο στρατόπεδα σωτηρία δὲ τοῖς ἑτέροις ἦν τὸ τοὺς ἑτέρους φθάσαι καὶ τὰς μὲν ἡμέρας ἐν αἵματι διῆγον τὰς δὲ νύκτας δέει χαλεπωτέρας καὶ γὰρ ἀπεσκευάσθαι τοὺς Ἰουδαίους δοκοῦντες ἕκαστοι τοὺς ἰουδαΐζοντας εἶχον ἐν ὑποψίᾳ καὶ τὸ παρ᾽ ἑκάστοις ἀμφίβολον οὔτε ἀνελεῖν τις προχείρως ὑπέμενεν καὶ μεμιγμένον ὡς βεβαίως ἀλλόφυλον ἐφοβεῖτο.

However, the Syrians were upon the lesser number of Jews whom they killed; for even they killed those whom they caught in their cities, and that not only out of hatred they bare them, as before, but to prevent the danger under which might rouse from them; so that the disturbances in all of Syria were terrible, and every city was divided into two armies pitted one against another, and the deliverance of the one party was through the destruction of the other. This had the result that the daytime was spent in the spilling of blood and the night in terror, which was of the two the more terrible. Yet when the Syrians thought they had annihilated the Jews, they still held the judaizers in suspicion since each side did not care to kill those whom they only suspected of being on the other side, and so they held grave fear when they were mingled with the other, as if they were certainly foreigners (author's trans.).

c. *Antiquities* 20.34–35, 38–46

Καθ᾽ ὃν δὲ χρόνον ὁ Ἰζάτης ἐν τῷ Σπασίνου χάρακι διέτριβεν Ἰουδαῖός τις ἔμπορος Ἀνανίας ὄνομα πρὸς τὰς γυναῖκας εἰσιὼν τοῦ βασιλέως ἐδίδασκεν αὐτὰς τὸν θεὸν σέβειν ὡς Ἰουδαίοις πάτριον ἦν καὶ δὴ δι᾽ αὐτῶν εἰς γνῶσιν ἀφικόμενος τῷ Ἰζάτῃ κἀκεῖνον ὁμοίως συνανέπεισεν μετακληθέντι τε

ὑπὸ τοῦ πατρὸς εἰς τὴν Ἀδιαβηνὴν συνεξῆλθεν κατὰ πολλὴν
ὑπακούσας δέησιν συνεβεβήκει δὲ καὶ τὴν Ἑλένην ὁμοίως
ὑφ᾽ ἑτέρου τινὸς Ἰουδαίου διδαχθεῖσαν εἰς τοὺς ἐκείνων
μετακεκομίσθαι νόμους … Πυθόμενος δὲ πάνυ τοῖς Ἰουδαίων
ἔθεσιν χαίρειν τὴν μητέρα τὴν ἑαυτοῦ ἔσπευσε καὶ αὐτὸς εἰς
ἐκεῖνα μεταθέσθαι νομίζων τε μὴ ἂν εἶναι βεβαίως Ἰουδαῖος
εἰ μὴ περιτέμνοιτο πράττειν ἦν ἕτοιμος μαθοῦσα δ᾽ ἡ μήτηρ
κωλύειν ἐπειρᾶτο ἐπιφέρειν αὐτῷ κίνδυνον λέγουσα βασιλέα
γὰρ εἶναι καὶ καταστήσειν εἰς πολλὴν δυσμένειαν τοὺς
ὑπηκόους μαθόντας ὅτι ξένων ἐπιθυμήσειεν καὶ ἀλλοτρίων
αὐτοῖς ἐθῶν οὐκ ἀνέξεσθαί τε βασιλεύοντος αὐτῶν Ἰουδαίου
μετὰ ταῦτα δέ τὴν γὰρ ἐπιθυμίαν οὐκ ἐξεβεβλήκει παντάπασιν
Ἰουδαῖός τις ἕτερος ἐκ τῆς Γαλιλαίας ἀφικόμενος Ἐλεάζαρος
ὄνομα πάνυ περὶ τὰ πάτρια δοκῶν ἀκριβὴς εἶναι προετρέψατο
πρᾶξαι τοὐργον ἐπεὶ γὰρ εἰσῆλθεν ἀσπασόμενος αὐτὸν καὶ
κατέλαβε τὸν Μωυσέος νόμον ἀναγινώσκοντα λανθάνεις εἶπεν
ὦ βασιλεῦ τὰ μέγιστα τοὺς νόμους καὶ δι᾽ αὐτῶν τὸν θεὸν ἀδικῶν
οὐ γὰρ ἀναγινώσκειν σε δεῖ μόνον αὐτούς ἀλλὰ καὶ πρότερον
τὰ προστασσόμενα ποιεῖν ὑπ᾽ αὐτῶν μέχρι τίνος ἀπερίτμητος
μενεῖς ἀλλ᾽ εἰ μήπω τὸν περὶ τούτου νόμον ἀνέγνως ἵν᾽ εἰδῇς
τίς ἐστιν ἡ ἀσέβεια νῦν ἀνάγνωθι ταῦτα ἀκούσας ὁ βασιλεὺς
οὐχ ὑπερεβάλετο τὴν πρᾶξιν μεταστὰς δ᾽ εἰς ἕτερον οἴκημα
καὶ τὸν ἰατρὸν εἰσκαλεσάμενος τὸ προσταχθὲν ἐτέλει καὶ
μεταπεμψάμενος τήν τε μητέρα καὶ τὸν διδάσκαλον Ἀνανίαν
ἐσήμαινεν αὐτὸν πεπραχέναι τοὐργον.

Now during the time when Izates resided at Charax Spasini, a certain
Jewish merchant named Ananias visited the king's wives and taught them
to worship God after the manner of the Jewish tradition. It was through
their agency that he was brought to the notice of Izates, whom he similarly
won over with the cooperation of the women … When Izates had learned
that his mother was very much pleased with the Jewish religion, he was
zealous to convert to it himself; and since he considered that he would
not be genuinely a Jew unless be was circumcised, he was ready to act
accordingly. When his mother learned of his intention, however, she tried
to stop him by telling him that it was a dangerous move. For, she said, he
was a king; and if his subjects should discover that he was devoted to
rites that were strange and foreign to themselves, it would produce much
dissatisfaction, and they would not tolerate the rule of a Jew over them
… He, in turn, reported her arguments to Ananias … The king, could, he
[Ananias] said, worship God even without being circumcised if indeed

he had fully decided to be a devoted adherent of Judaism, for it was this that counted more than circumcision. He told him, furthermore, that God himself would pardon him if, constrained thus by necessity and by fear of his subjects, he failed to perform this rite. And so, for the time, the king was convinced by his arguments. Afterwards, however, since he had not completely given up his desire, another Jew, named Eleazar, who came from Galilee and who had a reputation for being extremely strict when it came to the ancestral laws, urged him to carry out the rite. For when he came to him to pay his respects and found the law of Moses, he said: "In your ignorance, O king, you are guilty of the greatest offense against the law and thereby against god. For you ought not merely to read the law but also, and even more, to do what is commanded in it. How long will you continue to be uncircumcised? If you have not yet read the law concerning this matter, read it now, so that you may know what an impiety it is that you commit." Upon hearing these words, the king postponed the deed no longer (LCL).

d. *Against Apion* 2.123

τῶν Ἑλλήνων δὲ πλέον τοῖς τόποις ἢ τοῖς ἐπιτηδεύμασιν ἀφεστήκαμεν ὥστε μηδεμίαν ἡμῖν εἶναι πρὸς αὐτοὺς ἔχθραν μηδὲ ζηλοτυπίαν τοὐναντίον μέντοι πολλοὶ παρ᾽ αὐτῶν εἰς τοὺς ἡμετέρους νόμους συνέβησαν εἰσελθεῖν καί τινες μὲν ἐνέμειναν εἰσὶ δ᾽ οἳ τὴν καρτερίαν οὐχ ὑπομείναντες πάλιν ἀπέστησαν.

From the Greeks we are severed more by our geographical position than by our institutions, with the result that we neither hate nor envy them. On the contrary, many of them have agreed to adopt our laws; of whom some have remained faithful, while others, lacking the necessary endurance, have again seceded (LCL).

e. *Against Apion* 2.210

ὅσοι μὲν γὰρ θέλουσιν ὑπὸ τοὺς αὐτοὺς ἡμῖν νόμους ζῆν ὑπελθόντες δέχεται φιλοφρόνως οὐ τῷ γένει μόνον ἀλλὰ καὶ τῇ προαιρέσει τοῦ βίου νομίζων εἶναι τὴν οἰκειότητα τοὺς δ᾽ ἐκ παρέργου προσιόντας ἀναμίγνυσθαι τῇ συνηθείᾳ οὐκ ἠθέλησεν.

To all who desire to come and live under the same laws with us, he [Moses] gives a gracious welcome, holding that it is not family ties alone which constitute relationship, but agreement in principles of conduct. On the other hand, it was not his pleasure that casual visitors should be admitted to the intimacies of our daily life (LCL).

f. Against Apion 2.261

τῆς πολιτείας οὔτε τῆς παρ᾽ αὐτοῖς μετεδίδοσαν διατριβῆς ἡμεῖς δὲ τὰ μὲν τῶν ἄλλων ζηλοῦν οὐκ ἀξιοῦμεν τοὺς μέντοι μετέχειν τῶν ἡμετέρων βουλομένους ἡδέως δεχόμεθα καὶ τοῦτο ἂν εἴη τεκμήριον οἶμαι φιλανθρωπίας ἅμα καὶ μεγαλοψυχίας.

We, on the contrary, while we have no desire to emulate the customs of others, yet gladly welcome any who wish to share our own. That I think, may be taken as a proof both of humanity and magnanimity (LCL).

g. Against Apion 2.282

οὐ μὴν ἀλλὰ καὶ πλήθεσιν ἤδη πολὺς ζῆλος γέγονεν ἐκ μακροῦ τῆς ἡμετέρας εὐσεβείας οὐδ᾽ ἔστιν οὐ πόλις Ἑλλήνων οὐδητισοῦν οὐδὲ βάρβαρον οὐδὲ ἓν ἔθνος ἔνθα μὴ τὸ τῆς ἑβδομάδος ἣν ἀργοῦμεν ἡμεῖς τὸ ἔθος [δὲ] διαπεφοίτηκεν καὶ αἱ νηστεῖαι καὶ λύχνων ἀνακαύσεις καὶ πολλὰ τῶν εἰς βρῶσιν ἡμῖν οὐ νενομισμένων παρατετήρηται.

The masses have long since shown a keen desire to adopt our religious observances; and there is not one city, Greek or barbarian, nor a single nation, to which our custom of abstaining from work on the seventh day has not spread, and where the fasts and the lighting of lamp, and many of our prohibitions in the matter of food are not observed (LCL).

h. Life 1.112–113

Κατὰ τοῦτον τὸν καιρὸν ἀφικνοῦνται πρός με δύο μεγιστᾶνες τῶν ὑπὸ τὴν ἐξουσίαν τοῦ βασιλέως ἐκ τῆς τῶν Τραχωνιτῶν χώρας ἐπαγόμενοι τοὺς ἑαυτῶν ἵππους καὶ ὅπλα χρήματα δ᾽ ὑποκομίζοντες τούτους περιτέμνεσθαι τῶν Ἰουδαίων ἀναγκαζόντων εἰ θέλουσιν εἶναι παρ᾽ αὐτοῖς οὐκ εἴασα βιασθῆναι φάσκων δεῖν ἕκαστον κατὰ τὴν ἑαυτοῦ προαίρεσιν τὸν θεὸν εὐσεβεῖν ἀλλὰ μὴ μετὰ βίας χρῆναι δὲ τούτους δι᾽ ἀσφάλειαν πρὸς ἡμᾶς καταφυγόντας μὴ μετανοεῖν πεισθέντος

δὲ τοῦ πλήθους τοῖς ἥκουσιν ἀνδράσιν τὰ πρὸς τὴν συνήθη
δίαιταν ἅπαντα παρεῖχον δαψιλῶς

About this time there came to me from the region of Trachonitis two
nobles, subjects of the king, bringing their horses, arms, and money
which they had smuggled out of their country. The Jews would have
compelled them to be circumcised as a condition of residence among
them. I, however, would not allow any compulsion to be put upon
them, declaring that everyone should worship God in accordance with
the dictates of his own conscience and not under constraint, and that
these men, having fled to us for refuge, ought not to be made to regret
that they had done so. Having brought over the people to my way of
thinking, I liberally supplied our guests with all things necessary to their
customary manner of life (LCL).

4. Philo

a. *Virtues* 102–104

νομοθετήσας δὲ περὶ τῶν ὁμοεθνῶν καὶ τοὺς ἐπηλύτας
οἴεται δεῖν προνομίας τῆς πάσης ἀξιοῦσθαι, γενεὰν μὲν τὴν
ἀφ᾽ αἵματος καὶ πατρίδα καὶ ἔθη καὶ ἱερὰ καὶ ἀφιδρύματα
θεῶν γέρα τε καὶ τιμὰς ἀπολελοιπότας καλὴν δ᾽ ἀποικίαν
στειλαμένους τὴν ἀπὸ τῶν μυθικῶν πλασμάτων πρὸς τὴν
ἀληθείας ἐνάργειαν καὶ τὸν σεβασμὸν τοῦ ἑνὸς καὶ ὄντως ὄντος
θεοῦ, κελεύει δὴ τοῖς ἀπὸ τοῦ ἔθνους ἀγαπᾶν τοὺς ἐπηλύτας, μὴ
μόνον ὡς φίλους καὶ συγγενεῖς ἀλλὰ καὶ ὡς ἑαυτούς, κατά τε
σῶμα καὶ ψυχήν, κατὰ μὲν σῶμα ὡς οἷόν τε κοινοπραγοῦντας,
κατὰ δὲ τὴν διάνοιαν τὰ αὐτὰ λυπουμένους τε καὶ χαίροντας,
ὡς ἐν διαιρετοῖς μέρεσιν ἓν εἶναι ζῷον δοκεῖν, ἁρμοζομένης
καὶ συμφυὲς ἀπεργαζομένης τῆς κατ᾽ αὐτὸ κοινωνίας. οὐκέτ᾽
ἂν εἴποιμι λέγω περὶ σιτίων καὶ ποτῶν καὶ ἐσθῆτος καὶ τῶν
ἄλλων ὅσα περὶ δίαιταν καὶ τὰς ἀναγκαίας χρείας, ἃ τοῖς
ἐπηλύτοις δίδωσιν ὁ νόμος παρὰ τῶν αὐτοχθόνων· ἕπεται γὰρ
ταῦτα πάντα θεσμοῖς τοῖς τῆς εὐνοίας τοῦ στέργοντος ὁμοίως
ἀγαπῶντος τὸν ἐπήλυτον ὡς ἑαυτόν.

He [Moses] holds that the incomers [proselytes] too should be
accorded every favor and consideration as their due, because
abandoning their kinsfolk by blood, their country, their customs and
the temples and images of their gods, and the tributes and honors

paid to them, they have taken the journey to a better home, from idle
fables to the clear vision of truth and the worship of the one and truly
existing God. He [Moses] commands all members of the nation to
love the incomers, not only as friends and kinsfolk but as themselves
both in body and soul; in bodily matters, by acting as far as may be for
their common interest; in mental by having the same griefs and joys,
so that they may seem to be the separate parts of a single living being
which is compacted and unified by their fellowship in it. I will not
go on to speak of the food and drink and raiment and all the rights
concerning daily life and necessary needs, which the law assigns to
incomers as due from the native born, for all these follow the statues,
which speak of the friendliness shown by him who loves the incomer
even as himself (LCL).

b. *Virtues* 179

τί δ᾽ ἂν εἴη τῶν ὄντων ἄριστον ἢ θεός, οὗ τὰς τιμὰς προσένειμαν
τοῖς οὐ θεοῖς, ἐκείνους μὲν ἀποσεμνύνοντες πλέον τοῦ μετρίου,
τοῦ δὲ εἰς ἅπανπᾶς οἱ κενοὶ φρενῶν ἐκλαθόμενοι. πάντας οὖν,
ὅσοι τὸν κτίστην καὶ πατέρα τοῦ παντὸς εἰ καὶ μὴ ἐξ ἀρχῆς
σέβεινσέβω ἠξίωσαν ἀλλ᾽ ὕστερον μοναρχίαν ἀντὶ πολυαρχίας
ἀσπασάμενοι, φιλτάτους καὶ συγγενεστάτους ὑποληπτέον, τὸ
μέγιστον εἰς φιλίαν καὶ οἰκειότητα παρασχομένους θεοφιλὲς
ἦθος, οἷς χρὴ καὶ συνήδεσθαι, καθάπερκαθά ἂν εἰ καὶ
τυφλοὶ πρότερον ὄντες ἀνέβλεψαν ἐκ βαθυτάτου σκότους
αὐγοειδέστατον φῶς ἰδόντες.

All these who did not at the first acknowledge their duty to reverence
the Founder and Father of all, yet afterwards embraced the creed of one
instead of a multiplicity of sovereigns, must be held to be our dearest
friends and closest kinsmen. They have shown the godliness of heart
which above all leads up to friendship and affinity, and we must rejoice
with them, as if though blind at the first they had recovered their sight
and had come from the deepest darkness to behold the most radiant light
(LCL).

c. *Questions in Exodus* 2.2

προσήλυτός ἐστιν, οὐχ ὁ περιτμηθεὶς τὴν ἀκροβυστίαν ἀλλ᾽ ὁ
τὰς ἡδονὰς καὶ τὰς ἐπιθυμίας καὶ τὰ ἄλλα πάθη τῆς ψυχῆς.

The proselyte is not the one who has circumcised his uncircumcision, but
the one who has circumcised the pleasures and the desires and the other
passions of the soul (LCL).

d. *Special Laws* 1.320–323

τί γάρ, εἰ καλὰ ταῦτ' ἐστίν, ὦ μύσται, καὶ συμφέροντα,
συγκλεισάμενοι ἑαυτοὺς ἐν σκότῳ βαθεῖ τρεῖς ἢ τέτταρας
μόνους ὠφελεῖτε, παρὸν ἅπαντας πᾶς ἀνθρώπους ἐν ἀγορᾷ
μέσῃ τὰ τῆς ὠφελείας προθέντας, ἵνα πᾶσιν ἀδεῶς ἐξῇ
βελτίονος καὶ εὐτυχεστέρου κοινωνῆσαι βίου; φθόνος
γὰρ ἀρετῆς διῴκισται. οἱ μὲν γὰρ τὰ βλαβερὰ πράττοντες
αἰσχυνέσθωσαν καὶ καταδύσεις ἐπιζητοῦντες καὶ γῆς μυχοὺς
καὶ βαθὺ σκότος ἐπικρυπτέσθως τὴν πολλὴν ἀνομίαν αὐτῶν
ἐπισκιάζοντες ὡς μηδεὶς ἴδοι· τοῖς δὲ τὰ κοινωφελῆ δρῶσιν
ἔστω παρρησία καὶ μεθ' ἡμέραν διὰ μέσης ἴτωσαν ἀγορᾶς
ἐντευξόμενοι πολυανθρώποις ὁμίλοις, ἡλίῳ καθαρῷ τὸν ἴδιον
βίον ἀνταυγάσοντες καὶ διὰ τῶν κυριωτάτων αἰσθήσεων
τοὺς συλλόγους ὀνήσοντες, ὁρῶντας μὲν ἡδίστας ὁμοῦ καὶ
καταπληκτικωτάτας ὄψεις, ἀκούοντας δὲ καὶ ἑστιωμένους
λόγων ποτίμων, οἳ τὰς διανοίας τῶν μὴ σφόδρα ἀμούσων
εἰώθασιν εὐφραίνειν. ... εἶτ' οὐκ ἐχρῆν καὶ ἡμᾶς ἑπομένους
τοῖς ἐκείνης βουλήμασι πάνθ' ὅσα ἀναγκαῖα καὶ χρήσιμα
προτιθέναι πᾶσι τοῖς ἀξίοις ἐπ' ὠφελείᾳ;

For tell me, ye mystics, if these things are good and profitable, why do
you shut yourselves up in profound darkness and reserve their benefits
for three or four alone, when producing them in the midst of the market-
place you might extend them to every man and thus enable all to share in
security a better and happier life? For virtue has no room in her home
for a grudging spirit. Let those who work mischief feel shame and seek
holes and corners of the earth and profound darkness, there lie hid to
keep the multitude of their iniquities veiled out of the sight of all. But
let those whose actions serve the common weal use freedom of speech
and walk in daylight through the midst of the market-place, ready to
converse with crowded gatherings, to let the clear sunlight shine upon
their own life and through the two most royal senses, sight and hearing,
to render good service to the assembled groups, who through the one
behold spectacles as marvelous as they are delightful, and through the
other feast on the fresh sweet draught of words which are wont to
gladden the minds of such as are not wholly averse to learning . . . Were

it not well, then, that we should follow her intentions and display in public all that is profitable and necessary for the benefit of those who are worthy to use it (LCL)?

5. NEW TESTAMENT

a. Matthew 23:15

Οὐαὶ ὑμῖν, γραμματεῖς καὶ Φαρισαῖοι ὑποκριταί, ὅτι περιάγετε τὴν θάλασσαν καὶ τὴν ξηρὰν ποιῆσαι ἕνα προσήλυτον, καὶ ὅταν γένηται ποιεῖτε αὐτὸν υἱὸν γεέννης διπλότερον ὑμῶν.

Woe to you, scribes and Pharisees, hypocrites! For you cross sea and land to make a single convert, and you make the new convert twice as much a child of hell as yourselves (NRSV).

b. Acts 15:1–5

Καί τινες κατελθόντες ἀπὸ τῆς Ἰουδαίας ἐδίδασκον τοὺς ἀδελφοὺς ὅτι, ἐὰν μὴ περιτμηθῆτε τῷ ἔθει τῷ Μωϋσέως, οὐ δύνασθε σωθῆναι. γενομένης δὲ στάσεως καὶ ζητήσεως οὐκ ὀλίγης τῷ Παύλῳ καὶ τῷ Βαρναβᾷ πρὸς αὐτούς, ἔταξαν ἀναβαίνειν Παῦλον καὶ Βαρναβᾶν καί τινας ἄλλους ἐξ αὐτῶν πρὸς τοὺς ἀποστόλους καὶ πρεσβυτέρους εἰς Ἰερουσαλὴμ περὶ τοῦ ζητήματος τούτου. Οἱ μὲν οὖν προπεμφθέντες ὑπὸ τῆς ἐκκλησίας διήρχοντο τήν τε Φοινίκην καὶ Σαμάρειαν ἐκδιηγούμενοι τὴν ἐπιστροφὴν τῶν ἐθνῶν καὶ ἐποίουν χαρὰν μεγάλην πᾶσιν τοῖς ἀδελφοῖς. παραγενόμενοι δὲ εἰς Ἰερουσαλὴμ παρεδέχθησαν ἀπὸ τῆς ἐκκλησίας καὶ τῶν ἀποστόλων καὶ τῶν πρεσβυτέρων, ἀνήγγειλάν τε ὅσα ὁ θεὸς ἐποίησεν μετ᾽ αὐτῶν. Ἐξανέστησαν δέ τινες τῶν ἀπὸ τῆς αἱρέσεως τῶν Φαρισαίων πεπιστευκότες λέγοντες ὅτι δεῖ περιτέμνειν αὐτοὺς παραγγέλλειν τε τηρεῖν τὸν νόμον Μωϋσέως.

Then certain individuals came down from Judea and were teaching the brothers, "Unless you are circumcised according to the custom of Moses, you cannot be saved." And after Paul and Barnabas had no small dissension and debate with them, Paul and Barnabas and some of the others were appointed to go up to Jerusalem to discuss this question with the apostles and the elders. So they were sent on their way by the church, and as they passed through both Phoenicia and Samaria, they reported the conversion of the Gentiles, and brought great joy to all the believers. When they came to Jerusalem, they were welcomed by the church and the apostles and the elders, and they reported all that God had done with them. But some believers who belonged to the sect of the Pharisees stood up and said, "It is necessary for them to be circumcised and ordered to keep the law of Moses" (NRSV).

6. PAGAN AUTHORS

a. Horace, *Sermones* 1.4.139–143

... Hoc est mediocribus illis
ex vitiis unum; cui si concedere nolis,
multa poetarum veniat manus, auxilio quae
sit mihi: nam multo plures sumus, ac veluti te
Iudaei cogemus in hanc concedere turbam.

This is one of those lesser frailties I spoke of, and if you should make no allowance for it, then would a big band of poets come to my aid—for we are the big majority—and we, like the Jews, will compel you to make one of our throng (Stern, *GLAJJ* 1: §127 [LCL]).

b. Seneca, *De Superstitione* cited in Augustine, *City of God* 6.11

Cum interim usque eo sceleratissimae gentis consuetude convaluit, ut per omnes iam terras recepta sit; victi victoribus leges dederunt.

Meanwhile the customs of this accursed race have gained such influence that they are now received throughout all the world. The vanquished have given laws to their victors (Stern, *GLAJJ* 1: §186 [LCL]).

c. Epictetus, *Dissertationes* 2.9.20

οὐχ ὁρᾷς πῶς ἕκαστος λέγεται Ἰουδαῖος, πῶς Σύρος, πῶς Αἰγύπτιος; καὶ ὅταν τινὰ ἐπαμφοτερίζοντα ἴδωμεν, εἰώθαμεν λέγειν «οὐκ ἔστιν Ἰουδαῖος, ἀλλ᾽ ὑποκρίνεται». ὅταν δ᾽ ἀναλάβῃ τὸ πάθος τὸ τοῦ βεβαμμένου καὶ ᾑρημένου, τότε καὶ ἔστι τῷ ὄντι καὶ καλεῖται Ἰουδαῖος.

Do you not see in what sense men are severally called Jew, Syrian, or Egyptian? For example, whenever we see a man halting between two faiths, we are in the habit of saying, "He is not a Jew, he is only acting the part."

But when he adopts the attitude of the mind of the man who has been baptized and has made his choice, then he is both a Jew in fact and is also called one (Stern, *GLAJJ* 1: §254 [LCL]).

d. Tacitus, *Histories* 5.5

Hi ritus quoquo modo inducti antiquitate defenduntur: cetera instituta, sinistra foeda, pravitate valuere. Nam pessimus quisque spretis religionibus patriis tributa et stipes illuc congerebant, unde auctae Iudaeorum res, et quia apud ipsos fides obstinata, misericordia in promptu, sed adversus omnis alios hostile odium. Separati epulis, discreti cubilibus, proiectissima ad libidinem gens, alienarum concubitu abstinent; inter se nihil inlicitum. Circumcidere genitalia instituerunt ut diversitate noscantur. Transgressi in morem eorum idem usurpant, nec quicquam prius imbuuntur quam contemnere deos, exuere patriam, parentes liberos fratres vilia habere. Augendae tamen multitudini consulitur; nam et necare quemquam ex agnatis nefas, animosque proelio aut suppliciis peremptorum aeternos putant: hinc generandi amor et moriendi contemptus. Corpora condere quam cremare e more Aegyptio, eademque cura et de infernis persuasio, caelestium contra. Aegyptii pleraque animalia effigiesque compositas venerantur, Iudaei mente sola unumque numen intellegunt: profanos qui deum imagines mortalibus materiis in species hominum effingant; summum illud et aeternum neque imitabile neque interiturum. Igitur nulla simulacra urbibus suis, nedum templis sistunt; non regibus haec adulatio, non Caesaribus honor. Sed quia sacerdotes eorum tibia tympanisque concinebant, hedera vinciebantur vitisque aurea templo reperta, Liberum patrem coli, domitorem Orientis, quidam arbitrati sunt, nequaquam congruentibus institutis. Quippe Liber festos laetosque ritus posuit, Iudaeorum mos absurdus sordidusque.

This worship, however introduced, is upheld by its antiquity; all their other customs, which are at once perverse and disgusting, owe their strength to their very badness. The most degraded out of other races, scorning their national beliefs, brought to them their contributions and presents. This augmented the wealth of the Jews, as also did the fact, that among themselves they are inflexibly honest and ever ready to shew compassion, though they regard the rest of mankind with all the hatred of enemies. They sit apart at meals, they sleep apart, and though, as a nation, they are singularly prone to lust, they abstain from intercourse with foreign women; among themselves nothing is unlawful. Circumcision was adopted by them as a mark of difference from other men. Those who come over to their religion adopt the practice, and have this lesson first instilled into them, to despise all gods, to disown their country, and set at nought parents, children, and brethren. Still they provide for the increase of their numbers. It is a crime among them to kill any newly-born infant. They hold that the souls of all who perish in battle or by the hands of the executioner are immortal. Hence a passion for propagating their race and a contempt for death. They are wont to bury rather than to burn their dead, following in this the Egyptian custom; they bestow the same care on the dead, and they hold the same belief about the lower world. Quite different is their faith about things divine. The Egyptians worship many animals and images of monstrous form; the Jews have purely mental conceptions of Deity, as one in essence. They call those profane who make representations of God in human shape out of perishable materials. They believe that Being to be supreme and eternal, neither capable of representation, nor of decay. They therefore do not allow any images to stand in their cities, much less in their temples. This flattery is not paid to their kings, nor this honor to our Emperors. From the fact, however, that their priests used to chant to the music of flutes and cymbals, and to wear garlands of ivy, and that a golden vine was found in the temple, some have thought that they worshipped father Liber, the conqueror of the East, though their institutions do not by any means harmonize with the theory; for Liber established a festive and cheerful worship, while the Jewish religion is tasteless and mean (Stern, *GLAJJ* 2: §281 [LCL]).

e. Juvenal, *Saturae* 15.96–106

Quidam sortiti metuentem sabbata patrem
nil praeter nubes et caeli numen adorant,
nec distare putant humana carne suillam,
qua pater abstinuit, mox et praeputia pronunt;
Romans autem soliti contemneres leges
Iudaicum ediscunt et servant ac metunnt ius,
tradidit arcano quodcumque volumine Moyses:
non monstrare vias eadem nisi sacra colenti,
quaesitum ad fontem solos deducere verpos.
Sed pater in causa, cui septima quaeque fuit lux
ignava et partem vitae non attigit ullam.

Some who have had a father who reveres the Sabbath, worship nothing but the clouds, and the divinity of the heavens, and see no difference between eating swine's flesh, from which their father abstained, and that of man; and in time they take to circumcision. Having been wont to flout the laws of Rome, they learn and practice and revere the Jewish law, and all that Moses handed down in his secret tome, forbidding to point out the way to any not worshipping the same rites, and conducting none but the circumcised to the desired foundation. For all which the father was to blame, who gave up every seventh day to idleness, keeping it apart from all the concerns of life (Stern, *GLAJJ* 2: §301 [LCL]).

f. Suetonius, *Domitian* 12.2

Praeter ceteros Iudaicus fiscus acerbissime actus est; ad quem deferebantur, qui vel[ut] inprofessi Iudaicam viverent vitam vel dissimulata origine imposita genti tributa non pependissent. Interfuisse me adulescentulum memini, cum a procuratore frequentissimoque consilio inspiceretur nonagenarius senex, an circumsectus esset.

Besides other taxes, that on the Jews was levied with the utmost vigour, and those were prosecuted who without publicly acknowledging that faith yet lived as Jews, as well as those who concealed their origin and did not pay the tribute levied upon their people. I recall being present in my youth when the person of a man ninety years old was examined before the procurator and a very crowded court, to see whether he was circumcised (Stern, *GLAJJ* 2: §320 [LCL]).

INSCRIPTIONS

a. God-Fearer at Deliler, Lydia

[T]ῇ ἁγιστ[άτῃ] [σ]υναγωγῃ τῶν Ἑβραίων Εὐστάτιος ὁ θεοσεβὴς ὑπὲρ μνίας τοῦ ἀδελφοῦ Ἑρμοφίλου τὸν μασκαύλην ἀνέθηκα ἅμα τῇ νύμφ[ῃ] μου Ἀθανασίᾳ.

To the most holy synagogue of the Hebrews, Eustatios God-fearer, in remembrance of brother Hermophilos, I have dedicated the wash-basin together with my bride [or sister-in-law] Athanasia (Levinskaya 1996, 60; Frey, *CIJ* 2: §754).

b. God-Fearer at Miletus

τόπος Εἰδέων τῶν καὶ θεοσεβίον.

Place of the Jews who are also called God-fearers (Trebilco 1991, 157–58; Frey, *CIJ* 2: §748).

c. Proselyte at Sebaste

Ἰουδέα προσή[λυτος . . . θ]εοσεβής.

Ioudea a proselyte [and] God-fearer (Frey, *CIJ* 1: §202).

d. Proselyte at Rome

Εἰρήνη [θ]ρε[ζ]πτὴ προσήλυτος πατρός καὶ μητρὸς Εἰουδέα Ἰσδραηλίτης ἔζησεν [ἔ]τ[η] γʹ μ[ῆνας] ζʹ ἡμ[έ]ρ[αν] αʹ.

Eirene, a foster-child, a convert to Judaism through her father and mother, a Jewess and an Israelite, has lived for three years and one day (Williams 1998, 172; Frey, *CIJ* 1: §21).

e. Palestinian Proselyte Ossuary

Ἰούδατος Λαγανίωνος προσηλύτου.

[The ossuary of] Judas son of Laganion, a proselyte (Frey, *CIJ* 2: §1385).

RABBINIC LITERATURE

a. Mishnah, *Pesahim* 8.8

הָאוֹנֵן טוֹבֵל וְאוֹכֵל אֶת
פִּסְחוֹ לָעֶרֶב אֲבָל לֹא בְּקָדָשִׁים
הַשּׁוֹמֵעַ עַל מֵתוֹ וְהַמְ ת לַקֵּט
בְּעֲצָמוֹת טוֹבֵל וְאוֹכֵל בְּקָדָשִׁים גֵּר
שֶׁנִּתְגַּיֵּר עֶרֶב פְּסָחִים בֵּית שַׁמַּי אוֹ
טוֹבֵל וְאוֹכֵל אֶת פִּסְחוֹ לָעֶרֶב וּבֵית
הִלֵּל אוֹ הַפּוֹרֵשׁ מִן הָעוֹרְלָה כְּפוֹרֵשׁ
מִן הַקֶּבֶר:

A. One who has suffered a bereavement of a close relative immerses and eats his Passover offering in the evening,

B. but [he may not eat any other] Holy Things [in that evening],

C. He who hears word [of the death of a close relative], and he who is gathering up bones [for secondary burial] immerses and eats Holy Things.

D. A proselyte who converted on the eve of Passover [the fourteenth of Nisan]—

E. the House of Shammai say, "He immerses and eats his Passover offering in the evening."

F. And the House of Hillel say, "He who takes his leave of the foreskin is as if he took his leave of the grave [and must be sprinkled on the third and seventh day after circumcision as if he had suffered corpse uncleanness]" (Neusner).

b. Babylonian Talmud, *Niddah* 13b

A. *Our rabbis have taught on Tannaite authority:*

B. Proselytes and those who "play" with children postpone the coming of the Messiah.

C. *Now the statement with respect to proselytes poses no problems, since it is in accord with what R. Helbo said.* For said R. Helbo, "Proselytes are as hard for Israel as a scab" (Neusner).

c. Babylonian Talmud, *Shabbath* 145b–6a

AA. "How come gentiles lust?"

BB. "Because they didn't stand at Mount Sinai. For when the snake had sexual relations with Eve, he dropped into her a filthy drop [of lust]. When the Israelites stood at Mount Sinai, their lust came to an end, but since the gentiles did not stand at Mount Sinai, their lust did not come to an end."

CC. *Said R. Aha b. Raba to R. Ashi, "So how about converts?"*

DD. *He said to him, "Even though they weren't there, their stars were there:* 'Neither with you only do I make this covenant and this oath, but with him who stands here with us this day before the Lord our God and also with him who doesn't stand here with us this day' (Deut 29:14–15)."

EE. *This differs from R. Abba bar Kahana, for said* R. Abba bar Kahana, "For three generations lust didn't come to an end for our fathers. After all, Abraham begat Ishmael, Isaac begat Esau, but Jacob begat the twelve tribal progenitors, in whom there was no flaw at all" (Neusner).

BIBLIOGRAPHY

PRIMARY SOURCES

BIBLE

The Greek New Testament. Edited by Barbara Aland, Kurt Aland, Carlo
M. Martini, Johannes Karavidopoulos, and Bruce M. Metzger. 4th
ed. UBS: Deutsche Stuttgart, 1998 [1993].
*The Holy Bible: New Revised Standard Version: Containing the Old Tes-
tament and the New Testament with Apocrypha.* Nashville, Tenn.:
Thomas Nelson, 1993.
The New English Bible with the Apocrypha. Oxford: Oxford/Cambridge
University Press, 1970 [1961].
Septuaginta. Edited by Alfred Rahlfs. 2 vols.; Stuttgart: Württember-
gische Bibelanstalt, 1935.

JEWISH LITERATURE

Josephus. Edited by J. Thackeray, R. Marcus, A. Wikgren and L. H.
Feldman. 9 vols.; LCL; Cambridge: Harvard University Press,
1929–1953.
Josephus. Edited by Steve Mason. "Life of Josephus." In *Flavius Josephus:
Translation and Commentary.* Leiden: Brill, 2001.
Philo. Edited by F. H. Colson, G. H. Whitaker, J. W. Earp and R. Mar-
cus. 12 vols.; LCL; London/Cambridge: Harvard University Press/
William Heinemann, 1929–1953.
Dead Sea Scrolls. Translated by Geza Vermes. *The Complete Dead Sea
Scrolls in English.* 4th ed. London: Penguin, 1997 [1962].

Dead Sea Scrolls. Translated by Michael Wise, Martin Abegg, Jr. and Edward Cook. *The Dead Sea Scrolls: A New Translation.* Australia: Hodder & Stoughton, 1996.

The Old Testament Pseudepigrapha. Edited by James H. Charlesworth. 2 vols.; ABRL; New York: Doubleday, 1983–1985.

Isaiah Targum. Translated by Bruce D. Chilton. *The Isaiah Targum.* The Aramaic Bible; Collegeville: Michael Glazier, 1990 [1987].

Mishnah. Translated by Jacob Neusner. *The Mishnah.* New Haven/London: Yale University, 1988.

Talmud, Babylonian. Translated by I. Epstein. 18 vols.; London: Soncino Press, 1948.

Talmud, Babylonian. Edited by J. Neusner. *The Babylonian Talmud: A Translation and Commentary.* 22 vols.; Peabody, Mass.: Hendrickson, 2005.

Tosefta. Translated by Jacob Neusner. 6 vols.; New York: Ktav Publishing House, 1977–1986. Repr., 2 vols.; Peabody, Mass.: Hendrickson, 2002.

Midrash. Edited by Reuven Hammer. *The Classic Midrash: Tannaitic Commentaries on the Bible.* New York: Paulist Press, 1995.

Inscriptions. Edited by J. B. Frey. *Corpus inscriptionum judaicarum.* 2 vols.; New York: Ktav Publishing, 1975 [1936–1952].

Christian Writings

The Apostolic Fathers. Edited by J. B. Lightfoot, J. R. Harmer and Michael W. Holmes. 2d ed. Grand Rapids, Mich.: Baker, 1989.

The Nag Hammadi Library. Edited by James M. Robinson. Leiden: Brill, 1988 [1978].

New Testament Apocrypha. Edited by W. Schneemelcher and R. McL. Wilson. 2 vols.; London: Lutterworth, 1965 [1964].

The Apocryphal New Testament. Edited by J. K. Elliot. Oxford: Clarendon, 1993.

Eusebius: The History of the Church. Translated by G. A. Williamson. London: Penguin, 1965.

Church Fathers. The Ante-Nicene Fathers. Edited by Alexander Roberts and James Donaldson. 10 vols.; Grand Rapids, Mich.: Eerdmans, 1979 [1885].

Pagan Writings

Greek and Latin Authors on Jews and Judaism: Edited with Introductions, Translations and Commentary. Edited by Menahem Stern. 3 vols.; Jerusalem: Israel Academy of Sciences and Humanities, 1974–1984.

Inscriptions. Inscriptiones Judaicae Orientis: II Kleinasien. Edited by Walter Ameling. TSAJ 99; Tübingen: Mohr/Siebeck, 2004.

Inscriptions. The Ancient Near East: An Anthology of Texts and Pictures. Edited by J. B. Pritchard. Princeton: Princeton University Press, 1971 [1958].

The Greek Magical Papyri in Translation. Edited by H. D. Betz. 2d ed. Chicago: Chicago University Press, 1992.

Tacitus: The Annals of Imperial Rome. Translated by Michael Grant. Rev. ed.; England: Penguin, 1971 [1956].

Tacitus: The Histories. Translated by Kenneth Wellesley. England: Penguin, 1972 [1964].

Secondary Literature

Allison, Dale C. *Resurrecting Jesus: The Earliest Christian Tradition and Its Interpreters.* London: T&T Clark/Continuum, 2005.

Arnold, Clinton E. *The Colossian Syncretism: The Interface between Christianity and Folk Belief in Colossae.* Grand Rapids, Mich.: Baker, 1996.

Aune, David E. "Expansion and Recruitment among Hellenistic Religions: The Case of Mithraism." Pages 39–56 in *Recruitment, Conquest, and Conflict.* Edited by Peder Borgen, Vernon K. Robbins, and David B. Gowler. Atlanta: Scholars, 1998.

Avni, Gideon, and Zvi Greenhut. *The Akeldama Tombs: Three Burial Caves in the Kidron Valley, Jerusalem.* Jerusalem: Israel Antiquities Authority, 1996.

Bamberger, B. J. *Proselytism in the Talmudic Period.* 2d ed. Cincinnati/New York: Hebrew Union College/Ktav, 1968.

Barclay, J. M. G. *Jews in the Mediterranean Diaspora from Alexander to Trajan (323 BCE–117 CE).* Edinburgh: T&T Clark, 1996.

————. "Apologetics in the Jewish Diaspora." Pages 129–48 in *Jews in the Hellenistic and Roman Cities.* Edited by John R. Bartlett. London/New York: Routledge, 2002.

Barnett, Paul. *Jesus and the Rise of Early Christianity: A History of New Testament Times*. Downers Grove, Ill.: InterVarsity, 1999.

———. "The Jewish Mission in the Era of the New Testament and the Apostle Paul." Pages 263–83 in *The Gospel to the Nations*. Edited by P. Bolt and M. Thompson. FS Peter O'Brien; Sydney: Apollo, 2000.

Baron, Salo. "Population." Pages 866–903 in *Encyclopedia Judaica*. Edited by Cecil Roth. 16 vols.; New York: Macmillan, 1971. Vol. 13.

Bauckham, Richard. "The Parting of the Ways: What Happened and Why." *ST* 47 (1993): 135–51.

Becker, U. "προσήλυτος." *NIDNTT* 1.359–62.

Bedell, Clifford H. "Mission in Intertestamental Judaism." Pages 21–29 in *Mission in the New Testament: An Evangelical Approach*. Edited by William J. Larkin Jr. and Joel F. Williams. New York: Maryknoll, 1998.

Bird, Michael F. "Matthew 23:15—The Case of the Proselytizing Pharisees." *JSHJ* 2 (2004): 117–37.

———. "Mission as an Apocalyptic Event: Reflections on Luke 10:18 and Mark 13:10." *EQ* 76 (2004): 117–34.

———. "'A Light to the Nations' (Isa 49:6): Inter-textuality and Mission Theology in the Early Church." *RTR* 65 (2006): 122–31.

———. *Jesus and the Origins of the Gentile Mission*. LNTS 331; London: T&T Clark/Continuum, 2006.

———. *The Saving Righteousness of God: Studies on Paul, Justification and the New Perspective*. Milton Keynes, U.K.: Paternoster, 2007.

———. *Colossians and Philemon*. New Covenant Commentary Series; Eugene, Ore.: Wipf & Stock, forthcoming 2009.

———. "The Early Christians, the Historical Jesus, and the Salvation of the Gentiles." In *Jesus from Judaism to Christianity*. Edited by Tom Holmén. WUNT; Tübingen: Mohr/Siebeck, forthcoming.

Bird, Michael F., and Preston M. Sprinkle. "Jewish Interpretation of Paul in the Last Thirty Years." *CBR* 6 (2008): 355–76.

Birnbaum, Ellen. *The Place of Judaism in Philo's Thought: Israel, Jews, and Proselytes*. Providence: Brown University Press, 1996.

Blaschke, Andreas. *Beschneidung: Zeugnisse der Bible und verwandter Texte*. TANZ 28; Tübingen/Base: Francke, 1998.

Borgen, Peder. "The Early Church and the Hellenistic Synagogue." *ST* 37 (1983): 55–78.

———. *Early Christianity and Hellenistic Judaism*. Edinburgh: T&T Clark, 1996.

————. "Proselytes, Conquest, and Mission." Pages 57–77 in *Recruitment, Conquest, and Conflict*. Edited by Peder Borgen, Vernon K. Robbins, and David B. Gowler. Atlanta: Scholars, 1998.

Bowers, Paul. "Paul and Religious Propaganda in the First Century," *NovT* 22 (1980): 316–23.

Braude, W. G. *Jewish Proselytizing in the First Five Centuries of the Common Era: The Age of the Tannaim and Amoraim*. Providence: Brown University Press, 1940.

Burchard, C. "Joseph and Aseneth." Pages 177–247 in *OTP*. Edited by James H. Charlesworth. 2 vols.; ABRL; New York: Doubleday, 1985. Vol. 2.

Caird, G. B. *The Apostolic Age*. London: Duckworth, 1955.

Caragounis, C. C. "Aristeas, Epistle of." Pages 114–18 in *DNTB*. Edited by Stanley E. Porter and Craig A. Evans. Downers Grove, Ill.: InterVarsity, 2000.

Chesnutt, Randall D. *From Death to Life: Conversion in Joseph and Aseneth*. JSPSup; Sheffield: Sheffield Academic Press, 1995.

Cohen, S. J. D. *Josephus in Galilee and Rome: His Vita and Development as a Historian*. Leiden: Brill, 1979.

————. "Respect for Judaism by Gentiles according to Josephus." *HTR* 80 (1987): 409–30.

————. "Crossing the Boundary and Becoming a Jew." *HTR* 82 (1989): 13–33.

————. "Adolf Harnack's 'The Mission and Expansion of Judaism': Christianity Succeeds Where Judaism Fails." Pages 163–69 in *The Future of Early Christianity: Essays in Honor of Helmut Koester*. Edited by Birger A. Pearson. Minneapolis: Fortress, 1991.

————. "Was Judaism in Antiquity a Missionary Religion?" Pages 14–23 in *Jewish Assimilation, Acculturation and Accommodation*. Edited by M. Mor. Lanham, Md.: University Press of America, 1992.

————. *The Beginnings of Jewishness: Boundaries, Varieties, Uncertainties*. Berkeley: University of California, 1999.

————. *Why Aren't Jewish Women Circumcised: Gender and Covenant in Judaism*. Berkeley: University of California Press, 2005.

Collins, John. J. "A Symbol of Otherness: Circumcision and Salvation in the First Century." Pages 163–86 in *To See Ourselves as Others See Us: Christians, Jews, Others in Late Antiquity*. Edited by J. Neusner and E. S. Frerichs. Chico, Calif.: Scholars Press, 1985.

————. *Between Athens and Jerusalem: Jewish Identity in the Hellenistic Diaspora*. BRS; Grand Rapids, Mich.: Eerdmans, 1999.

Conzelmann, Hans. *Gentiles—Jews—Christians: Polemics and Apologetics in the Greco-Roman Era*. Translated by M. Eugene Boring. Minneapolis: Fortress, 1992 [1981].

Crook, Zeba A. *Reconceptualising Conversion: Patronage, Loyalty, and Conversion in the Religions of the Ancient Mediterranean*. BZNW 130; Berlin/New York: Walter de Gruyter, 2004.

Crossan, John Dominic. *The Historical Jesus: The Life of a Mediterranean Jewish Peasant*. San Francisco: Harper Collins, 1991.

Crossley, James G. *Why Christianity Happened: A Sociohistorical Account of Christian Origins (26–50 CE)*. Louisville: Westminster John Knox, 2006.

Dalbert, Peter. *Die Theologie der hellenistisch-jüdischen Missionsliteratur unter Ausschluss von Philo und Josephus*. Hamburg: Herbert Reich, 1954.

Daube, David. "Conversion to Judaism and Early Christianity." Pages 1–47 in *Ancient Jewish Law: Three Inaugural Lectures*. Leiden: Brill, 1981.

Davies, Graham. "The Destiny of the Nations in the Book of Isaiah." Pages 93–120 in *The Book of Isaiah*. Edited by J. Vermeylen. Leiden: Brill, 1989.

Davies, W. D., and Dale C. Allison, Jr. *The Gospel According to Saint Matthew*. 3 vols.; ICC; Edinburgh: T&T Clark, 1988–1997.

Deines, Roland. "Die Abwehr der Fremden in den Texten aus Qumran: Zum Verständnis der Fremdenfeindlichkeit in der Qumrangemeinde." Pages 59–91 in *Die Heiden: Juden, Christen und das Problem des Fremden*. Edited by Reinhard Feldmeier and Ulrich Heckel. WUNT 70; Tübingen: Mohr/Siebeck, 1994.

Dickson, John P. *Mission-Commitment in Ancient Judaism and in the Pauline Communities: The Shape, Extent and Background of Early Christian Mission*. WUNT 2.159; Tübingen: Mohr/Siebeck, 2003.

Donaldson, Terence L. *Paul and the Gentiles: Remapping the Apostle's Convictional World*. Minneapolis: Fortress, 1997.

————. *Judaism and the Gentiles: Jewish Patterns of Universalism (to 135 CE)*. Waco, Tex.: Baylor University Press, 2007.

Dunn, James D. G. "The Colossian Philosophy: A Confident Jewish Apologia." *Bib* 76 (1995): 153–81.

————. *The Epistles to the Colossians and to Philemon*. NIGTC; Grand Rapids, Mich.: Eerdmans, 1996.

Evans, Craig A. "From 'House of Prayer' to 'Cave of Robbers': Jesus' Prophetic Criticism of the Temple Establishment." Pages 417–42 in *The Quest for Context and Meaning: Studies in Biblical Interpretation in Honor of James A. Sanders*. Edited by Craig A. Evans and Shemaryahu Talmon. FS James A. Sanders; BIS 28; Leiden: Brill, 1997.

———. "Scripture-Based Stories in the Pseudepigrapha." Pages 57–72 in *Justification and Variegated Nomism: Volume 1—The Complexities of Second Temple Judaism*. Edited by D. A. Carson, Peter T. O'Brien, and Mark A. Seifrid. Grand Rapids, Mich.: Baker, 2001.

Feldman, Louis H. "Jewish 'Sympathizers' in Classical Literature and Inscriptions." *TAPA* 81 (1950): 200–208.

———. "Was Judaism a Missionary Religion in Ancient Times?" Pages 24–37 in *Jewish Assimilation, Acculturation and Accommodation*. Edited by M. Mor. Lanham, Md.: University Press of America, 1992.

———. *Jew and Gentile in the Ancient World: Attitudes and Interactions from Alexander to Justinian*. Princeton: Princeton University Press, 1993.

Feldman, Louis H., and Gōhei Hata, eds. *Josephus, Judaism, and Christianity*. Detroit: Wayne State University Press, 1987.

Feldman, Louis H., and Meyer Reinhold. *Jewish Life and Thought among Greeks and Romans: Primary Readings*. Minneapolis: Fortress, 1996.

Figueras, P. "Epigraphic Evidence for Proselytism in Ancient Judaism." *Immanuel* 24/25 (1990): 194–206.

Finn, T. M. "The God-fearers Reconsidered." *CBQ* 47 (1985): 75–84.

———. *From Death to Rebirth: Ritual and Conversion in Antiquity*. New York: Paulist, 1997.

Fredriksen, Paula. "Judaism, the Circumcision of Gentiles, and Apocalyptic Hope: Another Look at Galatians 1 and 2." *JTS* 42 (1991): 532–64.

Frey, J. "Paul's Jewish Identity." Pages 285–321 in *Jewish Identity in the Greco-Roman World*. Edited by J. Frey, D. R. Schwartz, and S. Gripentrog. AJEC 71. Leiden: Brill, 2007.

Fuller, Michael E. *The Restoration of Israel: Israel's Regathering and the Fate of the Nations in Early Jewish Literature and Luke-Acts*. BZNW 138; Berlin: Walter de Gruyter, 2006.

Gager, John. *Reinventing Paul*. Oxford: Oxford University Press, 2000.

Gaston, Lloyd. *Paul and the Torah*. Vancouver, B.C.: University of British Columbia Press, 1987.

Gaventa, Beverly Roberts. *From Darkness to Light: Aspects of Conversion in the New Testament*. Philadelphia: Fortress, 1986.

Georgi, Dieter. *The Opponents of Paul in Second Corinthians*. Edinburgh: T&T Clark, 1986.

Gibson, Elizabeth Leigh. *The Jewish Manumission Inscriptions of the Bosporus Kingdom*. Tübingen: Mohr/Siebeck, 1999.

Goldenberg, Robert. *The Origins of Judaism: From Canaan to the Rise of Islam*. Cambridge: Cambridge University Press, 2007.

Goodman, Martin. "Proselytising in Rabbinic Judaism." *JJS* 40 (1989): 175–85.

————. "Jewish Proselytizing in the First Century." Pages 53–78 in *The Jews among Pagans and Christians in the Roman Empire*. Edited by J. Lieu, J. L. North, and T. Rajak. London: Routledge, 1992.

————. *Mission and Conversion: Proselytizing in the Religious History of the Roman Empire*. Oxford: Clarendon, 1994.

————. "The Emergence of Christianity." Pages 7–24 in *A World History of Christianity*. Edited by Adrian Hastings. London: Cassell, 1999.

————. "Galilean Judaism and Judaean Judaism." Volume 3, pages 596–617 in *The Cambridge History of Judaism*. Edited by William Horbury, W. D. Davies and John Sturdy. 3 vols.; Cambridge: Cambridge University Press, 1999.

Goppelt, L. "Der Missionar des Gesetzes. Zu Röm. 2,21 f." In *Christologie und Ethik. Aufsätze zum Neuen Testament*. Göttingen: Vandenhoeck & Ruprecht, 1968.

Grabbe, Lester L. *Judaism from Cyrus to Hadrian*. London: SCM, 1992.

Green, Michael. *Evangelism in the Early Church*. Grand Rapids, Mich.: Eerdmans, 1970.

Gruen, Erich S. *Diaspora: Jews amidst Greeks and Romans*. Cambridge, Mass.: Harvard University Press, 2002.

Hagner, D. A. *Matthew*. 2 vols.; WBC; Dallas, Tex.: Word, 1993–1995.

Hahn, F. *Mission in the New Testament*. Translated by Frank Clarke. London: SCM, 1965 [1963].

Hanson K. C., and Douglas Oakman. *Palestine in the Time of Jesus: Social Structures and Social Conflicts*. Minneapolis: Fortress, 1998.

Harland, Philip A. *Associations, Synagogues, and Congregations: Claiming a Place in Ancient Mediterranean Society*. Minneapolis: Fortress, 2003.

Harnack, Adolf von. *The Expansion of Christianity in the First Three Centuries*. Translated by James Moffatt. 2 vols. London/New York: Williams & Norgate/G. P. Putnam's Sons, 1904–1905.

Hayes, C. E. *Gentile Impurities and Jewish Identities: Intermarriage and Conversion from the Bible to the Talmud*. Oxford: Oxford University Press, 2002.

Hayward, Robert. "Abraham as Proselytizer at Beer-Sheba in the Targums of the Pentateuch." *JJS* 49 (1998): 24–37.

Hengel, Martin. *Judaism and Hellenism*. Translated by John Bowden. 2 vols.; London: SCM, 1974.

Hengel, Martin, and Anna Maria Schwemer. *Paul between Damascus and Antioch*. Translated by John Bowden. London: SCM, 1997.

Hooker, Morna D. "Were There False Teachers in Colossae?" Pages 121–36 in *From Adam to Christ*. Cambridge: Cambridge University Press, 1990.

Hvalvik, Reidar. *The Struggle for Scripture and Covenant: The Purpose of the Epistle of Barnabas and Jewish-Christian Competition in the Second Century*. WUNT 2.82; Tübingen: Mohr/Siebeck, 1996.

————. "In Word and Deed: The Expansion of the Church in the Pre-Constantinian Era." Pages 265–87 in *The Mission of the Early Church to Jews and Gentiles*. Edited by Jostein Adna and Hans Kvalbein. WUNT 127; Tübingen: Mohr/Siebeck, 2000.

Jeremias, Joachim. *Jesus' Promise to the Nations*. Translated by S. H. Hooke. SBT 24. London: SCM, 1958 [1956].

Jossa, Giorgio. *Jews or Christians?* Translated by Molly Rogers. WUNT 202; Tübingen: Mohr/Siebeck, 2006.

Kähler, Martin. *Schriften zur Christologie und Mission*. Munich: C. Kaiser, 1971 (1908).

Kasher, Aryeh. *Jews, Idumaeans and Ancient Arabs*. Tübingen: Mohr/Siebeck, 1988.

Koester, Helmut. "Strugnell and Supersessionism: Historical Mistakes Haunt the Relationship of Christianity and Judaism," *BAR* 21 (1995): 26–27.

Köstenberger, Andreas J., and Peter T. O'Brien. *Salvation to the Ends of the Earth: A Biblical Theology of Mission*. NSBT 11; Downers Grove, Ill.: InterVarsity, 2001.

Kraabel, A. Thomas. "The Disappearance of the God-Fearers." *Numen* 28 (1981): 113–26.

————. "The Roman Diaspora: Six Questionable Assumptions." *JJS* 33 (1982): 445–64.

————. "Immigrants, Exiles, Expatriates, and Missionaries." Pages 71–88 in *Religious Propaganda and Mission Competition in the New Testament World: Essays Honoring Dieter Georgi*. Edited by L. Bormann, K. Del Tredici, and A. Standhartinger. FS Dieter Georgi; Leiden: Brill, 1994.

Kraemer, Ross S. "On the Meaning of the Term 'Jew' in Greco-Roman Inscriptions." *HTR* 82 (1989): 35–53.

Kraft, Robert A., and George W. E. Nickelsburg, eds. *Early Judaism and Its Modern Interpreters*. Atlanta: Scholars, 1986.

Kroll, John H. "The Greek Inscriptions of the Sardis Synagogue." *HTR* 94 (2001): 5–55.

Kuhn, K. G. "προσήλυτος." *TDNT* 6.727–44.

Kumar, P. Pratap, ed. *Religious Pluralism in the Diaspora*. Leiden: Brill, 2006.

Lake, Kirsopp. "Proselytes and God-Fearers." Pages 75–96 in *The Beginnings of Christianity*. Edited by F. J. Foakes Jackson and Kirsopp Lake. 5 vols.; London: Macmillan, 1922–1933. Vol. 5.

Lattke, Michael. "The Call to Discipleship and Proselytizing." *HTR* 92 (1999): 359–62.

Leon, Harry J. *The Jews of Ancient Rome*. Peabody, Mass.: Hendrickson, 1995 [1960].

Levinskaya, Irina. *The Book of Acts in Its First Century Setting 5: The Book of Acts in Its Diaspora Setting*. Grand Rapids/Carlisle: Eerdmans/ Paternoster, 1996.

Levison, Nahum. "The Proselyte in Biblical and Early Post-Biblical Times." *SJT* 10 (1957): 45–56.

Lieu, Judith M. "Circumcision, Women and Salvation." *NTS* 40 (1994): 358–70.

————. "The Race of God-fearers." *JTS* 46 (1995): 483–501.

Löhr, M. *Der Missionsgedanke im Alten Testament: Ein Beitrag zur alttestamentlichen Religionsgeschichte*. Freiburg: J. C. B. Mohr, 1896.

MacMullen, Ramsay. *Christianizing the Roman Empire (A.D. 100–400)*. New Haven: Yale University Press, 1986.

Malherbe, Abraham J. *Social Aspects of Early Christianity*. 2d ed. Eugene, Ore.: Wipf & Stock, 2003.

Marshall, I. Howard. "Who Were the Evangelists?" Pages 251–63 in *The Mission of the Early Church to Jews and Gentiles*. Edited by

Jostein Adna and Hans Kvalbein. WUNT 127; Tübingen: Mohr/ Siebeck, 2000.

Martin, Luther H. "Performativity, Narrativity, and Cognition: 'Demythologizing' the Roman Cult of Mithras." Pages 187–217 in *Rhetoric and Reality in Early Christianities*. Edited by Willi Braun. Toronto: Wilfrid Laurier University Press, 2005.

Mason, Steve. "The *Contra Apionem* in Social and Literary Context: An Invitation to Judean Philosophy." Pages 187–228 in *Josephus' Contra Apionem: Studies in its Character and Context with a Latin Concordance to the Portions Missing in Greek*. Edited by Louis H. Feldman and John R. Levison. Leiden: Brill, 1996.

———. "Jews, Judaeans, Judaizing, Judaism: Problems of Categorization in Ancient History." *JSJ* 38 (2007): 457–512.

McEleney, N. J. "Conversion, Circumcision and the Law." *NTS* 20 (1974): 319–41.

McGing, Brian. "Population and Proselytism: How Many Jews Were There in the Ancient World?" Pages 88–106 in *Jews in the Hellenistic and Roman Cities*. Edited by John R. Bartlett. London/New York: Routledge, 2002.

McKnight, Scot. *A Light among the Gentiles: Jewish Missionary Activity in the Second Temple Period*. Minneapolis: Fortress, 1991.

Meeks, Wayne A. *The First Urban Christians: The Social World of the Apostle Paul*. New Haven, Conn.: Yale University Press, 1983.

Meier, John P. *Matthew*. Wilmington: Michael Glazier, 1986 (1980).

Mitchell, Stephen. "The Cult of Theos Hypsistos between Pagans, Jews and Christians." Pages 83–148 in *Pagan Monotheism in Late Antiquity*. Edited by P. Athanassiadi and M. Frede. Oxford: Oxford University Press, 1999.

Mommsen, T. *Römische Geschichte V: Die Provinzen von Caesar bis Diocletian*. 5th ed. Leipzig: Weidmann, 1904.

Moore, G. F. *Judaism in the First Centuries of the Christian Era: The Age of the Tannaim*. 3 vols.; Cambridge, Mass.: Harvard University Press, 1927–1930.

Munck, Johannes. *Paul and the Salvation of Mankind*. Translated by Frank Clarke. London: SCM, 1959 [1954].

Murphy-O'Connor, Jerome. "Lots of God-Fearers? Theosebeis in the Aphrodisias Inscription." *RB* 99 (1992): 418–24.

Nanos, Mark D. *The Irony of Galatians: Paul's Letter in First-Century Context*. Minneapolis: Fortress, 2002.

Neusner, Jacob. "The Conversion of Adiabene to Judaism: A New Perspective." *JBL* 83 (1964): 60–66.

———. *Judaism and Its Social Metaphors: Israel in the History of Jewish Thought.* Cambridge: Cambridge University Press, 1989.

Nickelsburg, George W. E. *Jewish Literature between the Bible and the Mishnah: A Historical and Literary Introduction.* London: SCM, 1981.

Nock, A. D. *Conversion: Old and the New in Religion from Alexander the Great to Augustine of Hippo.* Oxford: Oxford University Press, 1933.

Nolan, Patrick, and Gerhard Lenski. *Human Societies: An Introduction to Macrosociology.* 9th ed. Boulder, Colo.: Paradigm, 2004.

Nolland, John. "Proselytism or Politics in Horace *Satires* 1,4,138–143." *VC* 33 (1979): 347–55.

———. "Uncircumcised Proselytes?" *JSJ* 12 (1981): 173–94.

Overman, J. Andrew. "The God-Fearers: Some Neglected Features." Pages 253–62 in *New Testament Backgrounds.* Edited by Craig A. Evans and Stanley E. Porter. Sheffield: Sheffield Academic Press, 1997 (1988).

———. *Church and Community in Crisis: The Gospel according to Matthew.* Valley Forge, Penn.: TPI, 1996.

Paget, J. C. "Jewish Proselytism at the Time of Christian Origins: Chimera or Reality?" *JSNT* 62 (1996): 65–103.

———. "Jewish Christianity." Pages 731–75 in *Cambridge History of Ancient Judaism.* Edited by W. D. Davies. 3 vols.; Cambridge: Cambridge University Press, 2002. Vol. 3.

Plummer, Robert L. *Paul's Understanding of the Church's Mission: Did the Apostle Paul Expect the Early Christian Communities to Evangelize?* PBM; Bletchley: Paternoster, 2006.

Porter, Stanley E. *Idioms of the Greek New Testament.* 2d ed. Sheffield: Sheffield Academic Press, 1994.

Porton, Gary. *The Stranger within Your Gates: Converts and Conversion in Rabbinic Judaism.* Chicago: University of Chicago Press, 1994.

Rajak, Tessa. "The Jewish Community and Its Boundaries." Pages 9–28 in *The Jews among Pagans and Christians in the Roman Empire.* Edited by Judith Lieu, John North, and Tessa Rajak. London: Routledge, 1992.

Rambo, L. R. *Understanding Religious Conversion.* New Haven, Conn.: Yale University Press, 1993.

Reed, Jonathan L. "Population Numbers, Urbanization, and Economics: Galilean Archaeology and the Historical Jesus." Pages 203–19 in *SBL Seminar Papers 1994*. Edited by Eugene H. Lovering, Jr. Atlanta: Scholars, 1994.

Reynolds, J., and R. Tannenbaum. *Jews and God-fearers at Aphrodisias: Greek Inscriptions with Commentary*. Cambridge: Cambridge Philological Society, 1987.

Riesner, Rainer. "A Pre-Christian Jewish Mission." Pages 211–50 in *The Mission of the Early Church to Jews and Gentiles*. Edited by J. Ådna and H. Kvalbein. Tübingen: Mohr/Siebeck, 2000.

Rokéah, D. "Ancient Jewish Proselytism in Theory and in Practice." *TZ* 52 (1996): 206–24.

Rutgers, Leonard Victor. *The Jews in Late Ancient Rome: Evidence of Cultural Interaction in the Roman Diaspora*. Leiden: Brill, 1995.

Safrai, S. and M. Stern, eds. *The Jewish People in the First Century: Historical Geography, Political History, Social, Cultural and Religious Life and Institutions*. 2 vols.; Amsterdam: Van Gorcum, 1974–1976.

Sanders, E. P. *Jewish Law from Jesus to the Mishnah: Five Studies*. London: SCM, 1990.

Sandmel, Samuel. *The First Christian Century in Judaism and Christianity: Certainties and Uncertainties*. New York: Oxford University Press, 1969.

Sappington, Thomas J. *Revelation and Redemption at Colossae*. JSNTSup 53; Sheffield: JSOT Press, 1991.

Schiffman, Lawrence H. "The Conversion of the Royal House of Adiabene in Josephus and Rabbinic Sources." Pages 293–312 in *Josephus, Judaism, and Christianity*. Edited by Louis H. Feldman and Gōhei Hata. Detroit: Wayne State University Press, 1987.

———. "Non-Jews in the Dead Sea Scrolls." Pages 153–71 in *The Quest for Context and Meaning: Studies in Biblical Intertextuality in Honor of James A. Sanders*. Edited by Craig A. Evans and Shemaryahu Talmon. BIS 28; Leiden: Brill, 1997.

Schnabel, Eckhard J. "Jesus and the Beginnings of the Mission to the Gentiles." Pages 37–58 in *Jesus of Nazareth, Lord and Christ*. Edited by Joel B. Green and Max Turner. Grand Rapids, Mich.: Eerdmans, 1994.

———. *Urchristliche Mission*. Wuppertal: R. Brockhaus, 2002.

———. *The Early Christian Mission*. 2 vols.; Downers Grove, Ill.: InterVarsity, 2004.

Schürer, Emil. *The History of the Jewish People in the Age of Jesus Christ*. Edited by G. Vermes, F. Millar, and M. Black. 3 vols.; Edinburgh: T&T Clark, 1973–1987.

Schwartz, Daniel R. "Doing Like Jews or Becoming a Jew? Josephus on Women Converts to Judaism." Pages 93–109 in *Jewish Identity in the Greco-Roman World*. Edited by J. Frey, D. R. Schwartz, and S. Gripentrog. AJEC 71, Leiden: Brill, 2007.

———. "'Judaean' or 'Jew'? How Should We Translate *Ioudaios* in Josephus?" Pages 3–27 in *Jewish Identity in the Greco-Roman World*. Edited by J. Frey, D. R. Schwartz, and S. Gripentrog. AJEC 71, Leiden: Brill, 2007.

———. "God, Gentiles, Jewish Law: On Acts 15 and Josephus' Adiabene Narrative." Pages 263–81 in *Jewish Identity in the Greco-Roman World*. Edited by J. Frey, D. R. Schwartz, and S. Gripentrog. AJEC 71, Leiden: Brill, 2007.

Scott, J. J., Jr. *Customs and Controversies: Intertestamental Jewish Backgrounds of the New Testament*. Grand Rapids, Mich.: Baker, 1995.

Segal, Alan F. "The Cost of Proselytism and Conversion." Pages 336–69 in *SBL 1988 Seminar Papers*. Edited by D. Hull. Atlanta: Scholars Press, 1988.

Smith, Carl B. *No Longer Jews: The Search for Gnostic Origins*. Peabody, Mass.: Hendrickson, 2004.

Smith, Ian. *Heavenly Perspective: A Study of the Apostle Paul's Response to a Jewish Mystical Movement in Colossae*. LNTS 326; London: Continuum, 2006.

Smith, Morton. "The Gentiles in Judaism 125 BCE–CE 66." Pages 192–249 in *The Cambridge History of Judaism: Volume Three*. Edited by W. D. Davies, William Horbury, and John Sturdy. Cambridge: Cambridge University Press, 1999.

Stark, Rodney. *The Rise of Christianity: A Sociologist Reconsiders History*. Princeton: Princeton University Press, 1996.

———. *Cities of God: The Real Story of How Christianity Became an Urban Movement and Conquered Rome*. San Francisco: Harper Collins, 2006.

Stark, Rodney, and Roger Finke. *Acts of Faith: Explaining the Human Side of Religion*. Berkeley: University of California Press, 2000.

Stettler, Christian. "The Opponents at Colossae." Pages 167–200 in *Paul and His Opponents*. Edited by Stanley E. Porter. Leiden: Brill, 2005.

Stowers, Stanley K. *A Rereading of Romans: Justice, Jews, Gentiles*. New Haven: Yale University Press, 1994.

Strelan, Rick. *Paul, Artemis, and the Jews in Ephesus*. BZNW 80; Berlin: Walter de Gruyter, 1996.

Stuehrenberg, Paul F. "Proselyte." Pages 503–5 in *ABD*. Edited by David Noel Freedman. ABRL; 6 vols.; New York: Doubleday, 1992. Vol. 5.

Taylor, N. H. "The Social Nature of Conversion in the Early Christian World." Pages 128–36 in *Modelling Early Christianity: Social Scientific Studies of the New Testament in Its Context*. Edited by Phil F. Esler. London: Routledge, 1995.

Tcherikover, Victor. "Jewish Apologetic Literature Reconsidered." *Eos* 48 (1956): 169–93.

———. *Hellenistic Civilization and the Jews*. Translated by S. Applebaum. New York: Atheneum, 1970 [1959].

Tellbe, Mikael. "The Temple Tax as Pre-70 CE Identity Marker." Pages 19–44 in *The Formation of the Early Church*. Edited by Jostein Ådna. WUNT 183; Tübingen: Mohr/Siebeck, 2005.

Theissen, Gerd. *Sociology of Early Palestinian Christianity*. Translated by John Bowden. Philadelphia: Fortress, 1978 [1977].

Trebilco, Paul R. *Jewish Communities in Asia Minor*. Cambridge: Cambridge University Press, 1991.

Wallace, Daniel B. *Greek Grammar beyond the Basics*. Grand Rapids, Mich.: Zondervan, 1996.

Wander, Bernd. *Gottesfürchtige und Sympathisanten*. WUNT 104; Tübingen: Mohr/Siebeck, 1998.

Ware, James Patrick. *The Mission of the Church in Paul's Letter to the Philippians in the Context of Ancient Judaism*. Leiden: Brill, 2005.

Wasserstein, A. "The Number and Provenance of Jews in Graeco-Roman Antiquity: A Short Note on Population Statistics." Pages 307–17 in *Classical Studies in Honor of David Sohlberg*. Edited by R. Katzoff. FS David Sohlberg; Ramat Gan: Bar-Ilan University Press, 1996.

Watson, Francis. *Paul, Judaism and the Gentiles*. Cambridge: Cambridge University Press, 1986.

Webb, Robert L. *John the Baptizer and Prophet: A Socio-Historical Study*. JSNTSup 62; Sheffield: Sheffield Academic Press, 1991.

Weitzman, Steven. "Forced Circumcision and the Shifting Role of Gentiles in Hasmonean Ideology." *HTR* 92 (1999): 37–59.

Wellhausen, Julius. *Israelitische und Jüdische Geschichte*. 2d ed. Berlin: Walter de Gruyter, 1895.

White, L. Michael. "Visualizing the 'Real' World of Acts 16: Toward Construction of a Social Index." Pages 234–61 in *The Social World of the First Christians: Essays in Honor of Wayne A. Meeks*. Edited by L. Michael White and O. Larry Yarbrough. FS Wayne A. Meeks; Phildelphia: Fortress, 1995.

Wilcox, M. "The "God-fearers" in Acts: A Reconsideration." *JSNT* 13 (1981): 102–22.

Will, E., and C. Orrieux. *"Prosélytisme Juif"? Histoire d'une erreur*. Paris: Les Belles Lettres, 1993.

Williams, Margaret H. "'Θεοσεβὴς γὰρ ἦν'—The Jewish Tendencies of Poppaea Sabina," *JTS* 39 (1988): 97–111.

———. "The Meaning and Function of *Ioudaios* in Greco-Roman Inscriptions." *ZPE* 116 (1997): 249–62.

———. *The Jews among the Greeks and Romans: A Diasporan Sourcebook*. London: Duckworth, 1998.

Wilson, Stephen G. *Leaving the Fold: Apostates and Defectors in Antiquity*. Minneapolis: Fortress, 2004.

Wright, N. T. *The Epistles of Paul to the Colossians and to Philemon*. TNTC; Grand Rapids, Mich.: Eerdmans, 1986.

INDEX OF MODERN AUTHORS

Gager, J., 133
Gaston, L., 133
Gaventa, B. R., 41, 84
Georgi, D., 8, 52, 106, 122, 130
Gibson, E. L., 80
Goldenberg, R., 83
Goodman, M., 2, 7, 9–12, 15, 17, 19,
   45, 53, 68, 74, 94, 98, 105, 110,
   114, 117, 119, 120, 122, 126, 128,
   130, 131, 147, 151, 156
Goppelt, L., 9
Grabbe, L. L., 10, 58, 131
Green, M., 3
Greenhut, Z., 70
Gruen, E. S., 77, 128–29, 131

Hagner, D. A., 68
Hahn, F., 21, 136
Hanson, K. C., 13
Harland, P., 91
Harnack, A., 7, 8, 52, 53
Hata, G., 78
Hayes, C. E., 72
Hayward, R., 74, 75, 94
Hengel, M., 16, 35, 42, 81, 84, 88,
   106, 128
Hooker, M. D., 141
Hvalvik, R., 3, 10, 17, 52, 75, 103,
   147, 150

Jeremias, J., 9, 21, 67
Jossa, G., 16

Kähler, M., 2
Kasher, A., 57, 58, 60
Koester, H., 155
Köstenberger, A. J., 11, 21, 68
Kraabel, A. T., 10, 45, 49, 67, 156
Kraemer, R. S., 14
Kraft, R. A., 15
Kroll, J. H., 46–47, 49, 74
Kuhn, K. G., 8, 41, 44, 68
Kumar, P. P., 83

Lake, K., 37, 44, 50, 52
Lattke, M., 36–37

Lenski, G., 9
Leon, H. J., 8, 96, 122, 132, 157
Levinskaya, I., 10, 45–46, 49, 52, 67,
   68, 80–81, 122, 128, 131, 157
Levison, N., 41
Lieu, J. M., 42, 44, 52
Löhr, M., 67

Mackenzie, D. A., 4
MacMullen, R., 2
Malherbe, A. J., 2
Marshall, I. H., 3
Martin, L. H., 19
Mason, S., 7–8, 13, 95
McEleney, N., 25, 26, 39, 44
McGing, B., 53–54
McKnight, S., 9–12, 17, 18, 19, 21,
   52, 53, 54, 55, 67, 68–69, 97, 98,
   108, 109, 110, 114, 115, 125, 127,
   128, 131, 134
Meeks, W. A., 23
Meier, J. P., 67
Mitchell, S., 80
Mommsen, T., 8
Moore, G. E., 8, 9, 17, 21, 37, 52, 57
Munck, J., 9, 68
Murphy-O'Connor, J., 48

Nanos, M., 138–39
Neusner, J., 97, 98, 107
Nickelsburg, G. W. E., 15, 112, 114,
   118, 119
Nock, A. D., 8, 19, 21, 105, 119, 121
Nolan, P., 9
Nolland, J., 26, 27, 30, 39, 122

Oakman, D., 13
O'Brien, P. T., 11, 21, 68
Orrieux, C., 10, 68
Overman, J. A., 15, 46, 50, 52

Paget, J. C., 10, 17, 19, 52, 53, 54, 67,
   97, 111, 118, 120, 122, 128, 131, 134
Plummer, R., 3
Porter, S. E., 100
Porton, G., 74

INDEX OF SUBJECTS

INDEX OF ANCIENT SOURCES